Losing Twice

Losing Twice

Harms of Indifference in the Supreme Court

EMILY M. CALHOUN

OXFORD

UNIVERSITY PRESS

OXFORD
UNIVERSITY PRESS

Oxford University Press, Inc., publishes works that further
Oxford University's objective of excellence
in research, scholarship, and education.

Oxford   New York
Auckland   Cape Town   Dar es Salaam   Hong Kong   Karachi
Kuala Lumpur   Madrid   Melbourne   Mexico City   Nairobi
New Delhi   Shanghai   Taipei   Toronto

With offices in
Argentina   Austria   Brazil   Chile   Czech Republic   France   Greece
Guatemala   Hungary   Italy   Japan   Poland   Portugal   Singapore
South Korea   Switzerland   Thailand   Turkey   Ukraine   Vietnam

Published by Oxford University Press, Inc.
198 Madison Avenue, New York, New York 10016

www.oup.com

Oxford is a registered trademark of Oxford University Press

Library of Congress Cataloging-in-Publication Data
Calhoun, Emily M.
Losing twice : harms of indifference in the Supreme Court / Emily M. Calhoun.
p.   cm.
Includes bibliographical references and index.
ISBN 978-0-19-539974-5 (hardcover : alk. paper)
1. United States. Supreme Court—Decision making.   2. Equality before
the law—United States.   3. Apathy.   I. Title.
KF8748.C25 2010
347.73'26—dc22   2010012551

9 8 7 6 5 4 3 2 1
Printed in the United States of America
on acid-free paper

To my parents, John C. Calhoun Jr. and Ruth Huston Calhoun
I am forever grateful for your love and guidance

CONTENTS

A NOTE ON FORMAT

I have attempted to avoid burdening and diverting readers with voluminous footnote references. Brief footnote citations do accompany specific quotations and case references in each chapter, but readers who wish to delve more deeply into scholarly opinion relevant to a given chapter's themes should consult the bibliographic essays at the end of the book.

ACKNOWLEDGMENTS

The faculties of the University of Colorado and the University of Denver law schools hosted presentations of ideas developed in *Losing Twice*, as did the University of Colorado Center for Conflict Research and the Center for the Humanities and Arts. I thank them for engaging with my arguments and for their helpful suggestions. I also thank the University of Colorado Law School for indispensable research support.

Many colleagues have encouraged my work, but I especially recognize Jim Nickel, who has cheerfully helped me sort through ideas; Pierre Schlag and Ahmed White, who led faculty workshops on portions of the manuscript; Nan Goodman, whose enthusiasm for the field of rhetoric could not be resisted; Martha Fineman, whose generous advice on the publishing world was instrumental in moving the book project along; and Jane Thompson for exceptional research support.

I am indebted to students who have pitched in with assistance over the years. For contributions to the final stages of my project, I gratefully acknowledge Anna Gerlings, Natalie Stephenson, Jennifer McDonald, Paris Nelson, Alaina Stedillie, Sarah Novotny, and Anna Dronzek. Carin Ramirez and Jessica Anderson have my special thanks for last-minute assistance. I also thank Barbara Cooper who helped prepare the manuscript for publication.

Family enthusiasm has been steadfast. Thank you, Robert, for listening to me work through various versions of the arguments presented here, for patiently enduring the last few months of writing, and for suggesting a good title.

Finally, many thanks are owed to Cecelia Cancellaro for her initial faith in my voice and my ideas.

Losing Twice

Loving Three

Introduction

Losing Twice in Constitutional Rights Disputes

Losing Twice is about the people involved in the constitutional rights disputes that reach the Supreme Court of the United States. It is about justices who resolve rights disputes and about the losing stakeholders whose interests, values, and constitutional arguments justices reject. Most importantly, it is about the obligations of justices to avoid and ameliorate harm to losing stakeholders, the consequences of justices' failure to satisfy their obligations, and the enhancement of the Court's legitimacy when these obligations are fulfilled. It adds a missing, personalized perspective to the jurisprudential rhetoric and framework through which the role of the Court has been debated in recent years.

Harm-avoidance and harm-amelioration obligations of justices of the Supreme Court derive from a classically liberal view of the proper relationship between government and citizen. Because they are informed by an ethical sensibility rather than abstract jurisprudential theory, however, the obligations cannot facilely be categorized as either politically liberal or conservative. People owe harm-avoidance and harm-amelioration obligations to other people, not to liberal or conservative interests or philosophies. If the obligations are not satisfied, people—not political interests or issues—experience injustice. As you will see, no judicial philosophy immunizes any given justice against neglecting the obligations to avoid and ameliorate harm to constitutional losers. Any justice's breach of obligations to constitutional losers adds the fuel of deeply felt personal outrage to the fire of philosophical debate about liberal or conservative interpretations of the Constitution.

We can each probably name at least one constitutional rights decision of which we intensely disapprove either for practical reasons or on grounds of principle. Some readers may strongly object to abortion on moral grounds and be offended by the protection given abortion in *Roe v. Wade*.[1] Others may approve of *Roe*'s outcome but decry the fact that some justices, dubious about how women might exercise their rights, seemed ultimately to entrust the decision to the judgment of physicians, while other justices seemed to believe that women require special protection as rights-holders. Some readers may be angered by *Bowers v. Hardwick*,[2] which suggested not only that a state may criminalize private homosexual behavior but also that those who engage in such conduct deserve to be treated as immoral political outcasts. Others may be appalled that justices in *Lawrence v. Texas*[3] subsequently opened the door to arguments that homosexuals have a right to civil marriage and its benefits. African Americans may react with disbelief to justices in *Parents Involved in Community Schools v. Seattle School District No. 1*,[4] who invoked *Brown v. Board of Education*[5] as a justification for limiting voluntary governmental efforts to prevent the racial re-segregation of public schools. Some may angrily accuse justices in *Grutter v. Bollinger*[6] of approving an affirmative action program that harms, rather than benefits, African American students. Voters outraged at justices' invalidation of restrictions on corporate electioneering in *Citizens United v. Federal Election Commission*[7] may demand a constitutional amendment negating the decision.

Although few if any of us have ever been a formal party to a constitutional rights dispute, we are often constitutional stakeholders in such controversies, and we are deeply affected by how the Supreme Court resolves them. When someone secures injunctive relief to desegregate a public school system, for example, anyone who has an interest in schools will be affected. If justices forbid one school district from basing decisions on race, their written decision will be read carefully and be relied on by state and federal judges as they resolve other disputes involving different governmental uses of race. Governmental bodies will reformulate their policies in anticipation of the broader application of a given decision. Public interest groups will develop issue or litigation campaigns responding to the decision. Assumptions about our future lives and our expectations of government will be affected by a decision's interpretational shadow.

Because we are often constitutional stakeholders, we are also, potentially, what this book terms "constitutional losers." If a decision adversely affects us, no one will be surprised if we react with disappointment, anger, or sometimes outrage at our loss. We overlook something important, however, if we fail to recognize that our outrage may stem from something more than justices' rejection of our preferred constitutional interpretation. We may be outraged because, in effect, we lose twice.

When justices resolve a rights dispute, they are in a position to inflict harms on constitutional losers that exceed the harm inherent in losing a substantive constitutional argument. Justices might, for example, write an opinion suggesting that constitutional losers do not count equally, or at all, as We the People of the United States. Their opinion might characterize constitutional losers as valueless, as persons whose consent does not matter to judicial legitimacy, as wrongdoers rather than worthy and respected proponents of non-frivolous constitutional arguments. In doing so, the opinion might naturally be read as an invitation to other members of the political community to treat the constitutional losers in a similarly dismissive fashion. Such an opinion, which harms the constitutional stature of the losers in a rights dispute, violates justices' obligations to citizens. It exacerbates the harm constitutional losers experience simply by virtue of ending up with the short end of the constitutional stick, and it will thus be a source of outrage for many.

That justices might exacerbate the harms of constitutional losers should be of concern to all of us. In 1803, in *Marbury v. Madison*,[8] Chief Justice John Marshall defended the power of constitutional judicial review by reminding us that civil liberty consists of the right of every individual to use the legal system to redress injury. If justices, whose constitutional legitimacy is linked to the power to remedy harm, instead exacerbate harm, we would be well advised to take a close look at the judicial practices that result in harm.

Justices take an oath of office to "faithfully and impartially discharge and perform all the duties incumbent" upon them,[9] an oath that reminds us that justices assume important obligations as they accept the privilege of exercising significant power in our lives.[10] In this book I argue that justices owe a duty to avoid and to ameliorate the serious harms individuals may suffer when they become constitutional losers. The duty arises out of the special, constitutional stature of citizens and the proper relationship between them and their government. It does not derive from a judge-made doctrine, such as judicial minimalism, or from a grand theory of constitutional interpretation, such as originalism. I do not challenge these theories as an "embarrassing failure,"[11] as Judge Richard Posner has done, but I do know that they omit an important, personalized perspective that should be included in jurisprudential debate.[12] Conventional theories operate from the top down and encourage debate dominated by members of the legal profession, attorneys, law professors, and judges. They keep citizens at the periphery of a discussion in which citizens should be central participants.

By focusing on justices' obligations to constitutional losers, *Losing Twice* hopes to engage ordinary citizens, as well as members of the legal profession, in a discussion of the legitimacy of judicial review. As justices reminded us in disputes involving the status and treatment of alleged enemy combatants, judicial review is inextricably entwined with the rule of law and a government of separated powers.[13] Active judicial involvement in rights disputing is thus a permanent although often contested feature of our constitutional life. You will surely want to be included in meaningful debates about judicial review if you believe—encouraged by the Declaration of Independence—that your consent lends government its legitimacy. You will want to know whether justices are properly satisfying their obligations to you and other citizens as they go about their business.

Contemporary debate about the legitimacy of judicial review is often grounded in accusations that liberal judges are activists who make, rather than apply, the law. We are told that federal judges engage in a *"fin-de-siècle* jurisprudence, where [a] court serves as nothing more than an ad hoc arbiter of issues it finds too difficult to decide in a principled way."[14] Over the years, however, most of us have come to see that charges of judicial activism might be leveled against conservative as well as more liberal members of the Court. A disdain for judicial activism, for example, did not prevent Justices Scalia and Thomas, in *Bush v. Gore,*[15] from assuming a pivotal role in the 2000 presidential election dispute. Neither has their professed disapproval of judicial review prevented them from voting to limit congressional power to criminalize the possession of guns near public schools,[16] create remedies for crimes of violence based on gender,[17] or protect religious groups against unduly burdensome regulations.[18] Despite the narrow text of the Eleventh Amendment to the Constitution,[19] conservative justices have expansively interpreted it; and in their interpretation of the Second Amendment they have given the Court broad judicial powers to nullify gun-control measures.[20] In *Grutter v. Bollinger,* Justice Thomas even bitterly denounced the Court's *refusal* to judicially intervene in university decisions; despite traditional deference to academic freedom, he wanted more rather than less judicial scrutiny of the University of Michigan's conduct.[21]

The truth is that accusations of judicial activism, whether by liberals or by conservatives, shed little light on the question of judicial legitimacy. *Losing Twice* therefore sets them aside in order to focus on a neglected but quite useful way of thinking about the work of Supreme Court justices. It explores our justices' obligations to avoid or ameliorate harm to constitutional losers.

Most of us conduct our affairs understanding that we should not inflict harm on another person. If we are indifferent to our obligation to avoid inflicting harm, we are held accountable for harms that we cause. We have adopted comprehensive regimes of legal liability to ensure that persons who suffer unjustified harm will receive some form of redress. A person who causes a car accident must pay for resulting injuries unless, perhaps, the accident resulted from an emergency response to unforeseeable conditions or occurred despite all reasonable efforts to avoid it. Society sometimes excuses the infliction of harm by persons who play a particularly valuable institutional or professional role, but only under carefully defined circumstances. In war, for example, a soldier is permitted to kill and even to cause what is euphemistically termed "collateral" damage to civilians. Similarly, a defense attorney may zealously defend a murderer although doing so may lead to the murderer's freedom and a risk to others.

Military, legal, and other professionals have developed comprehensive codes of ethics to help them properly perform the special functions and roles that risk inflicting harm. In addition, members of a profession learn about their powers and role responsibilities by living within a given professional world and observing how their colleagues resolve difficult ethical issues. Those of us living within the legal profession, for example, pay close attention to the practices of legal actors such as judges and attorneys. We know that law arises from—or, more strongly put, *is*—these practices, and that harm-inflicting practices can undermine the legitimacy of law itself. We also understand that there are not always clear-cut rules for deciding when and when not to excuse harmful professional practices. For example, legal professionals debate whether the duty of client confidentiality is an absolute imperative or a more forgiving, contextual standard. They disagree about whether (or when) a criminal defense attorney should breach client-confidentiality obligations if she knows that her client has committed a murder for which someone else was convicted.

Judges, whose harmful practices especially risk undermining the legitimacy of law and legal institutions, confront similar dilemmas. Consider, for example, the nineteenth-century controversy over Judge Edward Loring. Acting under the authority of the federal Fugitive Slave Law, which provided no meaningful protection against fraudulent claims of slave ownership, Judge Loring delivered an African American into the custody of a person claiming ownership. Judge Loring challenged neither the flaws in statutory procedure nor the "cruel fate" of those rendered to slave owners.[22] He envisioned his responsibility to be only that of "a professional evaluator of proof" under the rules set forth in the statute.[23] Loring's actions generated passionate debate among his professional contemporaries and within the community. Boston abolitionists were outraged that Loring had enforced an immoral law and had not ruled it unconstitutional.[24] As a result of pressure from the community, Loring lost his job as a lecturer at Harvard Law School and was removed from his position as a probate judge for the State of Massachusetts.[25] The propriety of his conduct continues to be a subject of debate.

Given the importance the legal profession ascribes to role obligations governing potentially harmful conduct by legal actors, it may surprise you to learn that Supreme Court justices are bound by few explicit rules of professional conduct. Federal statutes prohibiting conflicts of interest[26] and the Supreme Court's own recusal policy[27] have a limited scope. The Code of Conduct for United States Judges[28] does not apply to justices. The ABA Model Code of Judicial Conduct addressing judicial impartiality, integrity, and independence covers justices,[29] but it is not enforceable through normal disciplinary processes; adherence is dependent on the discretion of individual justices.[30] In cases of judicial misbehavior, we are more likely to speak about deprivations of due process than violations of role obligations relevant to the legitimacy of judicial review.[31] In any event, rules applicable to Supreme Court justices do not speak to harm avoidance or harm-amelioration obligations to constitutional losers.

Too often, majority justices—whether described as conservative, liberal, or somewhere in between—appear indifferent to the harms inflicted on constitutional losers. They act as if the harms to losers are of no more consequence, are no more susceptible to change, than is the blueness of the sky. At times they even suggest that harm inflicted on constitutional losers is in some way deserved, that no one should take the losers or their interests seriously, that the losers are no different from blameworthy parties in garden-variety personal-injury litigation or contract disputes. As a rule, justices do not reflect on the possibility that they might owe something—perhaps a form of compensation or restitution, perhaps an apology or even a simple expression of public remorse—to constitutional losers whose interests and values are sacrificed as rights disputes are resolved.

Constitutional losers deserve better. Cavalier attitudes regarding harms are at odds with what we typically expect from people or institutions that inflict harm. That constitutional losers may have lost a debate about constitutional meaning does not relieve justices of the obligations they owe to losers, as citizens.

Losing Twice explains justices' obligations to constitutional losers. Chapters 1 and 2 locate the obligations in a particular citizen-to-justice relationship and in the presumptively equal constitutional stature shared by all citizens. Chapter 3 offers examples of rights decisions in which justices' harmful assertions about the losers' constitutional stature were so intertwined with the analysis of the merits of the dispute that the legitimacy of the decision is in doubt. Chapter 4 explains why untruthfulness about what is at stake for constitutional losers undermines constitutional stature. The argument in these chapters is that untruthfulness and direct attacks on constitutional stature inflict harms that are, for the most part, avoidable, and that justices have an obligation to avoid harming constitutional losers.

Chapters 5 and 6 turn to the more complicated proposition that justices have an obligation to ameliorate the harm unavoidably inflicted on constitutional losers by virtue of their defeat. The argument is that justices' harm-amelioration obligation can be satisfied if they take steps to properly acknowledge harms to losers and to affirmatively honor losers' constitutional stature. Because the harm-amelioration obligation ensures that justices maintain a proper relationship with constitutional losers, the obligation should not be trivialized as requiring merely an effort to avoid hurting a loser's feelings. Moreover, justices should not attempt to excuse harm by arguing that "this is the way we've always done it" (as a colleague once said to me). Chapter 7 explores failures to satisfy harm-amelioration and harm-avoidance obligations in two well-known abortion rights decisions.

Suggestions for avoiding harm to constitutional stature and for ameliorating harms inherent in a loss may run up against countervailing ideological currents, personal predilections, and entrenched judicial traditions. The majority opinions of justices who properly ameliorate harms will certainly look somewhat different from those with which you may be familiar. Chapter 8 addresses these matters by considering the system of precedent that figures so significantly in rights disputes. Chapter 9 continues the discussion of judicial traditions and countervailing ideological currents by looking at recent Roberts Court decisions that inflict double losses and fail to recognize how the fulfillment of harm-avoidance and harm-amelioration obligations might enhance judicial legitimacy.

Despite judicial tradition and troublesome ideological predispositions, there is reason to hope that harm-avoidance and harm-amelioration obligations will be taken seriously by justices. As the infliction of harm is a concern within the legal profession, identifying and satisfying role obligations with regard to harm should be a matter of routine, internal housekeeping for justices. The housekeeping project has deep historical roots, derived from *Marbury v. Madison*, where Justice Marshall recognized that he might most effectively guard the Supreme Court's independence and legitimacy by basing his decision on adherence to the justices' oath of office. Moreover, the internal perspective of the housekeeping project shares a respected pedigree with other professions. Physicians, for example, debate whether they fulfill their oath to do no harm if they assist in the administration of the death penalty. Justices are unlikely to be indifferent to a project that is so widely recognized as important to the legal and other professions, especially if they can fulfill their obligations without necessarily altering the substantive outcome of any given rights controversy.

Indeed, justices concerned with their own legitimacy would be well served by working a perspective on harm-amelioration and harm-avoidance obligations into debates about judicial review. An understanding of the obligations is accessible to citizens. No advanced degree is required to identify examples of judicial harm *unnecessarily* inflicted on constitutional losers or to understand how that harm might be avoided. Even the more complicated subject of how to ameliorate harms that unavoidably inure to constitutional losers is not limited to the thin air of academic dispute, and citizen accessibility is no small matter. The founding generation reportedly believed that liberty would be better secured through "little cases, brought within reach of the least citizens daily . . . rather than by great proceedings to which one never has recourse."[32] Similarly, judicial legitimacy might be better attained through case-by-case fulfillment of basic obligations to citizens rather than through invocation of grand jurisprudential theories.

Throughout my career as a professor of law, I have been struck by the remarkable determination of my students to sustain their belief in the legitimacy of the Supreme Court and practices of judicial review, despite controversial decisions such as *Roe v. Wade, or Bush v. Gore, or Parents Involved in Community*

Schools v. Seattle School District No. 1. Many citizens share that determination. Their desire to move beyond cynical or hypocritical accusations of judicial activism reflects a sophisticated understanding of the importance of the Supreme Court within our constitutional system. It is to be encouraged.

Losing Twice is thus not intended as a lecture to justices. Its primary audience consists of ordinary citizens. It explores a personalized jurisprudence in a voice that emphasizes the relationship between justices and citizens, and real-world judicial practices and harms. By introducing a new discussion framework, it hopes to help citizens become more effective participants in the valuable and forever unfinished business of realizing our constitutional ideals.

As we become active participants in ensuring judicial legitimacy rather than confused eavesdroppers listening to theoretical, academic debate, we will improve our understanding of justices' obligations and of the qualifications we should insist on when presidents nominate and senators confirm future justices. We would do well, for example, to question the implications of familiar, throwaway assertions about the role of justices of the Supreme Court, for how we are often invited to see justices reflects neither the power they exercise nor the harm they are capable of inflicting.

Does it make sense, for example, to think of justices as mere "umpires" in something akin to an athletic contest? Chief Justice John Roberts once stated, "Judges are like umpires. Umpires don't make the rules, they apply them. The role of an umpire and a judge is critical. They make sure everybody plays by the rules, but it is a limited role."[33] And, he continued, "nobody ever went to a ball game to see the umpire."[34] Most of us, however, know that Judge Richard Posner is right when he says that balls and strikes may not exist unless and until an umpire calls them. Are the justices of the Supreme Court Roberts umpires or Posner umpires? Are justices properly invisible to us? In any event, is it through an analogy to a sporting event that we should define the obligations of justices to citizens in constitutional rights disputes?

Similarly, we might question the validity of Justice Scalia's view that justices are nothing more than technocratic lawyers who do "essentially lawyers' [interpretational] work up here [at the Court]," a type of work that will ensure that "the public [will] pretty much [leave] us alone."[35] In keeping with this idea, justices occasionally resort to technical analyses that would put Charles Dickens's fictional lawyers in *Jarndyce v. Jarndyce*[36] to shame.[37] But does it make sense to think of the Court as a mere collection of nine lawyers doing lawyers' work, or should we instead see them as individuals who have voluntarily accepted great power—and taken on correspondingly great responsibility—in our constitutional system? Should justices be left alone even if they are not invisible? Are justices who do not conform to Justice Scalia's prescribed role truly a dreaded "Imperial Judiciary?"[38] Might not judicial imperialism consist, instead, of a wish that justices should not have to suffer intrusive interactions with the public?

Losing Twice offers a new perspective on these questions, our justices, and the effect that their work has on us and, in particular, on constitutional losers. Readers tempted to take a firm, ideological stance against its arguments should first consider three simple queries: Why should justices not avoid inflicting avoidable harm on the constitutional stature of those who have been guilty of nothing more than failing to persuade a majority of justices to interpret the Constitution as the losers would have liked? Why is it not worthwhile for justices to undertake simple, case-by-case efforts to honor the losers' constitutional stature and thereby ameliorate the harm inherent in defeat? Why is it that constitutional losers must suffer a second loss at the hands of justices?

Understanding the significance of constitutional stature in rights disputes is central to these questions. With constitutional stature, therefore, we will begin.

Notes

1. Roe v. Wade, 410 U.S. 113 (1973).
2. Bowers v. Hardwick, 478 U.S. 186 (1986).
3. Lawrence v. Texas, 539 U.S. 558 (2003).
4. Parents Involved in Cmty. Sch. v. Seattle Sch. Dist. No. 1, 551 U.S. 701 (2007).
5. Brown v. Bd. of Educ., 347 U.S. 483 (1954).
6. Grutter v. Bollinger, 539 U.S. 306 (2003).
7. Citizens United v. Federal Election Comm'n, 130 S. Ct. 876 (2010).
8. Marbury v. Madison, 5 U.S. (1 Cranch) 137 (1803).
9. 28 U.S.C.A. § 453.
10. As RICHARD WEISBERG, POETHICS AND OTHER STRATEGIES OF LAW & LITERATURE 210 (1992), comments about Shakespeare's Shylock: "People need law, at least decent systems of law, implemented fairly and not by recourse to self-interest or arbitrary declaration. If Shylock's reliance on promise and oaths seems 'primitive,' we must understand that this reliance is his only protection—and it may be ours as well."
11. RICHARD A. POSNER, HOW JUDGES THINK 375 (2008).
12. DAVID LUBAN, LEGAL ETHICS AND HUMAN DIGNITY 105 (2007).
13. Hamdan v. Rumsfeld, 548 U.S. 557 (2006) (refusing to interpret the Detainee Treatment Act of 2005 to eliminate enemy combatant access to federal habeas review); Boumediene v. Bush, 553 U.S. 723 (2008) (refusing to permit Congress to abolish habeas review through the Military Commissions Act of 2006).
14. Charles Fried, Editorial, Courting Confusion, *N.Y. Times*, Oct. 21, 2004, at A29.
15. Bush v. Gore, 531 U.S. 98 (2001).
16. United States v. Lopez, 514 U.S. 549 (1995).
17. United States v. Morrison, 529 U.S. 598 (2000).
18. City of Boerne v. Flores, 521 U.S. 507 (1997).
19. U.S. CONST. amend. XI ("The Judicial power of the United States shall not be construed to extend to any suit in law or equity, commenced or prosecuted against one of the United States by Citizens of another State, or by Citizens or Subjects of any Foreign State.").
20. *See* District of Columbia v. Heller, 554 U.S. 570 (2008).
21. *Grutter*, 539 U.S. 306 (Thomas, J., concurring in part and dissenting in part).
22. Ruth Wedgwood, *Ethics under Slavery's Constitution: Edward Loring and William Wetmore Story*, 17 CARDOZO L. REV. 1865, 1867 (1996).
23. *Id.*
24. Paul Finkelman, *Legal Ethics and Fugitive Slaves: The Anthony Burns Case, Judge Loring, and Abolitionist Attorneys*, 17 CARDOZO L. REV. 1893 (1996).

25. *Id.*
26. 28 U.S.C. § 455(a).
27. Press Release, United States Supreme Court, Statement of Recusal Policy (Nov. 1, 1993), reprinted in RICHARD E. FLAMM, JUDICIAL DISQUALIFICATION: RECUSAL AND DISQUALIFICATION OF JUDGES 1068–70 (1st ed. 1996). The Statement of Recusal policy is referenced in Justice Scalia's refusal to recuse himself in Cheney v. United States District Court for the District of Columbia, 541 U.S. 913, 915 (2004), but was not mentioned in Chief Justice Rehnquist's public letter to Senator Patrick Leahy regarding the same matter. According to the letter, each justice decides the matter of recusal for himself. See http://news.findlaw.com/hdocs/docs/scotus/rehnquist12604ltr.html.
28. Available at http://www.uscourts.gov/guide/vol2/ch1.html.
29. MODEL CODE OF JUDICIAL CONDUCT Canon 1 (2007).
30. Debra Lyn Bassett, *Recusal and the Supreme Court*, 56 HASTINGS L.J. 657 (2005).
31. *See, e.g.,* Caperton v. A.T. Massey Coal Co., 129 S. Ct. 2252 (2009).
32. ALEXIS DE TOCQUEVILLE, DEMOCRACY IN AMERICA 98–99 (Harvey C. Mansfield & Delba Winthrop eds. & trans., Univ. of Chicago Press 2000).
33. *Confirmation Hearing on the Nomination of John G. Roberts Jr. to Be Chief Justice of the United States before the S. Comm. on the Judiciary,* 109th Cong. 55 (2005) (statement of John G. Roberts Jr.).
34. *Id.*
35. *Planned Parenthood,* 505 U.S. at 1000 (Scalia, J., concurring in part and dissenting in part).
36. CHARLES DICKENS, BLEAK HOUSE (Oxford Univ. Press 1948) (1852–53).
37. *See, e.g., Heller,* 554 U.S. 570.
38. *Planned Parenthood,* 505 U.S. at 996 (Scalia, J., concurring in part and dissenting in part).

Chapter 1

Constitutional Stature in Rights Disputes

The concept of constitutional stature is central to the personalized perspective of *Losing Twice*. A person enjoying full constitutional stature presumptively possesses the traits and capabilities of an iconic constitutional citizen as she enters a rights dispute. She enjoys a moral and political agency equal to that of other citizens, she is a constitutional leader equal to others who participate in developing constitutional meaning, and her consent to judicial review matters equally. If justices do not respect a constitutional loser's stature, they will unjustly inflict harm or will improperly exacerbate the harms inherent in losing a rights dispute.

We typically focus on disagreements about substantive constitutional meaning, not constitutional stature, when we think about rights disputes that find their way to the Supreme Court. These disagreements are not merely fact-based arguments about the application of unchallenged legal doctrine. Rather, they are about parties' contradictory visions and interpretations of the Constitution. They exist because someone's constitutional aspirations and beliefs do not coincide with prevailing traditions or because someone challenges the correctness of accepted constitutional meaning.

The Supreme Court's voting rights decisions involving the principle of equality illustrate how a substantive debate about constitutional meaning unfolds over time. Consider first the straightforward equality principle that government violates the Constitution if it denies a person the right to vote because of race. A more complicated version of the voting rights equality principle was eventually needed to address concerns that congressional electoral districts with disparate populations might unfairly penalize voters residing in the more populous districts. Thus, the Court held that, although malapportioned districts deny no qualified elector the right to cast a vote, they do violate a one-person, one-vote equality principle.[1] Still later, the Court held that districting practices that "dilute" the voting rights of minorities might also violate the constitutional equality principle.[2] Multi-member districts preventing the election of representatives preferred by racial minorities might be unconstitutional, and single-member districts might be required. More recently, the Court suggested that the equality principle prohibits districting practices that lead elected representatives to neglect the interests of a racially defined subset of their constituency.[3] The debate about the meaning of constitutional equality has also been extended to disputes arising out of rampant political gerrymandering, where justices continue to grapple with how best to define the constitutional principle of equality and its implementing doctrines.[4]

A second debate, about whether stakeholders in rights disputes should be accorded "full citizenship stature" under the Constitution,[5] frequently accompanies arguments about substantive constitutional meaning. As Justice Ginsburg once noted, in the course of invalidating Virginia Military Institute's male-only admissions policy, the constitutional stature argument is a "prime part of the history of our Constitution...[and part of] the story of the extension of constitutional rights and protections to people once ignored and excluded."[6]

Debates about constitutional stature often proceed under the radar, as unacknowledged influences on substantive constitutional debate. When they surface, however, they require us to pay attention to presumptions about citizens that lie at the heart of our system of government. Individuals who assert full constitutional stature, for example, will draw on widely shared understandings that all citizens are presumed to be equal moral and political agents, that each citizen's consent matters equally to governmental legitimacy, and that each is equally entitled to share in the benefits of our constitutional system. When justices undermine or fail to honor these understandings, they send a message that certain people do not "count as citizens in our American democracy equal in stature,"[7] do not "count" in "We the People,"[8] and do not enjoy "equal-citizenship stature."[9] Such a message exacerbates the harms inherent in losing a substantive constitutional argument about, for example, the right to vote, a right of privacy, or a right of free speech.

Because real people with concrete, personal interests assert constitutional rights claims, constitutional stature is potentially a factor in every rights dispute, and two types of arguments about constitutional stature are commonly made. A party may remind justices that she is presumptively equal to other citizens in all respects relevant to citizenship and is therefore entitled to the same rights other citizens have traditionally enjoyed. In the alternative, a party may argue that a presumption of full constitutional stature requires affirmation of a previously unrecognized right.

The civil rights rhetoric of Martin Luther King Jr., which insisted that African Americans should be recognized as having full constitutional stature and therefore should be entitled to traditional rights, illustrates the first type of argument. Dr. King's address to supporters of the Montgomery bus boycott, for example, commenced with the assertion "We are here in a general sense, because first and foremost—we are American citizens—and we are determined to apply our citizenship—to the fullness of its means."[10] Emphasizing that boycotters relied on traditional values to which the broader community professed adherence, King stated:

> I want it to be known throughout Montgomery and throughout this nation that we are Christian people.... If we were trapped in the dungeon of a totalitarian regime—we couldn't do this. But the great glory of American democracy is the right to protest for right.... There will be no crosses burned at any bus stops in Montgomery.... There will be no white persons pulled out of their homes and taken out on some distant road and murdered. There will be nobody among us who will stand up and defy the Constitution of this nation.[11]

In other words, King enthusiastically endorsed prevailing constitutional values and asked that they be extended to African Americans, who, he argued, should be recognized as fully equal citizens.

Abortion disputes illustrate how views of an individual's constitutional stature may affect justices' recognition of a new constitutional right, the second type of argument. In *Roe v. Wade*,[12] justices recognized a substantive right for women to choose whether to bear a child or to terminate a pregnancy. *Roe* justices, however, entertained some doubts about women's full constitutional stature. They were apparently able to set aside concerns that women might make capricious, immoral decisions regarding abortion only because they assumed that licensed physicians would act competently and in accord with professional responsibilities in considering abortion as a medical option. Later, in *Thornburgh v. American College of Obstetricians and Gynecologists*,[13] justices invalidated a statute that interfered with the integrity of women's deliberations about abortion, and rejected the views of dissenting justices whose analysis conveyed the impression that pregnancy transforms a woman into a diminished constitutional individual. In *Planned Parenthood v. Casey*,[14] justices clearly described women as individuals of full constitutional stature. *Planned Parenthood* justices emphasized that the right to choose an abortion is at "the heart of [women's] liberty,"[15] "within the zone of conscience and belief,"[16] and part of the "right to define one's own concept of...the mystery of human life,"[17] and one's own "personhood."[18] They accepted women as "reasonable people"[19] capable of making responsible decisions about matters of great personal and public import. Consistent with their respect for women's full constitutional stature, justices identified liberty, not privacy, as the relevant constitutional principle underlying women's right of choice. In 2007, in *Gonzales v. Carhart*,[20] however, justices returned to a diminished view of women as rights holders as they held that statutory limitations on a specified dilation and evacuation (D&E) abortion procedure were not facially unconstitutional. In the abortion decisions the existence and scope of women's constitutional right of autonomy is clearly dependent on justices' view of women's constitutional stature. If women's constitutional stature rests on shaky ground, so does their substantive right.

Because constitutional stature is such an important issue in rights disputing, we need a solid understanding of just what a person accorded full constitutional stature looks like. Consider three perspectives that together form a picture of such a person. One perspective draws on liberal philosophy, a second on a trust metaphor, and a third on a concept of constitutional leadership.

The perspective drawn from liberal philosophy is a key and obvious element in arguments about constitutional stature. It grounds our system of individual rights on the assumption that individuals are equally capable of reasoning about political and moral matters. It embodies a "political conception of human dignity."[21] *Planned Parenthood*'s portrayal of women comes from this tradition.

A second perspective views constitutional stature through the lens of a trust metaphor. When a trust is established, one person gives property to another, who is obligated to manage that property for the beneficiaries of the trust. Think of the founding generation as creators of an agreement, the Constitution of the United States, which entrusted powers over important parts of your life to the government. You and I, along with other citizens, are the intended beneficiaries of that trust. Moreover, without our consent, the trust agreement will dissolve. Viewing rights disputes through the trust metaphor, we will recognize persons accorded full constitutional stature both as equal beneficiaries of the constitutional trust and as powerful persons whose consent is essential to the continuation of the trust arrangement.

The idea of a trust relationship between government and its citizens is implicit in political arguments that were influential in the eighteenth century, and it easily maps onto two documents central to our constitutional history. Thomas Jefferson's Declaration of Independence, for example, was modeled after a traditional plea to English chancellors of equity, who described their powers as a public trust.[22] The Declaration complained of harms suffered because of a breach of governmental obligations, and it emphasized consent and equality concepts that are central to the trust metaphor. It declared, for example, that all men are created equal and that government derives its just powers from the consent of the governed.[23] The structure and language of our Constitution also support an understanding that we exist within a trust relationship with government. James Madison's system of representative government, for example, was intended to ensure that elected officials, like good trustees, would act on behalf of all citizen beneficiaries rather than partially, for factions.[24] The Constitution's Preamble, in extending blessings to "Posterity,"[25] reminds us that trust beneficiaries include not only the founding generation but also the contemporary community.

Throughout our history, we have benefited from the trusteeship terminology that enriched political discourse at the time our country came into being.[26] Post-Revolution charters of state government embody provisions reflecting the trust concept. Federal laws adopted after the Civil War, such as those extending voting rights and establishing the Freedmen's Bureau, rested on a principle of public trusteeship and the right of all citizens to share equally in the benefits of society. The trust concept is so widely shared that it is a familiar feature of "Letters to the Editor" complaining about government officials who exploit and abuse their power over private citizens. We are reminded that a trust relationship exists with justices of the Supreme Court when, in debates about nominees to the Court, pleas are made for the president and Congress to remember that the Court belongs to all citizens, not to a single party or ideological point of view.[27]

If consent and equality are important to constitutional stature, so is respect for citizen participation in processes that test the legitimacy of government. The third perspective on constitutional stature attests to this aspect of constitutional stature. It asks us to imagine that each citizen accorded full constitutional stature is a "constitutional leader"[28] having the capacity to reason about constitutional principle and value, to come to independent conclusions about the justice of existing political relationships, and to serve as an advocate for a proper understanding of the Constitution.

As Frederick Douglass recognized, our failure to fully realize a given constitutional ideal takes many forms at different times in history. He noted, for example that slavery might be "called by a great many names, and it will call itself by yet another name; and you and I and all of us had better wait and see what new form this old monster will assume, in what new skin this old snake will come forth."[29] Constitutional leaders represent all of us in debates about old snakes, like slavery, or deprivations of equality, or infringements of liberty or free speech, that appear in their new skins over time. Or, to use a different metaphor, constitutional leaders, like the mythical Sisyphus, roll their rock up the judicial hill, again and again, as fundamental constitutional questions surface and resurface, over time and in new and different configurations. They work to redeem the Constitution's meaning and governmental legitimacy by reminding justices of principles neglected in earlier rights disputes.[30] Citizens accorded full constitutional stature are seen as making valuable contributions to constitutional meaning.

As you might imagine from this description of constitutional leadership, persons accorded full constitutional stature do not expect to be accused of wrongfully participating in rights disputes, even if their arguments are novel and even if they ultimately fail to persuade justices to accept their understandings of the Constitution. They have simply requested the type of judicial review that goes hand in hand with the Supreme Court's power to decide specific cases[31] in concrete settings.[32] Fact-based, case-by-case decision making leaves plenty of room for arguments about old snakes that, in different times and contexts, raise their heads in new skins.

Indeed, although the notion might seem heretical, justices even encourage constitutional leaders to test and redeem constitutional meaning. Consider here only one of a variety of things that justices do to encourage constitutional leadership: justices frequently decide rights disputes by a close, five-to-four vote and explain those decisions in independent, concurring opinions that offer different explanations for a given outcome. Justices in *Regents of University of California v. Bakke*,[33] for example, determined that a university's special admissions program for admitting minorities into medical school violated the Equal Protection Clause. They could not agree on a justification for the decision, however, and as a result subsequent debate arose as to whether Justice Powell's concurring, swing-vote opinion should govern subsequent affirmative action disputes. The disagreement predictably festered for a number of years and eventually surfaced in two disputes involving affirmative action at the University of Michigan. In the Michigan cases, Justice O'Connor, the swing voter responsible for the Court's five-to-four approval of the University's law school affirmative action plan and five-four invalidation of its undergraduate plan, observed that Powell's opinion should perhaps not be treated as controlling.[34] Ironically, however, Justice O'Connor's voting behavior created further uncertainty about the status of affirmative action under the Constitution. Justice Scalia was moved to complain that her votes had resulted in a "split double-header...perversely designed to prolong the controversy and litigation" over affirmative action.[35] Justice Scalia then pointedly invited future litigants to tailor their disputes to gaps left in the Court's resolution of the Michigan disputes. In the very paragraph in which he disparaged the two University of Michigan decisions for their alleged propensity to prolong constitutional litigation,[36] Justice Scalia encouraged future constitutional leaders to take up the apparently unlitigated issue of whether diversity actually provides specific educational benefits.

Constitutional leaders also have room to perform their valuable role of testing governmental legitimacy and redeeming constitutional meaning because—judicial encouragement notwithstanding—it is simply not possible for justices to provide perfect answers in rights disputes. To paraphrase Alasdair MacIntyre, principles given minor weight in one context may become quite important in another because no court "can ever rule out the future possibility [that a given constitutional holding will be]...shown to be inadequate in a variety of ways."[37]

Even constitutional principles that we might assume to be unvarying are susceptible to some debate among constitutional leaders. A familiar example might be the pronouncement that racially segregated schools cannot be equal.[38] Today most people take as a given that separate schools can never be equal, but that principle has not been rigorously enforced when it comes to sex-segregated public schools. Moreover, the Court has acted in ways that suggest it might be prepared to qualify the separate-isn't-equal principle even in cases dealing with racial segregation. In *United States v. Fordice*,[39] for example, African Americans sued to end discrimination in Mississippi's system of higher education. Some members of the African American community, believing that it would be impossible to integrate Mississippi's system of higher education, argued that equality for African Americans would be best served if historically black institutions were preserved. They were willing to live with racially distinct institutions of higher education as long as all institutions were allocated equal state resources. When *Fordice* was initially decided, the Supreme Court formally refused to question *Brown*'s separate-isn't-equal principle,[40] even though its refusal threatened the potential closing of some of Mississippi's historically black colleges. The State of Mississippi, however, eventually reached an agreement that provided substantially more resources to historically black colleges and effectively accommodated the separate-can-be-equal contingent of the African American community.[41] Ultimately, the Court permitted that agreement to go into effect.[42] That the proposition that separate can never be constitutionally equal is up for debate is evident in the Court's recent decision in *Parents Involved*,[43] where justices engaged in a vigorous, even rancorous, debate about voluntary efforts to keep public schools from re-segregating along racial lines.

Other principles that we might wish to believe are absolute are similarly contestable. The constitutional prohibition on slavery embodied in the Thirteenth Amendment, for example, might produce debates about whether a conscripted member of the military, or a woman who becomes inextricably enmeshed in the brutal prostitution industry, is held in slavery. If you doubt the almost unlimited opportunities for constitutional leaders to make reasonable but debatable arguments, only note how difficult it can be to predict how the Supreme Court will resolve a given rights controversy. Readers may recall, for example, initial and erroneous predictions of how the Court might react to Colorado's Amendment 2, a voter-approved initiative that prohibited any branch of state government from responding to "claim[s] of discrimination" against homosexuals.[44] Many believed that existing equality doctrines did not encompass the claims made by those who challenged Amendment 2; others assumed that the Court would adhere to its earlier refusal in *Bowers v. Hardwick* to extend robust constitutional protections to homosexuals.[45] Nonetheless, the Court invalidated Amendment 2 in *Romer v. Evans*.[46] Readers also may recall the 2000 presidential election controversy that led to the decision in *Bush v. Gore*.[47] It was wrongly assumed by many experts that the Court would defer to state court interpretations of state election law and refuse to get involved in matters that might put the Court's legitimacy at risk. More recently, controversies have arisen out of the detention of alleged enemy combatants after September 11, which many believed would result in deference by the Court's conservative majority both to presidential war powers and to Congress's removal of habeas jurisdiction over detainees' lawsuits. In *Hamdi v. Rumsfeld*,[48] *Hamdan v. Rumsfeld*,[49] and *Boumediene v. Bush*,[50] however, the Court refused to immunize enemy combatant designations from judicial review.

There are indeed many opportunities for constitutional leaders to make reasonable arguments about constitutional meaning, and the fact that constitutional leaders become constitutional losers does not transform them into wrongdoers. Consider, for example, a typical affirmative action dispute such as the Michigan controversy in *Grutter v. Bollinger*.[51] Barbara Grutter, a hard-working, white woman who had done quite well as an undergraduate student, wished to attend law school at the University of Michigan. When denied admission, she challenged the law school's affirmative action admissions program. To all appearances, Grutter had done nothing that could be construed as racist. She certainly was not personally responsible for the lingering effects of historical racism that continue to disadvantage African Americans and members of other minority groups. Similarly, members of racial minority groups on whose behalf the University of Michigan had adopted its affirmative action policies were innocent of personal wrongdoing. They also simply wanted to attend a good law school. The University of Michigan, a defendant in *Grutter*, has a corporate life that extends back in time and almost surely once participated in or supported at least some practices that disadvantaged racial minorities, but current officers and faculty of the university defended, as sincere constitutional leaders, their affirmative action plans as good efforts to prevent discrimination. They, no less than Barbara Grutter or members of minority groups, were due respect as they pressed the Court to adopt their preferred interpretation of the Constitution.

If justices are to accord persons full constitutional stature, they must recognize that even constitutional losers are innocent and worthy participants in an ongoing project to redeem constitutional meaning, are equal moral and political agents, are citizens whose consent matters equally to governmental legitimacy, and are equal beneficiaries of a constitutional trust relationship with justices. Unsuccessful advocacy in a rights dispute should have no necessarily adverse effect on constitutional stature. The point is crucial, for, as the history of rights litigation attests, wins and losses in rights disputes are fundamentally contingent: no stakeholder can always count on being a winner, and no one is forever consigned to the status of loser. In some rights decisions, however, justices not only reject a constitutional loser's arguments about constitutional meaning; they also inappropriately attack or undermine the loser's constitutional stature.

The many ways in which a given judicial opinion can diminish the constitutional stature of losers will become clearer once we have more fully explored the consent and equality expectations of justices that each citizen stakeholder in a constitutional rights dispute might reasonably have. Those expectations are the subject of the next chapter.

Notes

1. Baker v. Carr, 369 U.S. 186 (1962).
2. White v. Regester, 412 U.S. 755 (1973).
3. Shaw v. Reno, 509 U.S. 630 (1993).
4. See, e.g., Vieth v. Jubelirer, 541 U.S. 267 (2004); League of United Latin American Citizens v. Perry, 548 U.S. 399 (2006).
5. United States v. Virginia, 518 U.S. 515, 532 (1996).
6. *Id.* at 557.
7. *Id.* at 545.
8. Tennessee v. Lane, 541 U.S. 509, 536 (2004) (Ginsburg, J., concurring).
9. Id.
10. TAYLOR BRANCH, PARTING THE WATERS: AMERICA IN THE KING YEARS 1954–63, 138–39 (1988).
11. Id. at 140.
12. Roe v. Wade, 410 U.S. 113 (1973).
13. Thornburgh v. Am. Coll. of Obstetricians & Gynecologists, 476 U.S. 747 (1986).
14. Planned Parenthood of Se. Pa. v. Casey, 505 U.S. 833 (1992).
15. *Id.* at 851.
16. *Id.* at 852.
17. *Id.*
18. *Id.*
19. *Id.* at 853.
20. Gonzales v. Carhart, 550 U.S. 124 (2007). This decision will be discussed at more length in chapters 3 and 7.
21. W. Bradley Wendel, *Legal Ethics as "Political Moralism" or The Morality of Politics*, 93 CORNELL L. REV. 1413, 1420 (2009).
22. PETER CHARLES HOFFER, THE LAW'S CONSCIENCE: EQUITABLE CONSTITUTIONALISM IN AMERICA 42, 71–72 (1990).
23. See THE DECLARATION OF INDEPENDENCE (U.S. 1776).
24. THE FEDERALIST No. 10, at 63 (James Madison) (Edward Gaylord Bourne ed., 1901) (arguing that elected representatives should not use their powers on behalf of factions "adversed to the rights of other citizens, or to the permanent and aggregate interests of the community").
25. U.S. CONST. pmbl.
26. HOFFER, *supra* note 22, at 46.
27. *Confirmation Hearing on the Nomination of Samuel A. Alito Jr. to Be an Associate Justice of the Supreme Court of the United States before the S. Comm. on the Judiciary*, 109th Cong. 5 (2006) (statement of Sen. Patrick Leahy).
28. DAVID A. J. RICHARDS, CONSCIENCE AND THE CONSTITUTION: HISTORY, THEORY, AND THE LAW OF THE RECONSTRUCTION AMENDMENTS 257 (1993).
29. Frederick Douglass, *Speech to the American Anti-Slavery Society*, in THE AMERICAN READER: WORDS THAT MOVED A NATION 154, 156 (Diane Ravitch ed., 1990).
30. Cf. WILLIAM H. SIMON, THE PRACTICE OF JUSTICE: A THEORY OF LAWYERS' ETHICS 102 (1998) (describing how Frederick Douglass approached the issue of slavery and the status of African Americans under the Constitution).

31. Marbury v. Madison, 5 U.S. (1 Cranch) 137 (1803).
32. OWEN FISS, THE LAW AS IT COULD BE 8–9 (2003).
33. Regents of Univ. of Cal. v. Bakke, 438 U.S. 265 (1978).
34. Grutter v. Bollinger, 539 U.S. 306 (2003); Gratz v. Univ. of Mich., 539 U.S. 244 (2003).
35. *Grutter*, 539 U.S. at 348 (Scalia, J., dissenting).
36. *Id.* at 348–49.
37. ALASDAIR MACINTYRE, WHOSE JUSTICE? WHICH RATIONALITY? 361 (1988).
38. Brown v. Bd. of Educ., 347 U.S. 483 (1954).
39. United States v. Fordice, 505 U.S. 717 (1992).
40. *Id.* at 721.
41. See Mississippi Desegregation Suit Settled for $500 Million, WASH. POST, April 24, 2001, at A1.
42. Ayers v. Thompson, 543 U.S. 951 (2004).
43. Parents Involved in Cmty. Sch. v. Seattle Sch. Dist. No. 1, 551 U.S. 701 (2007).
44. COLO. CONST. art. II, § 30 (b).
45. Bowers v. Hardwick, 478 U.S. 186 (1986) (discussed at length in chapter 4).
46. Romer v. Evans, 517 U.S. 620 (1996).
47. Bush v. Gore, 531 U.S. 98 (2000).
48. Hamdi v. Rumsfeld, 542 U.S. 507 (2004).
49. Hamdan v. Rumsfeld, 548 U.S. 557 (2006).
50. Boumediene v. Bush, 553 U.S. 723 (2008).
51. *Grutter*, 539 U.S. 306.

Chapter 2

Constitutional Stature: Equality and Consent Expectations

In rights disputes, justices who call a loser's constitutional stature into question inflict significant harm. It is a serious failure of obligation, for example, for justices to write opinions that undermine a loser's equal moral and political agency, or a loser's claim to an equal share in a constitutional trust corpus. If justices' opinions do not respect a constitutional loser's power to withhold or grant consent to the constitutional trust agreement, a similarly serious failure has occurred. To suggest that constitutional losers forfeit their stature improperly gives judicial imprimatur to the view that losing stakeholders have a diminished and unequal place in our political community. The severity of such harms is best understood as a consequence of legitimate but unsatisfied consent and equality expectations held by constitutional losers' claiming full constitutional stature.

Before turning to examples of two rights decisions in which justices obviously harmed the constitutional stature of losing stakeholders, we would be well advised to think more deeply about the reasonable equality and consent expectations linked to constitutional stature. If we fully understand the traits and capabilities with which each of us, as a citizen, is presumptively endowed, we will be able to articulate reasons for the special outrage we sometimes experience as a constitutional loser. Only then will we be prepared to offer practical suggestions for ensuring that judicial opinions do not inflict double losses on losing stakeholders.

Consider first equality, which seems to be a rather uncomplicated concept. You have already been introduced to citizens' presumptively equal moral and political agency. The Declaration of Independence reflects this equality principle in its assertion that we are all "created equal."[1] As Alexis de Tocqueville once observed, citizens of the United States assume that "each individual ... [has been endowed with] the degree of reason necessary for him to be able to direct himself."[2] Although many people, such as women and African Americans, were treated quite unequally when the Declaration was issued, citizens take seriously

23

the affirmation of inherent equality. Over the years, we have incrementally redeemed the affirmation, and we can now accurately state that the presumed equal moral and political capacity of all citizens is a working principle of our government. In the language of the Supreme Court, citizens of the United States are recognized as "joint and equal sovereigns."[3]

A somewhat different expectation of equality is embodied in the promise of "Equal Justice Under Law," which is inscribed on the building in which the justices of the Supreme Court do their business, and in the judicial oath of office, which requires justices to do "equal right" and to discharge their duties impartially. We can easily recognize this equality expectation in Supreme Court decisions addressing access to courts. In *Romer v. Evans*, for example, Justice Kennedy concluded that Colorado's Amendment 2 was unconstitutional, in part because it prevented homosexuals from claiming judicial protection against arbitrary treatment.[4] According to Kennedy, Amendment 2's treatment of homosexuals was inconsistent with "the principle that government and each of its parts remain open on impartial terms to all who seek its assistance."[5] When the rights of citizens are at stake, he said, the Constitution "neither knows nor tolerates classes among citizens."[6] Similarly, Justice Kennedy's concurring opinion in *Vieth v. Jubelirer*[7] was premised on equality expectations regarding judicial access. Although some justices would have declared federal courts out of bounds to citizens with political gerrymandering claims, thus creating a discrete group of permanent citizen losers, Kennedy refused to do so. Recognizing that the particulars of a constitutional claim may differ depending on their factual records or current technological achievement, Kennedy stated that "[it] is not in our tradition to foreclose the judicial process…where it is alleged that a constitutional right is burdened or denied."[8] Notwithstanding occasional grumblings like those of plurality justices in *Vieth*, justices from very different ends of the political spectrum would surely agree, in principle, that they must give all citizens equal and impartial access to the judicial forum.

Losing Twice is concerned with equality in relation to the written opinions through which justices announce their decisions in rights disputes, and it is perhaps not immediately obvious how straightforward equal-treatment principles might apply to judicial opinions. We know that it is impossible for everyone to prevail in a rights dispute and, because someone must lose, an expectation of equality of outcomes is unrealistic. We also know that citizens are a heterogeneous group. They will inevitably disagree about constitutional meaning and about which interests are sufficiently valuable to be given constitutional protection. It would, therefore, be unrealistic to expect justices to resolve rights disputes in ways that satisfy us all, equally. It would not be unreasonable, however, for constitutional losers to expect justices to write opinions that manifest a respect for the equal moral and political agency of losers. Similarly, it would not be unreasonable to expect opinions to equally respect the contributions losers have made as constitutional leaders to constitutional meaning.

A conception of equality relevant to these expectations can be derived from James Madison, who believed that elected representatives should neither act as captured agents of "factions" nor use their powers "adverse[ ] to the rights of other citizens, or to the permanent and aggregate interests of the community."[9] Madison envisioned governmental structures that would make it difficult for elected officials to disregard the interests of, or to impose unequal burdens on, a subset of the political community. Citizens might thus expect "to have their interests valued equally with those of all other citizens" in the representative process[10] by officials acting in furtherance of what Madison labeled a "communion of interests."[11] Early in our constitutional history, the Supreme Court seemed to echo these sentiments, in asserting that "the [C]onstitution of the United States was designed for the common and equal benefit of all the people of the United States" and that "the judicial power was granted for the same benign and salutary purposes."[12] Any governmental institution, including the judiciary, which is captured or owned by a discrete subset of citizens would be incompatible with the communion-of-interests equality principle.

Of course, as a practical matter, the communion of interests is difficult to achieve. There is good reason to doubt that all interests and values of citizens in our pluralistic society are equally taken into account by government, that burdens are equally shared by a "democratic majority [that accepts]...what they impose [on others],"[13] or that elected officials equally subject themselves to laws governing ordinary citizens. Nonetheless, the equality aspiration is important, and justices of the Supreme Court have acknowledged its validity.

Justices, for example, made an effort to give the communion-of-interests equality principle meaning in *Shaw v. Reno*,[14] an important voting rights decision. In *Shaw*, white voters had challenged a racially gerrymandered electoral district designed to benefit African American voters. Because the districting scheme did not deny any white person a right to vote on the basis of race and did not dilute the political strength of white voters as a group, no recognized constitutional doctrine of equality applied to the white voters' claim. Nonetheless, justices determined that the districting scheme violated the "representative" ideal of the Constitution, the expectation that elected officials should serve all of their constituents rather than some factional subset.[15] The challenged district, said Justice O'Connor, had been "created solely to effectuate the perceived common interests of one racial group," and, as a result, elected officials were "likely to believe that their primary obligation [was] to represent only the members of that group, rather than their constituency as a whole."[16] According to O'Connor, such an effect on elected officials "is altogether antithetical to our system of representative democracy."[17] *Shaw* held, in effect, that equality under the Constitution embodies an obligation of elected representatives to listen to all constituents and forbids governmental structures captive to the interests of a faction of citizens.

Justices have adopted a number of doctrines or principles intended to identify instances in which elected officials have paid insufficient attention to the communion of interests. When laws embody race- or sex-based classifications and raise suspicions that legislators are captive to only a faction of citizens, for example, the Court requires a state to show a compelling justification for the laws. In the absence of a compelling justification, even a law adopted by a legitimate majority vote is unconstitutional. Some justices have expressly applied the communion-of-interests equality principle to themselves. In *Planned Parenthood v. Casey*,[18] for example, justices affirming *Roe v. Wade* asserted that they had an obligation to act on behalf of the nation as opposed to any faction in the abortion debate.[19]

What if we applied the communion-of-interests equality principle to opinions written by justices in rights disputes? What if we took seriously the metaphorical proposition that persons accorded full constitutional stature—including constitutional losers—are equal beneficiaries and owners of a trust corpus of Supreme Court decisions interpreting the Constitution? What would be required of justices to write opinions that even constitutional losers might recognize as belonging to Cicero's res publica, the property of the People, rather than to a special faction or subset of the political community? A few, preliminary possibilities suggest themselves.

Drawing on the concept of constitutional leadership, we might expect justices to give equal respect to all stakeholders who contributed to the constitutional meaning inscribed within it and who therefore have an ownership claim to it. You will recognize what a creator's claim to equal ownership might look like in the words of George Vaughn, who once closed a Supreme Court oral argument against racial discrimination in property transactions with the following words:

> Now I've finished my legal argument, but I want to say this before I sit down. In this Court, this house of the law, the Negro today stands outside, and he knocks on the door, over and over again, he knocks on the door and cries out, "Let me in, let me in, for I too have helped build this house."[20]

In exercising their presumptively equal capacity to discern and advocate for particular constitutional meanings, constitutional leaders help us define ourselves as citizens and as a nation. Those who challenge and those who defend the status quo, those who win and those who lose rights disputes, have built the resulting Supreme Court decision and have an equal ownership claim to it.

The principle of equal ownership is straightforward, but constitutional winners and losers are in a very different and unequal position when it comes to asserting their ownership claims to judicial opinions. Constitutional winners assert ownership of decisional law in familiar ways. Because declared constitutional meaning by definition reflects the interests and values of winners, winners easily claim favorable decisions as theirs. They rely on such decisions as controlling precedent in other rights disputes. Favorable decisions are a resource that winners also exploit in legislative and political debate and in daily activities that reinforce winners' values.

Constitutional losers are obviously unable to assert ownership in the foregoing fashion. If they are to be equal owners of decisional law in a way that comports with their constitutional stature, therefore, justices will need to take affirmative steps to facilitate meaningful ownership claims by citizens who have lost in constitutional debate. For example, justices might carefully craft opinions to honor the losers' constitutional stature. Such opinions would give constitutional losers some ability to use even unfavorable decisional law as a resource by acknowledging the legitimacy of the losers' continued participation in future debates about constitutional meaning. Or, justices might take pains to include in their opinions an accurate and respectful account of the values and views that, from the losers' perspective, shaped a decision. Constitutional losers could then draw on such an account to encourage others to pay attention to their values and interests in nonjudicial settings. Justices must at least give constitutional losers an ownership stake sufficient to enable losers to bring a decision into their lives, to recognize that it has the authority of law, and to base their actions on what it says.

Subsequent chapters will develop these and other ideas related to equality. For now, simply keep in mind this way of thinking about our equality expectations and constitutional stature, in relation to judicial opinions, as we turn to consent expectations.

As a general proposition, the consent expectations of persons who enjoy full constitutional stature are embodied in the familiar mantra that governmental legitimacy rests on the consent of the governed. But what consent expectations about decisional law can citizens reasonably have of justices? In resolving rights disputes, justices are supposed to be independent of the political processes through which consent is typically given or withheld from government. And, if our consent expectations are legitimate, how do we give or withhold consent to pronouncements of justices that tell us what the Constitution means?

Citizen consent expectations are as complicated as their equality expectations, so we need to think outside the box. We must not define consent literally, any more than we do when we talk about government by the consent of the governed in the political branches. I doubt, for example, that any one of us has actually consented to any given piece of legislation. We elect representatives by (typically) a majority vote, and those representatives, in turn, adopt statutes by (typically) a majority vote. If all processes work as intended, we choose to act as if legislative outcomes reflect the actual consent of each of us. In other words, we have decided as a nation that procedural regularity in the political branches, backed up by judicial checks on abuses of majority power, sufficiently honors our constitutional stature as joint and equal sovereigns in our representative democracy. The question is whether there is a similarly sufficient, albeit imperfect, means of assuring that judicial processes satisfy consent expectations linked to constitutional stature.

Although unelected justices have no immediately obvious, procedural way of supporting a claim that they act—either in specific cases or in their general practice of judicial review—with our consent, they nonetheless apparently agree that consent expectations apply to the judicial as well as to the political branches of government. Justices rely, for example, on a variety of discretionary abstention doctrines to help them avoid becoming involved in highly charged constitutional disputes with the potential to generate attacks on their legitimacy. They also resort to various prudential standing doctrines, and even a version of the political question doctrine that counsels judges not to become involved in controversial "political thickets."[21] Avoidance doctrines, however, are an imperfect response to consent expectations, because closing the courthouse door to controversial rights disputes likely retains the consent of only that faction of citizens who are happy with the status quo. Other citizens, those who wish to debate constitutional meaning but who are denied a hearing, will believe that justices have not honored consent expectations or constitutional stature.

Another imperfect approach to consent expectations is a rigid originalist method of constitutional interpretation. A justice committed to originalism will claim that judicial legitimacy derives from consent given at the time the Constitution or any of its amendments were adopted. The difficulty is that the consent of significant groups of citizens was irrelevant when much of our Constitution was ratified. We know, for example, that the original constitutional ratification process excluded women, most members of racial minorities, and even many people who did not own property.

Even more problematic is that strict originalism results in opinions that deprive contemporary citizens of full constitutional stature. In contrast to constitutional avoidance doctrines, strict originalism neglects the Court's need to secure the consent of contemporary generations to its practices and decisions. It thus threatens significant harm to the constitutional stature of those who believe that they are joint and equal sovereigns. Although justices are in charge of interpreting the Constitution and they are ultimately free to define away the relevance of contemporary consent, they behave unwisely if they do. The constitutional trust was first established through the consent of persons living in 1789, but it would surely dissolve—with the proverbial whimper or in Jeffersonian revolution—without the acquiescence of contemporary citizens. As justices writing the joint opinion in *Planned Parenthood* noted, "Our Constitution is a covenant running from the first generation of Americans to us and then to future generations.... [Its] written terms embody ideas and aspirations that must survive more ages than one."[22]

Perhaps because citizen consent expectations are so difficult to satisfy, justices often seem to try to shore up their legitimacy by including highly rationalized and technical constitutional analyses in their written opinions. In *Vieth v. Jubelirer*, for example, Justice Scalia argued that the Court should protect itself and its legitimacy by ensuring that decisional law be "principled, rational, and based upon reasoned distinctions."[23] In *Hein v. Freedom from Religion Foundation*, he firmly linked the rule of law to a "surrender to logic."[24] There is, however, no necessary cause-and-effect relationship between technical rationality and citizen consent expectations. Indeed, technical rationality conveys a sense of authority at odds with the understanding that legitimacy claims based on something other than actual consent are fragile. Liberal philosophers, for example, do not equate rationality and consent, nor do they believe that a technically rational resolution of a given dispute can relieve a court of its obligation to seek consent.

Many of us may have experienced the inability of technical rationality to satisfy our consent expectations or the expectations of anyone who is not predisposed to accept a particular outcome. A number of scholars have pointed to the failure of technical rationality to secure general acceptance of the outcome in *Brown v. Board of Education*.[25] The best recent example of the inability of technical rationality to serve as a substitute for consent may be *District of Columbia v. Heller*,[26] which recognized an individual right to gun possession. The *Heller* decision was cloaked in robes of technical logic pertaining to the text of the Second Amendment.[27] Ordinary citizens—not to mention a law professor—would understandably be mystified and unpersuaded by the hyper-technical, linguistic analysis that purported to resolve significant questions about constitutional meaning in *Heller*. As Owen Fiss once said about an earlier Supreme Court decision, the analysis "trivialize[d] and distort[ed] the judicial task."[28]

Subsequent chapters will more comprehensively explore practices that would help justices properly respond to consent expectations, but for now we might note at least a few attitudinal shifts that would be constructive. Justices might, for example, choose to follow the lead of liberal philosophers whose solution to the consent issue associates legitimacy with continuing conversations among equals about contested matters. In the view of these philosophers, decisions are legitimate only if justified by reasons of the sort that could be accepted by every person (who is presumed to possess equal reasoning capacities to all others) over time and as debates continue. If that view were accepted, justices would strive to write opinions reflecting an understanding that legitimacy requires but is not satisfied by hypertechnical reasoning. Justices might keep in mind the important principle that citizens are joint and *equal* sovereigns as, for example, they develop and apply discretionary avoidance doctrines such as abstention so as to better respect consent expectations of all citizens.

Writing an opinion that fulfills consent and equality expectations of losing stakeholders of full constitutional stature is an undeniably daunting task, as the following chapters will attest, yet it is one that justices cannot rightly shirk. The issue of constitutional stature instrinsic to rights disputes significantly raises the stakes for all stakeholders, and if justices pay insufficient attention to the issue they fail to satisfy an obligation that is essential to their legitimacy.

We can take some comfort in the fact that justices acknowledge both the importance of equality and consent expectations and their bearing on judicial legitimacy. It also bodes well that justices do not always define these expectations formally or literally. Equality, for example, embraces both a baseline expectation that justices will treat us equally, and the more conceptually complex idea that government works for a communion of interests. As for consent, the principle of joint and *equal* citizen sovereignty suggests that justices must respect the consent expectations of all citizens, both constitutional losers and constitutional winners, in deploying their imperfect substitutes for attaining actual consent. It is reassuring that, although justices have not yet succeeded— and quite likely will never succeed—in perfectly satisfying equality and consent expectations, they nonetheless have not abandoned the aspiration.

There is, however, much more work to be done. Justices do not deeply explore or consistently attend to citizen equality and consent expectations. For example, justices may occasionally accuse one another of being illegitimately beholden only to a subset of citizens—to majority public opinion[29] or to a potent gun lobby[30]—but their accusations are not grounded in a discussion of equality that draws on the communion of interests. Moreover, justices who link equality expectations to the communion of interests in one decision have been known to abandon the concept in another. In *Shaw v. Reno*,[31] Justice Scalia joined Justice O'Connor's opinion, which developed new understandings of the complex nature of the right to vote in a racial gerrymandering dispute and endorsed a constitutional understanding of equality linked to the communion of interests.[32] In *Vieth v. Jubelirer*, however, he argued that justices should absolutely preclude discussion of similar equality claims raised in the context of political gerrymandering.[33]

Most important, justices responsible for inflicting harm on constitutional losers, that is, justices who are not dissenters, simply do not pay sufficient attention to the losing stakeholders in rights disputes. Constitutional losers become the concern of only dissenting justices. Even when justices directly address values potentially associated with losing claims, they do not link their remarks to the constitutional stature of or their obligations to losing stakeholders. Consider, as an example, Justice O'Connor's argument in *BE & K Construction Co. v. NLRB*, which recognized that the Constitution protects the right of all persons to petition courts, that even unsuccessful lawsuits advance important interests, and that losers should not be sanctioned simply because they have lost.[34] O'Connor noted that losing constitutional claims "allow the public airing of disputed facts...and raise matters of public concern,"[35] that they "promote the evolution of the law by supporting the development of legal theories that may not gain acceptance the first time around,"[36] and that keeping the judicial doors open to potential losers "adds legitimacy to the court system as a designated alternative to force."[37] Her comments, although important, did not extend to recognition of the judicial obligations that flow from the constitutional stature of losing stakeholders.

As it now stands, persons who assume the mantle of constitutional leadership in a rights dispute put themselves at risk of suffering significant and unjust harm. Two decisions in which that risk became reality are the subject of the next chapter.

Notes

1. THE DECLARATION OF INDEPENDENCE para. 2 (U.S. 1776).
2. ALEXIS DE TOCQUEVILLE, DEMOCRACY IN AMERICA 381 (Harvey C. Mansfield & Delba Winthrop eds. & trans., Univ. of Chicago Press 2000).
3. Chisholm v. Georgia, 2 U.S. 419, 477 (1793).
4. Romer v. Evans, 517 U.S. 620 (1996).
5. *Id.* at 633.
6. *Id.* at 623 (quoting Plessy v. Ferguson, 163 U.S. 537, 559 (1896) (Harlan, J., dissenting)).
7. Vieth v. Jubelirer, 541 U.S. 267 (2004).
8. *Id.* at 309 (Kennedy, J., concurring).
9. THE FEDERALIST No. 10 at 63 (James Madison) (Edward Gaylord Bourne ed., 1901).
10. Rebecca L. Brown, *Liberty, The New Equality*, 77 N.Y.U. L. REV. 1491, 1497 (2002).
11. *Id.* (citing James Madison).
12. Martin v. Hunter's Lessee, 14 U.S. 304, 348 (1816).
13. Cruzan v. Dir., Mo. Dep't of Health, 497 U.S. 261, 300 (1990) (Scalia, J., concurring).
14. Shaw v. Reno, 509 U.S. 630 (1993).
15. *Id.* at 648–49.
16. *Id.* at 648.
17. *Id.*
18. Planned Parenthood of Se. Pa. v. Casey, 505 U.S. 833 (1992).
19. *Id.* at 851.
20. Quoted in Philip Elman & Norman Silber, *The Solicitor General's Office, Justice Frankfurter, and Civil Rights Litigation, 1946–1960: An Oral History*, 100 HARV. L. REV. 817, 820 (1987).
21. District of Columbia v. Heller, 554 U.S. 570, 128 S. Ct. 2784, 2846 n.39 (2008).
22. *Planned Parenthood*, 505 U.S. at 901.

23. *Vieth*, 541 U.S. at 278 (2004).

24. Hein v. Freedom from Religion Foundation, 551 U.S. 587, 127 S. Ct. 2553, 2573 (2007).

25. See, e.g., PAUL W. KAHN, THE CULTURAL STUDY OF LAW: RECONSTRUCTING LEGAL SCHOLARSHIP 13 (1999); Reva B. Siegel, *Equality Talk: Antisubordination and Anticlassification Values in Constitutional Struggles over Brown*, 117 HARV. L. REV. 1470 (2004).

26. *Heller*, 128 S. Ct. at 2783.

27. See, e.g., *id.* at 2789 ("The Second Amendment is naturally divided into two parts: its prefatory clause and its operative clause."); *id.* at 2790–97 (analyzing the meaning of "right," "the people," and "keep and bear arms"); *id.* at 2800 ("It is true that the term 'State' elsewhere in the Constitution refers to individual States, but the phrase 'security of a free state' and close variations seem to have been terms of art in 18th century political discourse, meaning a 'free country' or free polity.")

28. Owen M. Fiss, *The Other Goldberg, in* THE CONSTITUTION OF RIGHTS: HUMAN DIGNITY AND AMERICAN VALUES 229, 234 (Michael J. Meyer & William A. Parent eds., 1992) (discussing the appropriate test for a due process analysis).

29. See *Planned Parenthood*, 505 U.S. at 979–1001 (Scalia, J., concurring in part and dissenting in part).

30. See *Heller*, 128 S. Ct. at 2846 (Stevens, J., dissenting).

31. *Shaw*, 509 U.S. 630.

32. See *id.* at 633–49.

33. See *Vieth*, 541 U.S. at 282–306.

34. BE & K Constr. Co. v. NLRB, 536 U.S. 516 (2002).

35. *Id.* at 532 (citation omitted).

36. *Id.*

37. *Id.*

Chapter 3

Harm to Constitutional Stature
in *Bowers* and *Carhart*

On occasion, justices write opinions that seem comprehensively indifferent to the stature of constitutional losers. Although the losers in these opinions are citizens who presumptively enjoy full constitutional rights (unlike children, the mentally incompetent, prisoners, or foreign nationals), justices nonetheless refer to them as if they had a diminished constitutional stature. Justices write, for example, as if the losers possessed less than equal moral or political agency, or as if the consent of losers did not matter to the legitimacy of the justices' actions. They call into question the losers' constitutional leadership and the value of their contributions to constitutional meaning. As a result, justices exacerbate the harm inherent in losing the substantive merits of a rights claim, and the constitutional losers lose twice.

A 1986 decision, *Bowers v. Hardwick*,[1] and the more recent 2007 Roberts Court decision, *Gonzales v. Carhart*,[2] produced opinions that inflicted such harms on constitutional losers. In *Bowers*, justices did not merely refuse to recognize constitutional rights of privacy asserted by a gay man. Their analysis also conveyed a clear message that homosexuals could legitimately be viewed as lacking full constitutional stature. Similarly, in *Carhart*, justices did not merely deny a constitutional challenge to a limitation on abortion that included no exception to safeguard a woman's health. They also justified their conclusion by portraying women as persons of deficient constitutional stature. It is important to note, however, that justices in neither opinion formally declared that women or homosexuals were unequal to other adult citizens. In *Bowers* majority justices did not dispute Justice Stevens's assertion that it would have been "plainly unacceptable" to hold that "the persons to whom Georgia seeks to apply its statute do not have the same interest in 'liberty' that others have."[3] In *Carhart*, justices avoided a frontal assault on the constitutional stature of women in favor of a more evasive analysis that emphasized issues of medical ethics and fetal life.

Most discussions of *Bowers* and *Carhart* focus on matters of substantive constitutional interpretation. Do homosexuals enjoy a right of constitutional privacy that encompasses otherwise criminally forbidden sexual behavior? Does women's right of choice protect them against legislatures that would limit abortions even when a woman's health is at risk? The outcome of these substantive questions is of secondary concern to the argument made in *Losing Twice*. You may even assume that a plausible interpretation of the Constitution would lead one to answer "no" to both questions. But you should not assume that the answer "no" can properly be based on a portrayal of homosexuals or women as diminished citizens. Unless justices formally determine that individuals do not enjoy full constitutional stature, justices have an obligation to refrain from attacking stature in their opinions.

Bowers is a classic example of how careless justices can inflict harm on constitutional losers by undermining constitutional stature. The *Bowers* dispute arose after a gay man, Michael Hardwick, was arrested by Georgia officials for committing sodomy with another man in the privacy of his home. The arrest was made to enforce a state statute that criminalized consensual sodomy by homosexuals and heterosexuals. Hardwick, along with a heterosexual couple, argued that the Georgia statute was unconstitutional. The heterosexual partners, who had never been arrested or threatened with prosecution, were told they had no legal standing to challenge the statute. Hardwick, although never prosecuted, was allowed to sue, and his constitutional claim eventually found its way to the Supreme Court, which held that his claims were so insubstantial that they could be dismissed without a full hearing.

Justice White, who wrote the majority opinion in *Bowers*, was by all accounts an exceptionally good person, someone who did much to advance the cause of the civil rights movement in the 1960s. In *Bowers*, however, he and other justices joining the majority opinion inflicted significant harm on the stature of the constitutional losers. The substantive outcome in *Bowers* was not favorable to the losers, of course, but our concern here is with only the justices' message that gay men do not have full constitutional stature.

Majority justices conveyed their message primarily through implication, indifference, and telling omission. If, for example, one were looking for an acknowledgment of the equal moral and political agency of homosexuals in the *Bowers* majority opinion, one would search in vain. Only dissenting justices talked about gay men in terms of equal moral and political agency. Justice Stevens, for example, recognized that Hardwick was asserting the "moral fact that a person belongs to himself and not others."[4] Stevens also noted that Hardwick had invoked a right related to an individual's moral stature and to "the dignity of individual choice in matters of conscience."[5] Dissenting justices, in this regard, echoed the arguments of stakeholders allied with Hardwick, such as the Lesbian Rights Project, which asked the Court to see gays and lesbians as morally responsible human beings.[6]

Neither Justice White's majority opinion, nor the concurring opinions of Chief Justice Burger and Justice Powell, affirmed the equal moral agency of homosexuals in this way. Instead, their opinions invoked morality as a component of moral or religious dogma extending back through "millennia of moral teaching"[7] (according to Chief Justice Burger) or "hundreds of years" (according to Justice Powell).[8] Justice White's opinion even hinted that homosexuals are people who reject morality in general. In the latter portions of his opinion, for example, White suggested that Hardwick had claimed protection for "any kind of private sexual conduct between consenting adults,"[9] although Hardwick had done no such thing. Hardwick's brief and the briefs of supporting gay and lesbian organizations repeatedly stressed the narrowness of his claim, which was always limited to a plea for protection from criminal prosecution for harmless, private, noncommercial sexual conduct between consenting adults.[10] Indeed, Hardwick and his supporters rested many of their arguments on an appeal to moral principle. The brief of the Presbyterian Church (U.S.A.), for example, reminded the Court that Hardwick was simply asking the Court to require the State of Georgia to justify its statute with reference to moral principles.[11] To his credit, Justice White did not refer to bestiality or necrophilia, which the amicus brief of the Rutherford Institute did,[12] nor did he call homosexuality monstrous, as implied in Chief Justice Burger's concurring opinion.[13] Nonetheless, his opinion did suggest that homosexuals exist outside the moral community.

Similarly, majority justices questioned Hardwick's political agency and constitutional leadership by positioning him as an enemy of the existing political community and its values. Although Hardwick offered a plausible interpretation of the Constitution, one to which justices would later lend their support in *Lawrence v. Texas*,[14] Justice White accused Hardwick of, in effect, appealing to the Court to act outside the confines of the law, to declare the Georgia statute unconstitutional on the basis of "facetious" arguments backed by no remotely relevant precedent.[15] According to White, the consequence of acceding to Hardwick's allegedly law-defying claim would be a disintegration of social order;[16] judicial resistance to Hardwick's claim "should be, therefore, great."[17] Unlike Justice Blackmun, who endorsed Hardwick's constitutional leadership by reminding us that we all have a right "to differ as to things that touch the heart of the existing order,"[18] Justice White invited citizens to view the Court's rejection of Hardwick's claim as a heroic defense against an enemy, rather than as a judicious refusal to accept a plausible constitutional interpretation advanced by a worthy constitutional leader.

Dissenting justices accused their colleagues in the majority of sending a message that "homosexuals are so different from other citizens that their lives may be controlled" in ways that would be intolerable for heterosexuals.[19] Indeed, the majority and concurring opinions appeared almost willfully blind[20] to interests that homosexuals share with all other individuals.[21] Justice White, for example, refused to acknowledge that Hardwick's claim involved any relational rights important to all human beings. He did not discuss rights of intimate association, although Hardwick's brief and the briefs of supporting organizations heavily emphasized that intimate relationships are a basic human need of all persons, homosexual and heterosexual. Unlike dissenting justices, he did not acknowledge that his opinion would effectively consign homosexuals to live a life without sexual intimacy—a substantial harm, given that human beings depend on the emotional enrichment derived from intimate ties with others.[22] For Justice White, only reprehensible associations were at stake in the dispute, associations such as incest or adultery.[23] Chief Justice Burger trivialized Hardwick's interests as involving mere "personal 'preferences,' "[24] while Justice Powell acknowledged only Hardwick's interest in not being sentenced to too many years in prison.[25]

If justices are deeply indifferent to the full constitutional stature of citizen stakeholders in a rights dispute, we should not be surprised if they are also deeply indifferent to the practical consequences of their substantive constitutional interpretations. The most problematic consequence of *Bowers* was that Georgia homosexuals would enjoy human physical intimacy only at the discretionary whim of police and prosecutors. Evidence in *Bowers* had revealed that officials did not enforce Georgia's criminal sodomy statute against heterosexuals and only haphazardly applied it to homosexuals. Indeed, the record showed, the statute was enforced so infrequently against homosexuals that the number of prosecutions in the last fifty years could be counted on the fingers of one hand.[26] By leaving Georgia's statute in place, justices ensured that all gays and lesbians would be at risk of criminal prosecution, although everyone understood that only a very few, unfortunate individuals—in very rare circumstances—would actually be prosecuted. Justices seemed to have convinced themselves that it would be acceptable to treat homosexuals as arbitrarily as if they were part of a lottery.

Indeed, *Bowers* calls to mind the pernicious lottery that was once proposed as a solution to the plight of Africans who had been rescued from the pirate ship *The Antelope* in 1825.[27] The rescued Africans petitioned courts for their freedom but, under prevailing law, those who had been held as slaves before their capture by pirates were legally considered slaves; only those who had not been slaves could be freed. The difficulty was that no one could identify who had and who had not been a slave before the pirate capture. It was therefore unclear which Africans had a right to freedom. Faced with this identification dilemma, a federal judge decided that a lottery would be an appropriate method of sorting out who should be freed and who should be consigned to slavery. Noting that lotteries were a "proper way to distribute property which consisted in an...undifferenti-ated mass,"[28] the judge concluded that a lottery would also be a convenient and sensible means of making choices about Africans—whom the judge deemed to be property. When the dispute reached the Supreme Court, Francis Scott Key eloquently objected to subjecting the Africans to a lottery. Instead, he argued, justices should presume that all of the Africans were free and should put the burden of establishing individual "ownership" on anyone who claimed other-wise, asserting "The Africans] are men, of whom it cannot be affirmed, that they have universally and necessarily an owner...[and i]t would be manifestly unjust to throw the onus probandi upon them, to prove their birthright."[29]

Although Key's argument had an inconclusive effect in *The Antelope* dispute, it does help us identify one of the most troubling aspects of the *Bowers* decision. Having indulged in an analysis that treated gay men as diminished citizens, *Bowers* justices were willing to give permission to officials to enforce a criminal law that effectively operated as a lottery *vis à vis* homosexuals. As others have noted, using a lottery to determine a human being's fate enables us to be willfully ignorant of the character of the choices we make. We might arguably accept will-ful ignorance when we are dealing with property, but determining the fate of human beings and citizens by a roll of the dice should give us serious moral and constitutional qualms.

Intentionally or not, justices set themselves on their troubling path when they framed the merits of the *Bowers* dispute. According to majority justices, Hardwick was not asserting an individual right that was possessed by all citizens but that only happened to be invoked by a person of a homosexual orientation. The claim, as framed by Justice White, was simply that homosexuals have a fundamental right to engage in consensual sodomy.[30] As a result of this discretionary framing choice, justices gave themselves permission to ignore oth-erwise troublesome precedent, such as *Loving v. Virginia*,[31] in which the Court had invalidated traditional, religion-justified laws banning interracial marriage,[32] and they could also avoid having to discuss the constitutional implications of the Georgia statute for the consensual, private sexual relationships of all citizens. They could declare Hardwick's claim to be unique, facetious, and unworthy of respect as an exercise in constitutional leadership. They could, in other words, more easily justify their decision to dismiss Hardwick's arguments out of hand.

In thinking about the infliction of harm on constitutional stature in *Bowers*, it is important to recognize that justices could have explored the validity of Hardwick's constitutional claim without undermining the constitutional stature of gay men. There are undoubtedly, for example, distinctions that might be drawn between statutes prohibiting interracial marriage and those prohibiting consensual sodomy that would not require justices to deny the full constitu-tional stature of homosexuals. There are also arguments for limiting federal court intervention into state criminal processes and for justifying a limited judicial role that are clearly unrelated to the constitutional stature of homosexuals or any other group of citizens. Had justices employed an analysis that did not attack constitutional stature and yet concluded that the Georgia statute should be left in force, *Bowers* would not warrant inclusion in this chapter.

However, *Bowers*, as written, is a textbook case of significant harm to the constitutional stature of the losers. Although *Bowers* justices did not formally hold that gay men enjoy lesser rights than other citizens, they could reasonably be understood as putting everyone on notice that the Court might offer little protection against statutes that attempted to directly consign homosexuals to a constitutionally diminished status. Indeed, gays and lesbians warned justices that *Bowers* would have spillover effects.[33] And, although an avalanche of new statutes criminalizing homosexual sodomy did not occur after *Bowers*,[34] Colorado voters adopted an initiative popularly known as Amendment 2, which provided that governmental entities could not:

> enact, adopt or enforce any statute, regulation, ordinance or policy whereby homosexual, lesbian or bisexual orientation, conduct, practices or relationships shall constitute or otherwise be the basis of or entitle any person or class of persons to have or claim any minority status, quota preferences, protected status or claim of discrimination.[35]

Amendment 2 attempted to formalize in law the more indirect message of *Bowers* that homosexuals do not have full constitutional stature.

By the time Amendment 2 was challenged as unconstitutional, ten years had passed and justices had apparently recognized the failings of the *Bowers* decision. In *Romer v. Evans*, they declared Amendment 2 unconstitutional, and their majority opinion read as if it had been crafted by someone who wished to rectify the harms inflicted in *Bowers*.[36] In applying the Constitution's equality principle to the dispute over Amendment 2, for example, *Romer* justices reminded us that the Constitution does not tolerate classes among citizens, especially when the state's definition of a particular class is motivated only by animosity.[37] According to *Romer* justices, the state cannot make a class of persons—such as homosexuals—constitutional "strangers" to its laws,[38] and it cannot withhold access to normal political channels that the rest of us take for granted. "[G]overnment and each of its parts [must] remain open on impartial terms to all who seek its assistance,"[39] and the state cannot categorically deny its protection to homosexuals seeking to participate in a broad range of transactions respecting ordinary civic life.[40] Moreover, *Romer* justices' views of the constitutional stature of homosexuals had apparently changed so significantly since *Bowers* that they were unwilling to ignore the practical consequences of Amendment 2 for homosexuals. Despite the fact that the challenge to Amendment 2 was not squarely governed by constitutional precedent and despite the likelihood that they would be criticized for improperly exceeding their judicial role, justices nonetheless interpreted the Constitution so as to protect homosexuals from a formal declaration of second-class citizenship.

It took justices almost twenty years to confirm their repudiation of the attack on the constitutional stature of homosexuals that had occurred in *Bowers*. In *Lawrence v. Texas*,[41] Justice Kennedy made an effort to remove all constitutionally sanctioned "invitation to subject homosexual persons to discrimination both in the public and private sphere."[42] Instead of demeaning homosexuals by comparing their private, consensual relationships to adultery, prostitution, or bestiality,[43] Justice Kennedy treated homosexuals as persons seeking dignity and liberty. Moreover, he refrained from repeating the mistake made in *Bowers* and did not attack the constitutional stature of the new constitutional losers, who were committed to the preservation of traditional forms of marriage and to a right to disassociate themselves from homosexuals in their private lives. Justice Kennedy did not, for example, accuse supporters of the Texas statute criminalizing homosexual sodomy of "wanting to oppress" homosexuals.[44] He addressed them, with respect, as people holding "profound and deep convictions accepted as ethical and moral principles to which they aspire and which thus determine the course of their lives."[45] Indeed, he blamed the plight of homosexuals more on the Court, for failing to "appreciate the extent of the liberty at stake" in *Bowers*, than on anyone else.[46]

In an ideal constitutional world, we would not see repeated examples of *Bowers'* mistaken assault on constitutional stature. We can certainly be reassured that there have been no recent attacks on the constitutional stature of homosexuals as blatant as that which occurred in *Bowers*. Nonetheless, justices on occasion still do inflict unnecessary harm on constitutional stature as they review the merits of substantive constitutional claims. Two decisions, one involving homosexuals and one affecting women, illustrate the point.

In *Boy Scouts of America v. Dale*,[47] justices determined that a New Jersey law protecting homosexuals from discrimination violated the First Amendment when state courts applied the law so as to prohibit the Boy Scouts from discriminating against homosexual adult Scout leaders. The opinions of dissenting justices in *Dale* suggested that the majority's decision was premised on an implicit attack on constitutional stature. According to the dissenters, justices in the majority had relied on prejudices with ancient roots "nourished by sectarian doctrine," and had "caused serious and tangible harm to [homosexuals]."[48] The dissenters objected that the majority had permitted prejudice to become constitutional principle "to another's hurt,"[49] and pointed out that the harm of prejudice could "only be aggravated by the [Court's] creation of a constitutional shield for a policy that is ... the product of a habitual way of thinking about strangers."[50] They also complained that the majority had assumed that Dale—by virtue of his homosexuality—would not comply with Boy Scout rules prohibiting Scout leaders from advocating personal views to young Scouts, while heterosexuals, who could just as easily "advocate to the Scouts the view that homosexuality is not immoral," were permitted to remain adult leaders.[51] According to the dissenters,

> The only... explanation for the... [Court's] holding... is that homosexuals are simply so different from the rest of society that their presence alone—unlike any other individual's—should be singled out for special...treatment. Under the majority's reasoning, [a homosexual's]... openness is the sole and sufficient justification for his ostracism [and exclusion]. Though unintended, reliance on such a justification is tantamount to a constitutionally prescribed symbol of inferiority.[52]

Majority justices in *Dale* did not make as direct or comprehensive an assault on the constitutional stature of homosexuals as occurred in *Bowers*, but their opinion nonetheless manifests indifference to the constitutional stature of losing stakeholders in rights disputes.

More recently, justices allowed an indirect attack on the constitutional stature of women to influence their substantive analysis of women's reproductive freedom. As you will recall, justices have slowly moved to recognize women's full constitutional stature in their abortion decisions. Their recognition was most clearly expressed in the joint opinion in *Planned Parenthood v. Casey*,[53] where Justices O'Connor, Kennedy, and Souter characterized women as free individuals making significant choices about personhood and destiny. Thirteen years later, in *Gonzales v. Carhart*,[54] however, majority justices returned to a disturbing, pre–*Planned Parenthood* view of women.

The named plaintiffs in *Carhart* were physicians, not women. They challenged the constitutionality of the federal Partial-Birth Abortion Ban Act of 2003,[55] which threatens physicians, but not women, with criminal prosecution if they use a banned, "intact" D&E procedure to perform an abortion. Because the fundamental liberty rights of women were at stake, however, doctors were permitted to represent the interests of women in the dispute.[56] Ultimately, a majority of justices concluded that the federal statute was not on its face an unconstitutional burden on women's right of choice. There was no evidence, they said, that the statute would prohibit "the vast majority of D&E abortions,"[57] would be "a substantial obstacle to late-term, but previability, abortions,"[58] or would subject women to significant health risks.[59] Justices would withhold their power of judicial review unless and until such evidence appeared as the statute was applied to specific abortion decisions.

Although *Carhart* justices did not formally declare that women have diminished constitutional stature, they nonetheless inflicted significant harm on women's stature and, as a result, prompted a passionate dissent from Justice Ginsburg who has been instrumental in ensuring that women "count" among the people for whom the Constitution was written. On the merits, Ginsburg was alarmed that justices upheld a ban on an abortion procedure accepted by the American Council of Obstetricians and Gynecologists and that they questioned *Roe's* distinction between pre-viability and post-viability abortions.[60] Ginsburg also, however, faulted justices for undermining women's autonomy and equal citizenship,[61] and a careful reading of the *Carhart* majority opinion confirms that the opinion lacks any acknowledgment that women have a capacity for moral and political choice equal to the capacity of the iconic citizen of the Constitution. Rather, majority justices portrayed women as lesser and emotional individuals, needing governmental protection in matters of personal health.

Justices asserted, for example, that the Partial-Birth Abortion Ban Act would protect meaningful choices for women whose doctors might prefer not to disclose the details of the statutorily prohibited D&E procedure.[62] Ginsburg, however, pointed out that the statute did not require physicians to inform women about matters that would help them make a choice.[63] Instead, the statute actually deprived women of meaningful choice by banning a medically accepted abortion procedure and insisting on the use of an alternative that might threaten women's health.[64] Justice Kennedy exacerbated the consequences of his analytical misstep by assuring women that he had their interest in avoiding future psychological injury at heart; he apparently assumed that women would suffer such injury when they came to regret their choice to terminate a pregnancy. Ginsburg, characterizing as completely unfounded the "shibboleth" that women who have abortions will suffer emotional harm,[65] questioned the empirical validity of Kennedy's assumption.

Moreover, as Ginsburg rightly noted, justices' assumption that women require protection in matters of reproductive choice bearing on mental or physical health or morality undermined *Planned Parenthood's* recognition that, given the right of liberty, "the destiny of the woman must be shaped... on her own conception of her spiritual imperatives and her place in society."[66] *Carhart* justices apparently doubted the ability of women to responsibly exercise their right to liberty in matters of reproduction. They seemed even to dismiss the judgments of physician surrogates for women's choice, persons to whom they had deferred in *Roe v. Wade*.[67] For *Carhart* justices, it was essential to establish a constitutional principle that would permit government to guard against "abortion doctors"[68] who might simply "choose the abortion method he or she might prefer,"[69] as if physicians based medical judgments on personal preference rather than an assessment of maternal health risks in consultation with their patients.[70]

Just as justices chose to describe the *Bowers* dispute as one involving only the unique rights of homosexuals, *Carhart* justices also made a discretionary framing decision that set them on an analytical path destined to undermine the full constitutional stature of women. *Carhart* justices chose to treat the challenged statute as if it were no different from run-of-the-mill legislation regulating medical ethics and having no bearing on women's fundamental liberties,[71] and that therefore might be upheld as long as it had some rational basis.[72] This discretionary choice at best deflected attention from women and their important liberty interests and, at worst, represented a conscious effort to denigrate rights of reproductive choice important to women.

Carhart justices' willingness to accept the troubling practical consequences of their decision for women, whose full constitutional stature had been called into question, reflected the dismaying, cavalier spirit of indifference that animated *Bowers*. The Partial-Birth Abortion Ban Act was challenged because it does not contain an exception for cases in which the health of the mother is in jeopardy.[73] As Justice Ginsburg noted, justices' rejection of the constitutional challenge ignored the immediate plight of women who, in the judgment of their doctors, require an intact D&E because other procedures would place their health at risk.[74] Although these risks were documented in the opinions of three lower federal courts,[75] justices were willing to "see" or to take these risks into account only at some later date. In order to warrant judicial intervention, they said, there would need to be evidence that "in discrete and well-defined instances a particular condition [had occurred] or [was] likely to occur in which the [D&E] procedure ... [would have to] be used."[76] Perhaps, for example, identifiable women actually suffering harm to health or in the midst of an urgent care emergency would decide to sue. Perhaps physicians who had exercised their reasonable judgment to use the banned procedure and were then threatened with prosecution might sue.[77] As Ginsburg noted, some women facing serious health risks would not be protected if majority justices insisted on waiting for discrete events such as these to give rise to another constitutional challenge.[78]

More will be said about *Carhart* and its treatment of women's constitutional stature in chapter 7. The decision is introduced here simply to illustrate how justices can inflict significant harm on constitutional stature without formally declaring that any given citizen enjoys only second-class constitutional rights. *Carhart* is not included in this chapter because it arguably manifested an unconcealed hostility to abortion[79] or because it came close to imbuing the fetus with constitutional personhood. It is included only because *Carhart* justices attacked women's full constitutional stature.

Planned Parenthood had it right in recognizing that abortion controversies are not about abortion per se. Abortion controversies are about whether women will be respected as full agents of choice in matters of life and death. In other rights disputes, justices have presumptively accorded such respect to other citizens, for example, in recognizing an individual's Second Amendment right to possess a handgun in *District of Columbia v. Heller*.[80] Although citizens can use guns to kill other human beings, a presumption of responsible agency in the use of guns undergirded the decision to protect individual gun ownership in *Heller*. *Carhart* justices, however, did not rely on a similar presumption regarding women and their life-and-death choices.

The limits imposed on judicial review in *Carhart* and *Bowers* and the substantive outcomes of the cases are inextricably and improperly tainted by attacks on the constitutional stature of women and homosexuals, respectively. A presumption of responsible agency and full constitutional stature for all citizens lies at the heart of our system of government. If all citizens presumptively enjoy full constitutional stature, it is unacceptable for justices to relentlessly, albeit indirectly, undermine constitutional stature throughout their opinions. Justices may find it easier to reject substantive constitutional claims if, in subtle or blatant ways, they can distance themselves from constitutional losers,[81] but if they persist in doing so they will deter citizens from testing the legitimacy of constitutional relationships, from offering new insights into the Constitution's meaning, and from participating in a renewal of consent to our Constitution. And justices will inflict a double loss on constitutional losers.

Justices whose analysis of a rights dispute depends on an attack on constitutional stature would do well to take a close look at their opinion, for such an attack raises a red flag that legitimate justifications for a particular constitutional interpretation are lacking. Indeed, as subsequent chapters will argue, justices ought to do more than avoid attacks on constitutional stature. They ought to vigorously affirm and honor the constitutional stature of losers, especially in intractable rights disputes. Before turning to the topic of honoring constitutional stature, however, a brief discussion of untruthfulness in judicial opinions is in order.

Notes

1. Bowers v. Hardwick, 478 U.S. 186 (1986).
2. Gonzales v. Carhart, 550 U.S. 124 (2007).
3. *Bowers*, 478 U.S. at 218 (Stevens, J., dissenting).
4. *Id.* at 204 (Blackmun, J., dissenting) (quoting Thornburgh v. Am. Coll. of Obstetricians & Gynecologists, 476 U.S. 747, 777 n.5 (Stevens, J., concurring)).
5. *Id.* at 217 (Stevens, J., dissenting) (quoting Fitzgerald v. Porter Memorial Hosp., 523 F.2d 716, 719–20 (7th Cir. 1975), cert. denied, 425 U.S. 916 (1976)).

6. Brief Amicus Curiae for Lesbian Rights Project et al. at 21–21, *Bowers*, 478 U.S. 186 (No. 85-140), 1985 WL 667944.

7. *Bowers*, 478 U.S. at 197 (Burger, C. J., concurring).

8. *Id.* at 198 n.2 (Powell, J., concurring).

9. *Id.* at 191 (majority opinion) (emphasis added).

10. To understand how narrowly Hardwick's claim was consistently framed, see, for example, Brief Amicus Curiae for Lesbian Rights Project et al. at 11–12, 16–17, 20, *Bowers*, 478 U.S. 186 (No. 85-140), 1985 WL 667944; Brief of National Gay Rights Advocates et al., Amici Curiae, in Support of Respondents at 10–14, *Bowers*, 478 U.S. 186 (No. 85-140), 1985 WL 667946; Amicus Curiae Brief on Behalf of the Respondents by Lambda Legal Defense and Education Fund, Inc. et al. at 8–13, 24, *Bowers*, 478 U.S. 186 (No. 85-140), 1986 WL 720449; Brief Amicus Curiae of the Association of the Bar of the City of New York by Its Committee on Sex and Law in Support of Respondent Hardwick at 14, *Bowers*, 478 U.S. 186 (No. 85-140), 1986 WL 720444; and Brief of Amici Curiae the Presbyterian Church (U.S.A.) et al. at 5, 8–13, *Bowers*, 478 U.S. 186 (No. 85-140), 1986 WL 720447.

11. Brief of Amici Curiae the Presbyterian Church (U.S.A.) et al., *supra* note 10, at 14.

12. Brief of the Rutherford Institute et al., Amici Curiae, in Support of the Petitioner at 3, 27, *Bowers*, 478 U.S. 186 (No. 85-140), 1985 WL 667943.

13. *Bowers*, 478 U.S. at 196–97 (Burger, C. J., concurring).

14. Lawrence v. Texas, 539 U.S. 558 (2003).

15. *Bowers*, 478 U.S. at 194.

16. *Id.* at 196.

17. *Id.* at 195.

18. *Id.* at 211 (Blackmun, J., dissenting) (quoting W. Va. State Bd. of Educ. v. Barnette, 319 U.S. 624, 641–42 (1943)).

19. *Id.* at 200.

20. *Id.* at 205.

21. *Id.* at 218 (Stevens, J., dissenting).

22. *Id.* at 202 n.2 (Blackmun, J., dissenting). *Amici* argued that intimate relationships are a basic human need of all persons, homosexual and heterosexual. *See, e.g.,* Brief of National Gay Rights Advocates et al., Amici Curiae, in Support of Respondents, *supra* note 10, at 6, 9–10; Amicus Curiae Brief on Behalf of the Respondents by Lambda Legal Defense and Education Fund, Inc., et al., *supra* note 10, at 8–13. Justice White did discuss traditional marital, family, and parent–child relationships, *Bowers*, 478 U.S. at 190–91, but because homosexuals would find it difficult to achieve those relationships under existing laws, his discussion necessarily had little relevance to Hardwick's fate.

23. *Bowers*, 478 U.S. at 196 (majority opinion).

24. *Bowers*, 478 U.S. at 197 (Burger, C. J., concurring).

25. *Id.* at 197–198 (Powell, J., concurring).

26. *Id.* at 219 (Stevens, J., dissenting).

27. *See* JOHN T. NOONAN Jr., THE ANTELOPE: THE ORDEAL OF THE RECAPTURED AFRICANS IN THE ADMINISTRATIONS OF JAMES MONROE AND JOHN QUINCY ADAMS (1977).

28. *Id.* at 101.

29. *Id.* at 97.

30. *Bowers*, 478 U.S. at 191.

31. Loving v. Virginia, 388 U.S. 1 (1967).

32. See *Bowers*, 478 U.S. at 211, n.5 (Blackmun, J., dissenting).

33. See Brief Amicus Curiae for Lesbian Rights Project et al., *supra* note 6, at 21–27; Amicus Curiae Brief on Behalf of the Respondents by Lambda Legal Defense and Education Fund, Inc., et al., *supra* note 10, at 25–30.

34. *Lawrence*, 539 U.S. at 573.

35. COLO. CONST. art. II, § 30b.

36. Romer v. Evans, 517 U.S. 620 (1996).

37. *Id.* at 634–35.

38. *Id.* at 635.

39. *Id.* at 633.

40. *Id.* at 631.

41. Lawrence v. Texas, 539 U.S. 558 (2003).

42. *Id.* at 575.

43. *Id.* at 590 (Scalia, J., dissenting).

44. *Id.* at 600 (emphasis added).

45. *Lawrence,* 539 U.S. at 571.

46. *Id.* at 567.

47. Boy Scouts of Am. v. Dale, 530 U.S. 640 (2000).

48. *Id.* at 699–700 (Stevens, J., dissenting).

49. *Id.* at 687 (quoting Railway Mail Assn. v. Corsi, 326 U.S. 88, 98 (1945) (Frankfurter, J., concurring)).

50. *Id.* at 700.

51. *Id.* at 691 n.19.

52. *Id.* at 696.

53. Planned Parenthood of Se. Pa. v. Casey, 505 U.S. 833 (1994).

54. Gonzales v. Carhart, 550 U.S. 124 (2007).

55. 18 U.S.C. § 1531.

56. See, e.g., *Planned Parenthood,* 505 U.S. 833, and Webster v. Reprod. Health Servs., 492 U.S. 490 (1989) (both according physicians third-party standing to assert the rights of women).

57. *Carhart,* 550 U.S. at 156.

58. *Id.*

59. *Id.* at 161, 162, 166–67.

60. *Id.* at 170–71 (Ginsburg, J., dissenting).

61. *Id.* at 172.

62. *Id.* at 159–60 (majority opinion).

63. *Id.* at 184 (Ginsburg, J., dissenting).

64. *Id.*

65. *Id.* at 183.

66. *Id.* at 185 (internal citations omitted).

67. Roe v. Wade, 410 U.S. 113 (1973).

68. *Carhart,* 550 U.S. at 144, 154, 155, 161, 163.

69. *Id.* at 158.

70. See also *id.* at 134, 159 (referring to physician preference).

71. *Id.* at 163 ("The law need not...elevate [abortion doctors'] status above other physicians in the medical community.").

72. *Id.* at 166 (stating that in regulating medical ethics under the Commerce Clause, "[c]onsiderations of marginal safety, including the balance of risks, are within the legislative competence when the regulation is rational and in pursuit of legitimate ends").

73. *Id.* at 165 (majority opinion).

74. *Id.* at 183, 188–90 (Ginsburg, J., dissenting).

75. According to Kennedy, the statute would be unconstitutional if it subjected women to significant health risks, *id.* at 161 (majority opinion), but he contended that medical professionals disagree about the facts pertaining to those risks. Under the circumstances, he said, legislatures have discretion to ban the procedure at issue. *Id.* at 163.

76. *Id.* at 167. See also *id.* at 168 (a discrete case is required).

77. Kennedy stated that the health of the woman must be protected through an as-applied challenge, in a specific context: "It is neither our obligation nor within our traditional institutional role to resolve questions of constitutionality with respect to each potential situation that might develop." *Id.* at 167–68.

78. *Id.* at 190 (Ginsburg, J., dissenting).

79. *Id.* at 186–87.

80. District of Columbia v. Heller, 554 U.S. 570, 128 S. Ct. 2783, 2827 (2008) (Stevens, J., dissenting).

81. Mayo Moran, *Talking about Hate Speech: A Rhetorical Analysis of American and Canadian Approaches to the Regulation of Hate Speech,* 1994 WIS. L. REV. 1425, 1451–52 n.110 ("Judges [may] respond to the concerns of the losers by minimizing the adverse results of their decisions, and by refusing to grant them personhood... [thereby leaving] room for only one individual... the person who is *not* injured by the cases' results.") (emphasis added).

Chapter 4

Harms of Untruthfulness

Blatant attacks on constitutional stature such as those in *Bowers* and *Carhart* are relatively few and far between. But although justices more often than not manage to explain their decisions without directly challenging the losers' constitutional stature, they nonetheless find ways to call constitutional stature into question more subtly and indirectly. This chapter explores how judicial untruthfulness about what is at stake for constitutional losers puts constitutional stature at risk. In addition, the chapter bears on a second argument in *Losing Twice*, that the harms inherent in losing a rights dispute can be ameliorated if justices take affirmative steps to honor the constitutional stature of losing stakeholders. The objective, here, is limited. The chapter strives to present the phenomenon of judicial untruthfulness without becoming mired in debates about angels that dance on the head of a pin. It does not ask you to embrace a comprehensive, philosophical theory of truthfulness or to approve of a mechanistic test for evaluating judicial truthfulness. Instead, you will be asked only to consider why judicial truthfulness is important to constitutional stature and to become acquainted with features of conventional rights disputing that can put truthfulness at risk.

Justices often put us on notice that we should doubt the truthfulness of their accounts of rights disputes. Indeed, it is rather surprising how frequently they accuse one another of knowingly mischaracterizing the nature of a rights dispute, of being willfully ignorant of constitutional losers' interests, or of deliberately misusing precedent to achieve a predetermined outcome.

As an example, consider *Hill v. Colorado*, which involved a First Amendment challenge to a statute prohibiting abortion protesters from coming too close to patients entering medical clinics.[1] Justices determined that the so-called Bubble Bill was constitutional. In dissent, Justice Scalia accused the *Hill* majority of manipulating constitutional doctrine because of the abortion debate. According to Scalia, the majority had made abortion a "highly favored

practice" by employing a legal "ad hoc nullification machine" against any "doctrines of constitutional law [that stood] in the way" of abortion.[2] "The jurisprudence of this Court has a way of changing when abortion is involved,"[3] he
said, adding that it was "relentlessly proabortion."[4] "Does the deck seem
stacked?" he asked; and he answered, "You bet."[5] He added:

> The interest [in protecting citizens from unwanted speech] that the
> Court makes the linchpin of its analysis was not only unasserted by the
> State; it is not only completely *different* from the interest that the statute
> specifically sets forth; it was explicitly *disclaimed* by the State in its brief
> before this Court, and characterized as a "straw interest" ... served up in
> the hope of discrediting the State's case.[6]

Finally, Scalia accused the majority of displaying "a willful ignorance" about the
protesters' speech objectives.[7] Although the constitutional losers had described
themselves as sidewalk counselors wishing to speak softly, sympathetically, and
directly to individual women entering abortion clinics, majority justices asserted
that antiabortion protesters could achieve their objectives through means other
than face-to-face communication, such as leaflets, signs, or bullhorns. Scalia
chastised the majority for its assertion, stating that leafletting is not done the way
the majority had described it, and that "the Court [knew] it—or should."[8] Justice
Kennedy agreed, complaining that the majority had insulted protesters by telling
them that their interests could be protected by using a bullhorn.[9]

Similar complaints of untruthfulness were voiced in *Boy Scouts of America
v. Dale*, where Justice Stevens accused the majority of taking "an astounding view
of the law" in its endorsement of an "odd form" of independent, First Amendment
review consisting of "deferring entirely to whatever a litigant claim[ed]."[10] Justice
Stevens accused majority justices of misusing precedent in *District of Columbia
v. Heller.*[11] In *Parents Involved in Community Schools v. Seattle School District No. 1*,
majority and dissenting justices accused one another of altering the facts and mis-
handling established law in cases concerning race-based decision-making.[12]

We may have become so used to such accusations of judicial untruthfulness
that we dismiss them as irritating but not particularly significant family feuds
among justices. We should not do so. Citizens of full constitutional stature
rightly recognize that, if justices do in fact lie to each other, they also necessarily
lie to us. Citizens will also sense that acts of judicial untruthfulness can treat us
as less than equal or as persons whose true consent does not matter to judicial
legitimacy. In other words, citizens will recognize that judicial untruthfulness
can inflict significant harm on their constitutional stature.

Of course, truthfulness is a complicated issue, and being truthful to citizens
might arguably demand one or more of many different, even incompatible

behaviors. Being truthful might, for example, necessitate full disclosure. Proper truthfulness might be absolutely unforgiving of even white lies. It might only necessitate sincerely truthful statements made in good faith. The necessary elements of judicial truthfulness may be especially difficult to pin down because justices are not ordinary citizens. They have an institutional and professional role that arguably either imposes special truthfulness obligations or, in the alternative, gives justices dispensation to shade the truth to achieve important ends.

Consider some arguments that only scratch the surface of the many different perspectives that could be brought to bear on the requirements of judicial truthfulness. It might be asserted, for example, that shading, silence, or obfuscation is a good and legitimate way for justices to attain a national consensus on some matters. Traumatic national events such as the Civil War or the forcible removal of American Indians from their homelands might arguably warrant a degree of silence as a means of putting passionately fought controversies to rest. Some believe that acknowledging recent interrogation practices could do irreparable harm to the international reputation of the United States or might lead to retaliatory acts by Islamic extremists. It is also possible that truthful discussion of topics such as torture might have the perverse consequence of legitimizing conversation about practices that should be considered entirely off the discussion table. On the other hand, absolute truthfulness may be a prerequisite to political stability and consensus. The benefits of full disclosure have been a working assumption in countries such as South Africa and Argentina, which have employed truth commissions to expose the horrors of racial apartheid and the fate of Argentinian *desaparecidos*. Moreover, if we give justices unguided permission to be less than fully truthful, they may be tempted to routinely render decisions embodying a distorted version of past events.

Fortunately, we do not need to resolve these or similar arguments about truthfulness. We need only to keep our focus on the relationship of truthfulness to constitutional stature. To keep ourselves grounded, we might simply think of constitutional stature as embodying a political conception of dignity. According to David Luban, "Honoring human dignity means... listening to [the individual's story] and insisting that it be told."[13] In the language of *Losing Twice*, the argument would be that justices owe an obligation to listen to and take serious account of the values and interests identified as important by constitutional losers; otherwise, they will inflict harm on the losers' constitutional stature.[14]

We can surely recognize the harms to constitutional stature resulting from justices' failure to take truthful account of the values and interests promoted by constitutional losers in a rights dispute. An opinion that is untruthful about losers' values and interests, for example, will not manifest respect for either the losers' view of constitutional meaning or the losers' constitutional leadership. In addition, untruthfulness is incompatible with Cicero's res publica and constitutional losers' equal ownership of decisional law. If justices ignore constitutional losers' interests, values, and contributions to constitutional meaning, there will be no judicial witness or memorial to the legitimacy of interests to which losers might wish to appeal in other settings or times. Further, when justices are untruthful about the interests and values of constitutional losers, they violate Madison's communion-of-interests principle, which mandates equal—and presumably truthful—consideration of the interests of all citizens. Judicial opinions based on a false picture of constitutional losers' interests and values are akin to gerrymandered election-district boundaries. They signal that justices and other citizens may properly pay attention to only a faction of the political community.[15] Untruthfulness about the interests and values of constitutional losers denigrates the losers' constitutional stature by suggesting that the losers are not worthy political and moral agents or constitutional leaders, that they are not fit to be equal participants in debates about constitutional meaning, and that they do not have the right to test the legitimacy of government.

In other words, untruthful judicial opinions send a message that constitutional losers do not count as people to whom justices are responsible. Another way of stating the point is that untruthful opinions fail to satisfy the expectation that the consent of all citizens of full constitutional stature matters to the legitimacy of judicial review and constitutional meaning. In this regard, please note that untruthfulness defeats the consent expectations of constitutional winners in addition to the expectations of losers. Untruthful judicial opinions manipulate winners' acceptance of constitutional meaning, political arrangements, and views of fellow citizens which winners might otherwise reject were justices truthful about losers' interests and values. Untruthfulness thus disregards the consent expectations and puts at risk the constitutional stature not only of constitutional losers but of constitutional winners, too.

Of course, even if we recognize that untruthfulness inflicts grave harm on constitutional stature, we must confront the difficult issue of what justices should do to ensure that their opinions contain truthful accounts of the losers' values and interests. Regarding this issue, *Losing Twice* has a modest objective: to identify a few features of conventional rights disputing that create significant risks of *un*truthfulness, so that justices might better avoid indirect attacks on constitutional stature. As one example, this chapter first considers the formal structure of rights disputes and the multiplicity of interests that a given rights dispute will affect, both of which can compromise justices' ability to give a truthful account of constitutional losers' interests and values. It then shows how constitutional doctrines and metaphors can obscure truthfulness. Finally, it takes note of discretionary framing choices that can interfere with truthfulness.

As previously noted, a rights dispute affects multiple stakeholders, not merely the formal parties, and each stakeholder may have multiple interests in a single dispute. For example, although a government official is often named as the formal defendant in rights disputes, government is composed of many different individuals and entities, each interested in protecting its own budget or bureaucratic prerogatives in addition to accomplishing broader public goals. Moreover, a named official's personal preferences may not coincide with the interests advanced by a government policy. Colorado's governor, Roy Romer, for example, was required to defend Amendment 2, at issue in *Romer v. Evans*,[16] even though he had opposed placing the amendment on Colorado's initiative ballot. Similarly, public universities defending affirmative action policies do not always share the interests of the minorities who benefit from the policies. Minorities might not hesitate to show that a university has engaged in prior intentional discrimination as a constitutional defense of affirmative action, but a university will probably not wish to confess to past discriminatory behavior. Finally, although a legislator may have a stake in the resolution of a rights dispute—she may, for example, have voted for a challenged statute, or her future votes on government expenditures might be affected by a judicial order to spend more money to remedy a constitutional wrong—legislators will rarely be formal parties in rights disputes.

The multiplicity of stakeholders and interests makes it difficult for even the most willing of justices to take note of every single interest or value implicated in a given rights dispute. Consider, for example, the stakeholders and resolution of the dispute in *Rumsfeld v. Forum for Academic and Institutional Rights*.[17] The Forum for Academic and Institutional Rights (FAIR), the formal plaintiff in the dispute, was a membership corporation consisting of law schools, law professors, and law students. The formal defendants were the secretaries of the federal departments of defense, education, and homeland security.

FAIR contested the constitutionality of the Solomon Amendment, a federal statute that requires universities receiving federal funds to give military recruiters full access to campus placement services. If any unit or "subelement" of a university refuses access to military recruiters, the entire university risks being denied substantial federal funding. The Solomon Amendment poses a special difficulty for law schools and their parent institutions because law schools typically do not extend their placement services to prospective employers who discriminate on the basis of sexual orientation. Given the military's "don't ask, don't tell" policy regarding homosexuals, the military would typically be considered a discriminatory employer, and military recruiters barred from law school placement facilities.

Many interests other than federal funds were at stake in the *FAIR* litigation. For example, FAIR argued that the Solomon Amendment compromised free speech and academic freedom. It contended that the Solomon Amendment compromises the integrity of law schools by forcing them to act as tools of the government. It emphasized the importance of law school efforts to inculcate nondiscrimination values in law students, and the importance of ensuring that law students are judged on their merits rather than their sexual orientation. Numerous "declarations" of individuals agreeing with FAIR stressed the unique historical traditions of specific law schools and explained how those traditions are threatened by the Solomon Amendment. The record in *FAIR* also contained opposing perspectives. Law professors and law students supporting the Solomon Amendment claimed a right to resist imposition of the nondiscrimination views held by FAIR and its supporters. The government and military stressed that giving military recruiters access to law schools and law students is essential to maintaining national security.

Perhaps the best evidence of the many different interests and stakeholders implicated in the *FAIR* lawsuit is the voluminous record of amicus curiae briefs filed in the Supreme Court. These amicus briefs reflected the views and interests of law professors who had not joined FAIR, law students and student organizations, universities, placement officers and other law school administrators, human and civil rights organizations, legal advocacy and policy groups, the American Legion, the Judge Advocates Association, bar associations, the American Association of University Professors, a number of states, the Christian Legal Society, and the Boy Scouts of America. Each amicus curiae claimed to have an independent stake in the outcome of the litigation. As you can see, practical obstacles to complete truthfulness necessarily exist because of the multiplicity of stakeholder interests and values in a rights dispute.

Judge-made constitutional doctrine can also interfere with a truthful account of interests and values. Consider, for example, the doctrine that states must justify restrictions on First Amendment rights by showing that their policies are necessary to the protection of compelling state interests.

Truthfulness in *Boy Scouts of America v. Dale*[18] was undermined by the compelling state interest doctrine. James Dale initiated the dispute by asking a state court to use a state public accommodations law to protect his position as a Boy Scouts of America (BSA) leader, which the BSA had denied him because of his acknowledged homosexuality. In state court Dale's individual interest in being a Scout leader was front and center, and state courts gave Dale the protection he sought. When the BSA appealed the state court decision to the Supreme Court of the United States, however, the compelling state interest doctrine moved Dale's individual interests into the shadows of constitutional analysis. Dale was required to defend the state court decision by identifying compelling *state* interests for New Jersey's public accommodations law. Instead of looking directly at Dale's interests, therefore, justices viewed them through the prism of the state's concerns. They discussed Dale's interests only by proxy while, in contrast, they carefully considered and deferred to the BSA's interests in freedom to think, speak, and associate.

District of Columbia v. Heller offers another example of how doctrine can obstruct a truthful account of the interests of constitutional losers in rights disputes.[19] Dick Heller, who eventually prevailed in the dispute, argued that the District of Columbia's restrictive handgun possession laws violated his rights under the Constitution's Second Amendment. From Heller's point of view, the central issue was whether the Second Amendment protected an individual right to keep and bear arms or only a right to bear arms linked to military or militia activities. Defending its handgun prohibitions, the District of Columbia argued that even if the Second Amendment protected an individual right to bear arms unrelated to organized militia activities, the right was not absolute. It claimed that handgun prohibitions were justified by the District's compelling interest in protecting ordinary citizens of all ages from handgun violence and deadly force. All justices recognized that Heller's individual rights were at stake in the dispute, and they addressed his interests in their opinions. However, the interests of citizen stakeholders exposed to gun violence were taken into account in the written opinions of the justices—both majority and dissenting—only as empirical evidence on which legislators might have relied when they voted to adopt handgun restrictions. Relegated to the background of constitutional analysis by the doctrinal emphasis on the legitimacy of *state* interests in regulating handguns, ordinary citizens became statistical beings rather than living and breathing people exposed to concrete, lethal danger.

Many constitutional doctrines can obstruct truthfulness. Over the years, for example, pregnant women have argued that employee benefit plans lacking coverage for pregnancy-related medical care unconstitutionally discriminate against them on the basis of sex.[20] Justices, however, have chosen to analyze these claims using a doctrine that recognizes only two classes of people affected by a pregnancy-based policy: pregnant persons and non-pregnant persons. Because the class of non-pregnant persons includes both women and men, according to justices there is no sex discrimination.[21] Justices' decision to adhere to a formalist equality doctrine has ensured that truthfulness about the interests of women can be fully taken into account only in the legislative arena, not in constitutional rights litigation.[22]

Sometimes judge-made doctrine embodies constitutional metaphors that make it difficult for justices to speak truthfully about interests in a rights dispute. For example, although dissenting Justice Scalia described abortion protesters in *Hill v. Colorado* as sidewalk counselors wishing to establish an intimate relationship with misguided women, he referenced a First Amendment doctrine embodying a "marketplace of ideas" metaphor to support his argument.[23] A marketplace metaphor would make sense if applied to a political debate about abortion policies, but it is ill-suited to constitutional analysis of issues raised by one-on-one speech intended to inform a patient about the facts of a medical procedure. As applied to sidewalk counselors, it detracts from an accurate portrayal of the protesters' activities. Similarly, the use of a "fighting words" exception to the First Amendment to determine the constitutionality of prohibitions on sexually harassing workplace speech seems out of place. I venture to suggest that a fighting words concept has little meaning for women in general, much less women who confront harassing speech in their place of employment. In my experience, women rarely turn to physical violence when accosted by offensive speech, in contrast to what the fighting words exception would suppose. Nonetheless, Justice Scalia once invoked the fighting words doctrine to suggest that prohibitions on harassing workplace speech might withstand constitutional attack.[24] Even though his use of the fighting words exception may help women by providing a constitutional justification for regulation of sexually harassing speech, ultimately the doctrine will stand in the way of a truthful account of what is actually at stake for women facing such harassment.

Constitutional doctrine affects framing choices made in rights disputes, and accurate framing is central to truthfulness. In *Hein v. Freedom from Religion Foundation*,[25] for example, an organization opposed to government endorsement of religion challenged a presidential "faith-based initiative" program's use of federal tax dollars. Justices debated how to describe the harm suffered by the plaintiff stakeholders. The plaintiff organization had argued that the harm implicated liberty of conscience,[26] but only dissenting justices fully accepted this characterization. The plurality described the harm as an economic injury suffered by taxpayers.[27] Justice Scalia's concurring opinion argued against both the plurality's and the dissenters' descriptions. Scalia viewed the harm as a psychic injury rather than "a real dollars-and-cents-injury,"[28] as a "psychological consequence presumably produced by observation of conduct with which one disagrees," a "psychic frustration," a "psychological displeasure," and "mental angst."[29] The decision of majority justices to minimize the losers' interest in freedom of conscience was compatible with technical standing doctrine, but it undeniably resulted in opinions lacking truthfulness for the constitutional losers.

Just as framing choices are influenced by judge-made doctrine, so are they affected by the tendency of justices to focus their powers of judicial review on abstract constitutional debates about principle rather than on concrete dilemmas facing citizens involved in a given rights dispute. Each year, justices review only a few of the many rights disputes resolved by lower courts. Through their certiorari jurisdiction, they carefully select disputes using criteria that emphasize the importance of answering issues of great public importance or of resolving conflicting lower court interpretations of the Constitution. When justices focus on abstract debate, a given rights dispute can become a vehicle for academic discussion lacking a truthful account of what is at stake for the immediate stakeholders in the dispute.

Consider, as an example, the opinions written in the case of *Board of Education of Kiryas Joel Village School District v. Grumet.*[30] This rights dispute arose after the New York state legislature, in an effort to find a way of providing suitable education to handicapped children of the Satmar Hasidim religious community, authorized the creation of a public school district that precisely overlapped the boundaries of a village incorporated by Satmar Hasidim citizens.

Much was at stake in the *Kiryas Joel* dispute. For example, some state taxpayers objected to having their tax dollars support a public school district tied so closely to a religious community. Some Satmar Hasidim objected that their own community's decision to become involved in public school district affairs was an affront to the separatist tenets of their religion. On the other hand, parents of handicapped Satmar children supported a new school district as a means of protecting their vulnerable children from traumatic interactions with non-Satmar schoolchildren. A neighboring school district accepted the statute creating the district as a convenient solution to the difficulty and expense it faced in attempting to accommodate the needs of the handicapped Satmar children.

Justices' opinions in the *Kiryas Joel* dispute, however, framed the issues as if they were participating in a moot court debate about the continuing validity of prior Supreme Court decisions interpreting the Constitution's prohibition on the official establishment of religion by government. To be sure, some stakeholder interests were discussed in the opinions. Justices, for example, made the New York legislature the focus of its analysis and, in separate opinions, offered various views on the constitutionality of the legislature's interests in assisting the Satmar community. Justice Scalia insisted that the dispute was about cultural survival rather than religion,[31] while Justice Stevens objected to cultural separatism.[32] The dominant orientation and tone of most of the *Kiryas Joel* opinions, however, reflect the fact that justices who voted to review the dispute were perhaps more interested in reconsidering the Supreme Court's prior decisions in *Lemon v. Kurtzman*[33] and *Aguilar v. Felton*[34] than in addressing the concerns of living, breathing citizens confronting a constitutional problem unique to their circumstances. Justice Kennedy blamed *Aguilar* for giving rise to the Satmar dispute.[35] Justice O'Connor devoted much of her concurring opinion to the abstract debate and argued that the Court would be better served by a flexible constitutional doctrine adaptable to varying Establishment Clause controversies than by a "Grand Unified Theory."[36] Even Justice Souter, whose plurality opinion repeatedly emphasized that the dispute was unique,[37] did not transcend an abstracted constitutional frame of reference.

Kiryas Joel thus illustrates how justices can let one of the purposes of Supreme Court review—the clarification of abstract constitutional doctrine—dominate judicial opinions and stand in the way of truthfulness about citizen interests and values. Truthfulness about the values and interests of the handicapped children, the Satmar religious community, or other citizens took a back seat to the argument about whether *Lemon* and *Aguilar* were or were not reliable precedent. Moreover, justices' limited, abstract focus compromised any possibility that their opinions would adequately honor constitutional stature by voicing respect for the Satmar community.

On the other hand, justices may at times be so involved with specific citizen interests that their framing becomes an exercise in advocacy that also precludes a truthful account of opposing interests and values. Advocacy framing, for example, resulted in the disappearance of women from *Bray v. Alexandria Women's Health Clinic*.[38] The *Bray* plaintiffs had hoped to secure an injunction against antiabortion demonstrators using aggressive tactics to disrupt the activities of abortion clinics. They argued that the demonstrations prevented women from exercising their right to choose an abortion. For them, women and values associated with women's reproductive rights were central to the understanding of what was at stake in the dispute. Demonstrators objecting to an injunction, however, framed the dispute as one involving antiabortion activists wishing to intervene between an innocent victim (i.e., the "unborn child") and an abortionist (i.e., the doctor).[39] From their frame of reference, women were not even stakeholders in the dispute. Astonishingly, justices in the *Bray* majority adopted the demonstrators' frame. In a controversy having significant implications for women, women's interests, and women's rights, justices appropriated the rhetoric of one of the parties to the dispute and, in effect, removed women from the dispute.

Truth-obstructing conventions of rights litigation such as framing, and the practical difficulty of recognizing all interests at stake in a rights dispute, might cause us to question whether it makes any sense to imagine that justices have an obligation to be truthful regarding constitutional losers—until, that is, we recall the significant harms that untruthfulness can inflict on losers' constitutional stature. At its worst, as the disappearance of women from the *Bray* dispute illustrates, untruthfulness is as serious as the more direct attacks on constitutional stature in *Bowers* and *Carhart*. Moreover, as you will see in the chapters that follow, truthfulness is a prerequisite to ameliorating harms inherent in losing a rights dispute. Thus, justices should do what they can to minimize the risk of untruthfulness.

Because of the winnowing process through which rights disputes make their way to the Supreme Court, because parties generally do a good job of educating justices, and because of the participation of many *amici* in most rights disputes, justices are aware of the interests of stakeholders in rights disputes. Informed by stakeholder argument, justices should refuse to let prevailing constitutional doctrine and metaphors distort their descriptions of what is at stake in the real world. Even if justices do not believe that the interests of constitutional losers are sufficiently weighty to prevail in constitutional analysis, and even if substantive doctrine does not "see" those interests as directly relevant, justices can nonetheless truthfully inform us about those interests. In *Dale*, for example, the fact that state interests were at the forefront of constitutional analysis should not have ruled out an honest discussion of what was at stake for Dale and other persons of his sexual orientation. Similarly, although the *Hein* plurality would argue that its opinion was a legitimate, straightforward application of standing doctrine, justices might nonetheless have truthfully taken note of the importance of freedom of conscience to the losers.

At a minimum, justices should do a sufficiently acceptable job of coming to grips with what is at stake in a rights dispute that it will be impossible for them to accuse one another of lying, of knowingly mischaracterizing the nature of a dispute, of being willfully ignorant of constitutional losers' interests, or of deliberately misusing precedent to achieve a predetermined outcome. If a majority opinion is at risk of being accused of untruthfulness by dissenters, it is probable that constitutional losers will question its truthfulness, as well. Justices wishing to avoid harm to the losers' constitutional stature would, in that case, be well served by revising their written opinion.

Avoiding untruthfulness will be the first step needed if justices wish to ameliorate the normal harms inherent in losing a rights dispute. The next chapter turns to the challenging subject of justices' harm-amelioration obligation. Fulfilling that obligation requires justices to properly and truthfully acknowledge what is at stake but is lost to citizens who do not prevail in rights disputes.

Notes

1. Hill v. Colorado, 530 U.S. 703 (2000).
2. *Id.* at 741 (2000) (Scalia, J., dissenting).
3. *Id.* at 742.
4. *Id.* at 750.
5. *Id.* at 764.
6. *Id.* at 750.
7. *Id.* at 756.
8. *Id.* at 757–58.
9. *Id.* at 789 (Kennedy, J., dissenting).
10. Boy Scouts of Am. v. Dale, 530 U.S. 640, 686 (2000) (Stevens, J., dissenting).
11. District of Columbia v. Heller, 554 U.S. 570, 128 S. Ct. 2783, 2823–24 (2008) (Stevens, J., dissenting).

12. See, e.g., Parents Involved in Cmty. Sch. v. Seattle Sch. Dist. No. 1, 127 S. Ct. 2738, 2761 (2007).
13. DAVID LUBAN, LEGAL ETHICS AND HUMAN DIGNITY 79 (2007).
14. See ROBERT A. BURT, THE CONSTITUTION IN CRISIS 356 (1992) (stating that judges should defer to the subjective perception of losers themselves).
15. See Shaw v. Reno, 509 U.S. 630 (1993) (holding that the congressional district created by state's redistricting legislation was so irregular that the legislation could be viewed only as an effort to draw racial lines for the purpose of voting).
16. Romer v. Evans, 517 U.S. 620 (1996).
17. Rumsfeld v. Forum for Academic and Institutional Rights, 547 U.S. 47 (2006).
18. *Dale*, 530 U.S. 640.
19. *Heller*, 128 S. Ct. 2783.
20. See AT&T Corp. v. Hulteen, 129 S. Ct. 1962 (2009); General Elec. Co. v. Gilbert, 429 U.S. 125 (1976); Geduldig v. Aiello, 417 U.S. 484 (1974).
21. See *id.*
22. See the Pregnancy Discrimination Act of 1978, 42 U.S.C. sec. § 2000e.
23. *Dale*, 530 U.S. at 750–51 (Scalia, J., dissenting).
24. See R.A.V. v. City of St. Paul, 505 U.S. 377, 383–84 (1992).
25. Hein v. Freedom from Religion Found., 551 U.S. 587 (2007).
26. *Id.* at 2585 (Souter, J., dissenting).
27. *Id.* at 2559 (majority opinion).
28. *Id.* at 2574–75, 2578 (Scalia, J., concurring).
29. *Id.* at 2578, 2581–83.
30. Bd. of Educ. of Kiryas Joel Vill. Sch. Dist. v. Grumet, 512 U.S. 687 (1994).
31. *See id.* at 741–42 (Scalia, J., dissenting).
32. *See id.* at 711 (Stevens, J., concurring).
33. Lemon v. Kurtzman, 403 U.S. 602 (1971).
34. Aguilar v. Felton, 473 U.S. 402 (1985).
35. *See id.* at 723–24 (Kennedy, J., concurring).
36. *Id.* at 718–720 (O'Connor, J., concurring).
37. See, e.g., *Kiryas Joel*, 512 U.S. at 701 (plurality opinion).
38. Bray v. Alexandria Women's Health Clinic, 506 U.S. 263 (1993).
39. *Id.* at 268–69.

Chapter 5

Acknowledgment of Harm

Imagine, if you will, a constitutional leader who has not persuaded justices of the validity of her argument about constitutional meaning. She has participated in a rights debate in which she has made reasonable but unsuccessful constitutional arguments. Although justices have rejected her arguments, they have not attacked her constitutional stature. She and stakeholders who identify with her have not been consigned to the constitutional dustbin; neither they nor their interests have been effaced from justices' opinions. Justices have, in other words, not inflicted harm on her constitutional stature. Nonetheless, she is not a constitutional winner and, as a constitutional loser, has suffered the harm that is inherent in defeat. Have justices, by refraining from attacking constitutional stature, fulfilled all of their obligations to her and other constitutional losers like her? They have not.

Constitutional leaders do not act wrongfully when they participate in the development of constitutional meaning regarding, for example, voting rights, race discrimination, free speech, or abortion. Moreover, constitutional leaders do not become blameworthy simply because they fail to persuade justices to adopt their views and are declared constitutional losers. They remain joint and equal sovereigns under the Constitution. Constitutional losers end up holding the short end of the constitutional stick simply because justices must make a choice among passionately defended values and interests. The judicial choice is thus an essentially tragic choice, in which there are no unequivocally good or evil contenders but only competing stakeholders of full constitutional stature.[1] *Losing Twice* argues that, under these circumstances, justices owe a harm-amelioration obligation to the constitutional leaders whose arguments justices have rejected.

This chapter discusses why justices making a tragic choice have a harm-amelioration obligation to properly acknowledge their choice and its harmful consequences for constitutional losers. It will also offer some ideas about what proper acknowledgment might look like. As previously noted, truthfulness about what is at stake for all parties is a central requirement of proper acknowledgment. Truthfulness does not, however, fully satisfy the obligation. Something more is required. Drawing on the insights of scholars working outside the field of law, this chapter embarks on an exploration, from a multidisciplinary perspective, of justices' harm-amelioration obligation. Think of the exploration as if it were an excavation of an archeological site and the chapter an initial step in constructing an approach to justices' obligation out of shards of philosophical, literary, and other theories. Because these theories reflect shared cultural understandings, the contours of the harm-amelioration obligation should have a familiar feel. The obligation may not comport with all particulars of any given theory, and my description of the obligation will certainly be incomplete, but the chapter should offer a useful framework and language for thinking about justices' obligations.

With these cautions and qualifications in mind, consider the initial question of why justices of the Supreme Court might owe an obligation to properly acknowledge harms resulting from a tragic choice. Two reasons emerge if we dig into relevant scholarship. First, scholars believe that proper acknowledgment of an essentially tragic choice and its consequences will shore up the integrity and legitimacy of the person or institution making the choice. Second, proper acknowledgment honors the humanity and moral stature of the person harmed. In other words, scholars link proper acknowledgment both to the legitimacy of a maker of tragic decisions and to the preservation of the rightful stature of individuals adversely affected by a tragic choice.

The first point, that proper acknowledgment of a tragic choice and its consequences preserves the integrity and legitimacy of the person making the choice, is a theme in the work of Martha Nussbaum. Nussbaum, known for her eloquent analyses of Greek tragedy and its implications for the study of law, asserts that Greek tragedy repeatedly tells stories about people who become monstrous by making a tragic choice and then failing to acknowledge the nature of the choice or the inevitable harm to an innocent that results from it. She discusses, for example, one account of the decision of Agamemnon, King of Argos, to sacrifice his daughter Iphigeneia, in *Agamemnon*.[2] Nussbaum argues that Aeschylus condemned Agamemnon not because of the sacrifice itself but, rather, because Agamemnon insisted on describing his decision as a pious and unqualifiedly rightful act instead of a choice necessitated by a tragic "intersection of two divine demands."[3] Nussbaum draws a similar conclusion from Sophocles' depiction, in *Antigone*, of the conflict between Creon and Antigone over the burial of a man who had died fighting against the prevailing government of Thebes.[4] Creon, the ruler of Thebes, had prohibited burial; Antigone, the sister of the dead man, was determined to see burial occur. In Nussbaum's view, both Creon and Antigone faced difficult choices, Creon between competing obligations to the political community and to family, Antigone between similar obligations as well as an additional obligation rooted in religious precepts. Rather than properly acknowledging the nature and consequences of their choices, however, both Creon and Antigone tried to justified their choices in ways that denied the essentially tragic nature of their decisions and actions. Thus, according to Nussbaum, both Creon and Antigone were portrayed by Sophocles as "oddly inhuman beings."[5] They, like Agamemnon, forfeited their humanity.

Other scholars have a slightly more abstract and somewhat different approach to the proposition that those who inflict harm through a tragic choice are transformed and corrupted by a failure to properly acknowledge the harm. The philosopher Avishai Margalit, for example, posits that institutions and government must take proper account of harm if they are to avoid becoming tyrannical. According to Margalit, an institution or official who does not acknowledge harm but instead insists on forgetting it succumbs to "evil forces" that undermine morality and legitimacy. Such a person attempts to assert authoritarian control by "rewriting the past and controlling collective memory."[6] Philosophers who have studied truth and lying would recognize Margalit's link between tyranny, illegitimacy, and the refusal to truthfully acknowledge harms. Sissela Bok and Bernard Williams, for example, argue that falsehood puts a liar in a position of illegitimate power over others by depriving them of autonomy and choice.[7]

Each of these scholars—Nussbaum, Margalit, Bok, and Williams—would also recognize that a failure to properly acknowledge the existence of a tragic choice and its harm has deleterious effects that extend to anyone who is the object of a tragic choice. Nussbaum, for example, discerns in Greek tragedy a lesson that proper acknowledgment of harm honors the moral stature and dignity of a person whose legitimate claims are rejected in a tragic choice. Bok's arguments suggest that it may be permissible to lie to individuals who are enemies but not otherwise.[8] Applied to justices and their tragic choices, these ideas support the conclusion that a failure to properly acknowledge the harm of a tragic choice in a rights dispute will dishonor the constitutional stature of the person whose loss is ignored. The failure will send a signal that a constitutional loser is not a fellow citizen but, instead, no different from an enemy.

Judith Shklar offers an especially useful way of thinking about acknowledgment of harm and citizen stature, in her accessible and eloquent collection of essays entitled *The Faces of Injustice*.[9] For Shklar, a failure to properly acknowledge harm reflects an indifference that dehumanizes the person who is harmed.[10] While we may have no obligation to pay attention to people who suffer harm accidentally, by happening to be in the wrong place at the wrong time, Shklar says we cannot intentionally "administer people as if they were things" undeserving of proper explanations for conscious government choices that change lives.[11]

An obligation to properly acknowledge harms resulting from one's tragic choices thus derives from the need to avoid inflicting additional harms on the human and political stature of those adversely affected, and from the desire of the person making a tragic choice to attest to the legitimacy of that choice. There is no readily apparent reason that we should not apply these observations and arguments to tragic judicial choices. Insofar as justices of the Supreme Court are concerned, there would be two simple propositions. First, justices who do not properly acknowledge their tragic choices and the harms they inflict on constitutional losers put their legitimacy at risk. Second, justices' failure to acknowledge the choice and its harms will dishonor constitutional stature and inflict additional, unjust harm on constitutional losers.

This is all very well and good, you might say, but it does not help anyone figure out how, as a practical matter, justices might write their opinions so as to properly acknowledge harm. We need to uncover something in our conceptual dig that gives us an answer to that difficult question. Scholars who discuss tragic choices offer some useful options.

First, proper acknowledgment requires something more than truthfulness or respectfully nodding one's head to signify that someone suffering from a tragic choice has been heard. Martha Nussbaum suggests, for example, that proper acknowledgment of harm resulting from a tragic choice requires that the person who has inflicted harm send a message that she understands the significance of what she has done. The message might be sent in a number of ways. It might consist of the harming party making a pledge to attempt to avoid doing similar harm in other cases. It might be conveyed by avoiding doing or saying anything that would encourage others, citizens or legislators, for example, to ignore the losers' values in other circumstances. The harming party might also recognize the significance of harm through expressions of remorse or regret.

Consider the view that proper acknowledgment will embody a pledge to make efforts to avoid the same tragic choice in future cases. According to Nussbaum, persons harmed by a tragic choice hold values that are important. For that reason, people who make tragic choices should properly search for other circumstances in which they will find it possible to recognize sacrificed values.[12] Nussbaum even suggests that someone who makes a tragic choice should do something to "remake the world in such a way that [similar rights disputes and the necessity for additional tragic choices] more rarely arise."[13] Proper acknowledgment has the character of Avishai Margalit's moral witness: it reassures losers of this "sober hope: that in another place or another time there exists, or will exist," a community that will recognize the losers' claims.[14]

If we transpose these ideas to the world of rights disputing, we might conclude that justices should not only be truthful about the value of constitutional losers' claims but also write opinions honoring those values. Perhaps justices should make known their commitment to respect the claim in other contexts and circumstances. They should avoid writing opinions that might encourage others—constitutional winners, other citizens, other government officials—to be indifferent to the losing values and interests. Even if they do not affirmatively call for legislative action to avert or ameliorate future harm to the losers, they can surely avoid repeating the wrongheaded practices of *Bowers v. Hardwick*, which so contemptuously disparaged the losers and their interests that Colorado voters were arguably encouraged to try to write a group of citizens out of their state constitution.[15] Justices could point out that the reach of their decision is limited by the circumstances that gave rise to the dispute and that in other contexts or times the losers' interests might prevail. Although justices already write opinions that occasionally do some of these things—for example, they often note that their decisions are contextually bounded and leave doors open to re-litigation of previously losing claims—they do so as a matter of judicial minimalism or some other doctrine of judicial restraint, not as a gesture of respect for constitutional losers or because of a wish to fulfill harm-amelioration obligations.

Moreover, proper acknowledgment of the significance of a loser's harms arguably involves even more than sending messages that justices and others should try to honor losers' values in other circumstances and settings. Some scholars suggest that justices' recognition of a constitutional loser's interests and values should be sufficiently strong that it embodies, in effect, an expression of remorse or regret for the tragic choice and its harms. Bernard Williams, for example, reminds us that a loser is rarely able to *fully* accept the justification for a tragic choice that inflicts harm. Losers will almost inevitably feel wronged in some way by such a choice. For that reason, Williams argues, an explanation for a tragic choice must have a certain qualitative aspect. It should not only include full acknowledgment of all of its costs but also ought to be accompanied by regret.[16] Williams's view is also implicit in Judith Jarvis Thomson's statement that the "moral residue" of a tragic choice precludes someone who has made such a choice from washing her hands of responsibility for its consequences, even if those consequences can be justified by good reasons.[17]

Moving from the philosophical to the literary corner of this chapter's conceptual dig, we find suggestions that help us understand the specific quality of regret suited to proper acknowledgment of harm. Regret might, for example, have the qualities that Jahan Ramazani attributes to the modern elegy.[18] According to Ramazani, the traditional elegy was designed to help an audience detach itself from, or find a transcendent meaning in, a loss deemed part of the natural order of things. The traditional elegiac form, however, is not suited to the acknowledgment of losses that are not divinely ordained. In particular, Ramazani argues, the traditional form does not work well in a modern, pluralistic society where, by definition, specific losses cannot be attributed to a predetermined order or set of standards on which all agree. Contemporary elegists such as Auden and Yeats, therefore, have adopted a modified poetic form adapted to a world in which people have competing, legitimate claims and suffer for reasons that cannot be explained in terms of black-and-white standards of good and evil.[19]

Justices who decide rights disputes between competing, innocent constitutional leaders and whose explanations of constitutional meaning are contingent might be well served by applying Ramazani's ideas to their written opinions. They might be especially interested in Ramazani's discussion of how the modern elegy enables a poet to both honor and displace tradition. The modern elegiac form seeks to avoid betraying the dead (or, in our frame of reference, the constitutional loser) by pretending, as did the traditional elegy, that a loss and associated harms can somehow be transcended. It also does not merely take detached, bureaucratic, cost–benefit note of harms. The form of the modern elegist, according to Ramazani, finds its tangible counterpart in the Vietnam War Memorial. It is consciously non-transcendent and ambivalent. It does not attempt to ignore or convert losses into gains in order to mask them. In mirroring tragedy, it opens the door to sorrow. It employs communicative strategies that evoke irresolution, ambivalence, guilt, and anxiety. It uses fractured speech and lacks an autocratic tone.[20] These traits of the modern elegy are relevant to the proper acknowledgment of harm—including a manifestation of remorse—in a judicial opinion suited to a pluralistic world of constitutional disputing where the designation of losers and winners is not preordained.

If an expression of remorse is an element of proper acknowledgment of harm when a tragic choice is made, however, justices may need to substantially reorient their approach to opinion-writing. Ramazani's analysis suggests, for example, that justices would need to make adjustments in conventional judicial language and practices of justification. The language of logic, on its own, would be clearly seen as insufficient to the task of properly acknowledging harm, for it suggests an unrealistic inexorability and definitiveness in constitutional meaning. Similarly, the language of ideology, insofar as it purports definitively to declare winners and losers for all time without regard to context, would be called into question.

We might also unearth a bit of advice about proper acknowledgment if we spend a little bit of time reflecting on Robert Pogue Harrison's *Dominion of the Dead*.[21] Harrison discusses memorials to the dead and notes that proper memorials remind the living that their fate is bound up with that of the dead.[22] A proper memorial is constructed so as to ensure that the dead will not seek revenge or haunt the living.[23] Transposing Harrison's observations to opinions written in constitutional rights disputes, readers might think of Harrison's "living" individuals as the constitutional winners, the "dead" as constitutional losers, and the relevant memorials as the written opinions of Supreme Court justices.

Justices do sometimes think of death and burials when rendering a decision in a rights dispute. Justice Stevens reportedly has commented, for example, that if "[we are] overruling *Roe v. Wade*...[let's] give the case a decent burial," and Justice Blackmun once worried about *Roe*'s "passing."[24] But perhaps justices should also think about constructing their opinions to remind winners that they and losers have a shared constitutional fate and that losers' stature within the constitutional community must be respected. Whether justices refuse to give new meaning to general constitutional principles in a rights dispute or, alternatively, reject traditional constitutional meaning, the constitutional losers are like the dead discussed by Harrison. Constitutional losers do not go away even if efforts are made to make them disappear. They do not renounce their citizenship or their constitutional stature. They remain part of the community.

Constitutional losers continue to have equality and consent expectations that give them a rightful ownership claim to the Court's body of decisional law. Justices thus cannot afford to behave like the Sicilian baron described by Harrison, a baron who refused to allow peasants to bury their dead on his land lest the peasants "come to believe that the land belonged to them by natural right."[25] Justices cannot ignore the ownership claims of constitutional losers. Nor can they ignore the fact that the fate of constitutional winners is inextricably bound up with that of the losers, or that harms inflicted on constitutional losers can have deleterious effects on or haunt the rest of the political community. Justices wishing to properly acknowledge harm will wisely seek to memorialize the harm in such a way that the conjoined fate of winners and losers becomes an honored part of the political community rather than a source of distress or trouble.

To summarize, justices' acknowledgment of a tragic choice and its consequences for constitutional losers should arguably have a number of features and qualities. Justices should strive to be truthful respecting what is at stake for constitutional losers. They should convey an understanding of the significance of the harms inuring to losers. They should indicate a commitment to avoiding similar harms in future cases and in other areas of political life. They should not do anything that would invite others to cavalierly neglect the losers' values and harms done to them. They should manifest remorse for the necessity of their tragic choice and the consequences for constitutional losers. They should understand that their opinions are essentially cornerstones of a memorial to constitutional losers: the opinions may be structured so as to serve some traditional purposes of memorials but they must also take into account features of memorials (or elegies) suited to contemporary society.

An apology shares many of the features and qualities summarized above. Even if justices have no obligation to issue formal apologies to constitutional losers, we all—citizens and justices alike—can learn much of value from considering the elements of a valid apology. According to accepted theory, a valid apology is not merely a justification for or an explanation as to why a decision was appropriate. Instead, it conveys an understanding of the harm that has been inflicted and accepts full responsibility for that harm. It recognizes that a harmed person might legitimately resent or be offended by what has happened. It conveys remorse and a promise that every effort will be made to avoid a similar, future harm.

As Kathleen Gill has noted, apologies are especially important to governmental institutions that have the capacity to inflict substantial harm on citizens and that must secure the consent of different people across time and space.[26] According to Gill, such an institution has a self-interest in acknowledging the value of those who have been harmed and in at least implicitly promising that it will try to avoid doing harm in the future. An acknowledgment offered through an apology, says Gill, will reassure citizens that the institution is attempting to behave legitimately toward even the losers. Moreover, it may be the *only* way for an institution to sustain legitimacy as society changes over the years. Gill's argument is obviously relevant to justices, whose practices of judicial review and decisions depend on renewed citizen consent, over time, for their legitimacy.

Avishai Margalit makes an additional and important point relevant to apologies. Apologies solicit forgiveness; they ask injured parties to forget their harms and to restore broken relationships.[27] Thus, a valid apology signifies that injured parties are in control of whether a relationship will be restored, and under what terms. A constitutional loser who chooses to forgive and forget, for example, will *affirm* judicial legitimacy. In contrast, it is not within justices' power to buttress their legitimacy by forgiving themselves or forgetting the harm they have inflicted on losers.

A judicial opinion that offers only an extended and rationalized justification for, rather than a proper acknowledgment of, a tragic choice may reasonably be understood as a contemptible effort of justices to forgive and legitimate themselves. In the absence of proper acknowledgment of the harms done them, why should constitutional losers *not* withhold what only they can give: assurance that the infliction of harm has neither irreparably breached an important relationship nor destroyed judicial legitimacy? In contrast, a judicial opinion that reflects the elements of a valid apology would affirm that constitutional losers are in a superior position of power *vis à vis* justices, an affirmation that accords with full constitutional stature. An opinion embodying such an affirmation would lay a foundation for the restoration of relationships and for putting the world in proper alignment. It would, to paraphrase George Fletcher, build bridges between losers and winners and enable losers to continue to participate in the life of the nation.[28] It would send a message that constitutional losers matter to justices and to the rest of the political community.

A judicial opinion, of course, does not have to embody a formal apology to serve these purposes. As you will see in subsequent chapters, justices can properly acknowledge harms inflicted on constitutional losers in a variety of ways. Moreover, proper acknowledgment will require justices to make some tough judgment calls. The difficulty of knowing when to starkly remember and when to soften the truth of events, for example, has already been noted in chapter 4's discussion of truthfulness.[29] Compounding the difficulty is the fact that proper acknowledgment of the harms inherent in defeat will result in written opinions that may appear disturbingly ambiguous and thus less than authoritative. It is obvious, given these and other concerns addressed in subsequent chapters, that our quintessentially practical question—what must a *proper* acknowledgment consist of?—is not easy to answer.

Nonetheless, acknowledging the obligation and exploring the question has inestimable value. As citizens begin to recognize justices' obligations, we will read Supreme Court decisions differently. We will pay attention to the absence of a proper acknowledgment of harm and to what that absence might signify. If we encounter an opinion lacking the elements, attitudes, and commitments of an apology, for example, we might reasonably conclude that justices have intentionally sent a message that the losers do not count equally with other citizens, as constitutional leaders. Alternatively, we might decide that justices in a given opinion tried but were unable to find a way to construct the equivalent of a valid apology. In either event, we will be in a position to respond appropriately to a given opinion. If we decide that the absence of a proper acknowledgment stems from justices' belief that a constitutional loser does not enjoy equal stature, for example, we can assess the presumptively questionable validity of the justices' belief. In other words, we will have a satisfactory way of deciding whether justices have acted legitimately in resolving a rights dispute, of precisely describing identified judicial failures, of articulating the basis for our outrage at a given decision, and of constructing a useful response. We will have a powerful counterargument to those who would like us to believe that justices are entitled to act as legal technocrats or umpires immune from or invisible to pestering, distracting citizens.

The following chapters should assist citizens in developing their understanding of justices' obligations to properly acknowledge and thereby ameliorate harms to constitutional losers. They identify additional harm-amelioration practices, analyze a state court decision that might serve as a model for honoring the stature of constitutional losers, and explore whether justices have honored constitutional stature and thus ameliorated harm in abortion rights disputes.

Notes

1. Cf. Mark J. Osiel, *Ever Again: Legal Remembrance of Administrative Massacre*, 144 U. PA. L. REV. 463, 562 (1995) (describing such a choice as a "genuine tragedy").
2. MARTHA C. NUSSBAUM, THE FRAGILITY OF GOODNESS: LUCK AND ETHICS IN GREEK TRAGEDY AND PHILOSOPHY 33–38 (rev. ed. 2001).

3. *Id.* at 33.
4. See generally *id.* at 51–82.
5. *Id.* at 65.
6. AVISHAI MARGALIT, THE ETHICS OF MEMORY 83 (2002).
7. SISSELA BOK, LYING: MORAL CHOICE IN PUBLIC AND PRIVATE LIFE 18–20 (Vintage Books ed. 1989); BERNARD WILLIAMS, TRUTH AND TRUTHFULNESS: AN ESSAY IN GENEALOGY 221–23 (2002).
8. See BOK, *supra* note 7, at 134–45.
9. JUDITH N. SHKLAR, THE FACES OF INJUSTICE (1990).
10. *Id.* at 35–36, 119.
11. *Id.* at 119.
12. Martha C. Nussbaum, *Valuing Values: A Case for Reasoned Commitment,* 6 YALE J.L. & HUMAN. 197, 212–15 (1994).
13. *Id.* at 214.
14. MARGALIT, *supra* note 6, at 155.
15. Bowers v. Hardwick, 478 U.S. 186 (1986).
16. BERNARD WILLIAMS, MORAL LUCK: PHILOSOPHICAL PAPERS 1973–1980, at 37 (1981); BERNARD WILLIAMS, SHAME AND NECESSITY 135 (1993) (describing the "moral cost" of tragic choices).
17. JUDITH JARVIS THOMSON, THE REALM OF RIGHTS 84–86 (1990).
18. JAHAN RAMAZANI, POETRY OF MOURNING: THE MODERN ELEGY FROM HARDY TO HEANEY (1994).
19. *Id.* at 180–89.
20. *Id.* at 362.
21. ROBERT POGUE HARRISON, THE DOMINION OF THE DEAD (2003).
22. *Id.* at 70 ("The living share the mortal fate of the dead").
23. *Id.* at 69 (proper burials "appease the dead [and] secure their good will"); *id.* at 103 (being deprived of proper memorialization, "the dead [will] have their way with us" and be in control).
24. See, e.g., BERNARD SCHWARTZ, DECISION: HOW THE SUPREME COURT DECIDES CASES 26–27 (1996).
25. HARRISON, *supra* note 21, at 24.
26. Kathleen A. Gill, *The Moral Functions of an Apology, in* INJUSTICE AND RECTIFICATION 111, 118–19 (Rodney C. Roberts ed., 2002).
27. MARGALIT, *supra* note 6, at 205.
28. George P. Fletcher, *The Storrs Lectures: Liberals and Romantics at War: The Problem of Collective Guilt,* 111 YALE L.J. 1499, 1569 (2002).
29. See generally MARGALIT, *supra* note 6, at 13, 17 (arguing that an ethic for remembering harm must always be accompanied by standards or an ethic of forgetting).

Chapter 6

The Art of Harm Amelioration

The previous survey of relevant scholarship suggests that justices can and should ameliorate the harms inherent in losing a rights dispute by properly acknowledging the tragic nature of their choice and its harmful consequences for persons of full constitutional stature. Proper acknowledgment requires a truthful account of the interests and values held by constitutional losers; untruthfulness about these matters both interferes with acknowledgment of the tragic nature of the choice and also sends a message that losers and their values are not worthy of respect in future conversations about constitutional meaning. More broadly, proper acknowledgment requires honoring the constitutional stature of losers, which is perhaps the key to the art of harm amelioration.

If justices wish to honor constitutional stature, they must, of course, refrain from attacks on constitutional stature that undercut losers' equal moral and political capacity to participate in the development of constitutional meaning. Justices must, for example, refuse to treat losers as blameworthy if they wish to respect constitutional leadership. In addition, attacks on constitutional stature are an impediment to expressions of remorse or regret, the creation of a proper memorial to constitutional struggle, and the repair of fractured relationships.

Honoring constitutional stature and ameliorating harms inherent in losing a rights dispute, however, require more from justices than a mere refusal to attack constitutional stature. Honoring constitutional stature requires affirmative acts. The previous chapter, for example, argued that justices might consider writing opinions containing the elements of a valid apology if they wish to honor losers' constitutional stature and ameliorate the harms done to them. This chapter sets forth four specific recommendations compatible with that argument. Readers should understand, however, that justices cannot satisfy their harm-amelioration obligation merely by conforming to a checklist of cut-and-dried, do-and-don't rules. Properly accounting for harm in a manner that honors constitutional stature is as much an art as a science. For that reason, I have also included a discussion of an opinion issued by a state court judge in *Romer v. Evans*,[1] which complies, in its own fashion, with the recommendations made here. That opinion should help illustrate what a Supreme Court opinion might look like were justices to take affirmative steps to honor the constitutional stature of losers in rights disputes.

The first recommendation is that justices abandon the convention of relying on dissenting opinions to fully explain losers' interests and values. It is true that dissenting opinions can do a number of useful things relevant to the concerns expressed in this book. Dissents can, for example, carry a "judicial conversation through time" so that no citizen is forever declared a constitutional loser.[2] A good illustration is Justice Harlan's dissent in *Plessy v. Ferguson*,[3] which rejected racially separate but equal facilities but received general vindication only sixty years later, when the Court announced its landmark decision in *Brown v. Board of Education*.[4] On the other hand, because dissenting justices do not speak for the Court, they may incorporate "cantankerous expressions of individual prejudice" into the res publica.[5] Dissenters may also think of themselves as "gladiator[s] making a last stand against the lions"[6] and neglect the constitutional stature of winners. When they are not combative or personally snappish, dissents can become pro forma or simple statements affirming a particular justice's sense of personal integrity. In death penalty cases, for example, Justice Brennan repeatedly injected the terse statement: "Adhering to my view that the death penalty is in all circumstances cruel and unusual punishment prohibited by the Eighth and Fourteenth Amendments...I would grant certiorari and vacate the death sentence in this case."[7] Moreover, rights disputes do not always produce a dissent. Indeed, justices may strive to reach unanimous decisions, as Chief Justice Roberts reportedly encourages his colleagues to do.

Most importantly, even if every rights decision were to produce a dissenting opinion, a dissent cannot discharge the harm-amelioration obligation owed by the majority justices who have inflicted harm. By definition, dissenting opinions do not give majority justices—the justices who inflict harms through their tragic choice—a means of taking responsibility for what they have done. Dissenting opinions can neither repair relationships between majority justices and constitutional losers nor shore up the legitimacy of the Court. It is majority justices who must do the work of properly acknowledging and ameliorating the harms inflicted on constitutional losers by their tragic choice.

A second recommendation is, thus, that majority justices must accept responsibility for inflicting harm on constitutional losers. More specifically, they must not deflect their responsibility for harm by invoking ideology as an excuse. Ideology, according to William Simon, is an a priori judicial commitment to a political agenda that does not embody a universal principle, although its adherents would like us to believe otherwise.[8] From the perspective of the argument made in *Losing Twice*, an especially pernicious feature of an ideology is its displacement of a contextual approach to difficult questions of ethical obligation by rigid, categorical rules and analytical frameworks.[9] An ideology persistently denies the truth of many things that ordinary citizens know to be real.

Ideological justifications are most damaging to constitutional stature when justices invoke them to absolve themselves of any responsibility for their tragic choices and the resulting harms to constitutional losers. Ideological justifications seem to say to constitutional losers "don't blame me, the devil made me do it." They enable justices to, in effect, forgive themselves for the harms they inflict. You will recall that judicial self-forgiveness is associated with justices who are unwilling to acknowledge that the power of forgiveness resides in constitutional losers. Efforts at self-forgiveness send a message that misrepresents the relationship between justices and citizens—agents and principals, respectively—in our system of government. Opinions embodying ideological justifications that absolve justices are thus ill suited to repairing relationships with constitutional losers.

It can, of course, be difficult to determine whether justices have used ideological justifications to avoid proper acknowledgment of harm in a given rights dispute. Consider, as an example, one of Justice Kennedy's concurring opinions. *Texas v. Johnson* involved the prosecution of a protester who had burned an American flag.[10] Majority justices decided that the Texas statute on which the prosecution was based was unconstitutional as applied to flag-burning. Justice Kennedy noted that "this case, like others before [the Court] from time to time, exacts its personal toll."[11] He acknowledged, for example, that "among those who will be dismayed by our holding will be some who have had the singular honor of carrying the flag in battle."[12] He expressly stated, "The outcome can be laid at no door but ours,"[13] but then continued:

> Sometimes we must make decisions we do not like. We make them because...the law and the Constitution, *as we see them*, compel the result.... [E]xcept in the rare case, we do not pause to express distaste for the result, perhaps for fear of undermining a valued principle that dictates the decision.[14]

Did Kennedy claim that rigid doctrine made him inflict harm on the losing stakeholders who had carried the U.S. flag in battle, or did he accept responsibility for the losers' treatment and harms? You will have to decide for yourselves, but if you interpret Kennedy's opinion as an attempt at ideological self-forgiveness, then Kennedy did not properly honor the losers' constitutional stature or ameliorate the harm of defeat.

A third recommendation, closely related to the second, is that justices should convey humility in their opinions. The type of humility recommended here differs from the humility arguably reflected in a doctrine of judicial mini-malism that cautions justices to decide rights disputes on narrow grounds. For purposes of the harm-amelioration obligation, humility consists in part of a non-ideological attitude. Justices displaying humility recognize that they are making tragic and harmful choices and that in the world of constitutional rights "no one is [ever] finally defeated."[15] Humble justices will admit that they may misunder-stand what is at stake in a dispute, that their interpretations are fallible, that they might not have reached the proper outcome in a given dispute, and that acceptance of what they have done is ultimately in the hands of citizens. In effect, humble justices acknowledge the important role of citizen consent and constitu-tional leadership in the development of constitutional meaning, the potential validity of losers' values and interests in other settings and circumstances, and also that they are not owners but only trustees of constitutional meaning. This form of humility enables justices to express remorse for harms they have caused. Most important, it supports the restoration of a proper relationship between constitutional losers and justices.

Finally, opinions capable of restoring a proper relationship between justices and constitutional losers who suffer harm must be written with an understanding that language has the power not only to persuade but also to cause harm. Thus, justices should not only use words precisely and with an understanding of their nuances; they should also know *how* to speak in a manner suited to their rela-tionship with and obligations to citizen stakeholders in rights disputes. It is well beyond the scope of this book to review philosophies of language and rhetoric that address relevant ethical issues. However, one thing justices might do is simply develop better and richer understandings of what losing can entail in a rights dispute. For example, justices might begin to understand harms to losers as encompassing the state of "being lost" or not being seen or heard. Perhaps citizens are "lost" when they are not treated in accordance with their constitu-tional stature. Justices might also think of loss and harm as being uncertain about one's location, as sometimes happens when courts are not clear about where los-ing citizens fit in the constitutional world. They might begin to think of loss and harm as including a relational component, and recognize that constitutional losers are at risk of becoming unavailable to (i.e., of "being lost to") or having no influence on (i.e., "being lost on") others in the political community. If these perspectives on losing influenced their opinions, justices might more readily honor constitutional losers' leadership and stature within the political community.

These four simple rules—do not rely on dissenting opinions to discharge obligations to constitutional losers, do not use ideological justifications to excuse harms inflicted on losers, display humility suited to the proper relationship bet-ween justices and citizens, and use language carefully and with a proper ethical orientation—will optimize the possibility that justices will properly acknowledge the harms inflicted on constitutional losers, honor constitutional stature, and ameliorate the harms inherent in losing. However, it is worth repeating Judge Richard Posner's reminder that judges' work is as much art as science,[16] in addition to William Simon's caution that it is difficult to institutionalize an ethical system through rules.[17] Justices' obligations describe a way of living within the world of law. We may therefore recognize proper acknowledgment of harm and its amelioration more in the doing than through a checklist of abstract rules for writing judicial opinions.

For that reason, readers might find it helpful to look at an example of how one state court judge actually resolved a highly charged rights dispute while recognizing many of the obligations described in this and the preceding chapters. I am thinking of Judge H. Jeffery Bayless, who issued the first reported opinion in *Romer v. Evans*.[18] *Romer* has been discussed in previous chapters, so you may recall that it involved a challenge to Colorado's Amendment 2, a voter initiative that prohibited government from adopting or enforcing regulations or policies granting homosexuals protection against discrimination.[19]

According to the plaintiffs in *Romer*, Amendment 2 put homosexuals seeking equal rights and other legal protections at a disadvantage within normal governmental processes, a view eventually adopted by the Supreme Court.[20] Defenders of Amendment 2, however, interpreted it simply as a provision that prevented special preferences based on sexual orientation from threatening existing marriage laws and depleting limited state resources.[21] The conservative groups responsible for getting Amendment 2 on the election ballot tended to justify the amendment as a provision that would bar a special interest group, namely, gays, from seeking to attain "special protection" not possessed by other citizens.[22]

Judge Bayless seemed to understand judicial obligations related to constitutional stature, and his opinion is consistent with this chapter's recommendations. Consider only the first three paragraphs spoken by Judge Bayless to the persons gathered in his courtroom and to the wider audience of stakeholders in the dispute:

> The Court is prepared to rule and is going to rule at this time . . . and one side is going to perceive that they have won something, and the other side is going to perceive that they have lost something. And that might generate some emotions. And I understand that. As a matter of fact, I suspect there are strong emotions on both sides. And for those who perceive that they have won something, they may want to celebrate. For those who perceive they have lost something, they might want to express disagreement with that, and that's inappropriate in court. I didn't want it yesterday, I don't want it today. But having told everybody what

I want, I'm satisfied that this group will abide by the Court's request and maintain the decorum that's appropriate for a courtroom.

Now, the second thing I want to tell you, I decided this about 2:30 this morning. Since that time, with about four hours out to sleep, I have been writing. And what I've attempted to do is to understand and have my ruling reflect that I know the audience to whom I'm speaking. And I think the audience is made up of two distinct groups. One is a group of legally trained people. That is to say, counsel who have presented this, counsel who have been perhaps inside the bar who may not have presented evidence, and they are familiar with the case law, and they are familiar with the legal concepts, and there will be catch phrases and legal expressions, code I talk in, and they'll understand that. And so a part of it is written for them.

And both sides have told me very fairly, not at this hearing but before, that they anticipate that regardless of what I do, there might be another day and in another higher appellate court that something might be reviewed. So I have written for that audience as well. But I am aware of the interests in this case and the interests in this decision from non-legally trained folks, just the people of Colorado who voted on the Amendment. So what I have attempted to do in writing this is to write at two levels. One for the lawyers and one for the non-lawyers. And I hope not to insult either. And I hope to be clear to both. How well I have succeeded in that will be determined by someone other than me.[23]

Consider what Judge Bayless did in these three opening paragraphs. First, he forthrightly established the context for his decision. He recognized that he was faced with a win–lose decision and that the stakes were very high and passionately defended by all concerned. He acknowledged that stakeholders included persons other than the formal parties before him, for he addressed everyone in the courtroom in addition to all of the voters of Colorado. He recognized that his audience included lawyers, non-lawyers, and judges. He might even have been thinking about audiences as they exist in time when he noted that "there might be another day" when his decision would be questioned.[24] He noted the potential for outrage (or celebration) in response to his decision, and he indicated that he wanted and expected all stakeholders to accept what he would do without disrupting the institutional setting of the courtroom. He humbly expressed a hope that his opinion would not insult any stakeholder and that his reasoning would be transparent to all. Finally, he acknowledged that only "someone other than" himself—presumably the audiences he addressed—had the power to determine whether his opinion did what he hoped it would do.[25] Citizens, not the judge, were in the driver's seat in deciding whether his decision was legitimate.

If you read the following, substantive portion of the opinion, you will see that Judge Bayless made an effort to meet the goals he had set for himself. First, he explained that all people are important in a constitutional democracy. He carefully and respectfully reviewed the arguments made by all sides. Doing so was especially tricky in *Romer* because the governor of the State of Colorado, the named defendant, did not agree with the views of the Colorado voters who put Amendment 2 on the ballot. As Judge Bayless noted, the state had tried to distance itself from some of Amendment 2's more conservative and religiously fundamental supporters:

> Defendants then well and fairly argue there are several things here that have been discussed that have been presented that they strongly urge are not part of the case. Mr. Dailey [representing the state] did this very well, really, at the upfront part of his argument yesterday. He said Coloradans for Family Values isn't a party here. He said the Religious Right isn't a party here, nor the Political Right, nor whether Colorado could be deemed a hate state. That's not here, Judge. That's not what you are to decide.[26]

Judge Bayless nonetheless understood that persons other than the state had real interests in the outcome of the dispute, and he respectfully addressed those persons:

> As a matter of fact, I looked at what was presented to the Court in terms of the efforts that have been made on the part of Coloradans for Family Values and the Religious Right and the Political Right. And what I saw was a group of Colorado citizens who wanted to present an initiative to the voters. They said we would like the voters of Colorado to look at this. So they acquired signatures. They presented things to the state government. They followed the political process, and they got it on the ballot. And they lobbied for or were part of a lobbying effort for the passage of the Amendment, and that involved spending money and presenting their views.
>
> There is absolutely nothing wrong with that. As a matter of fact, that is exactly in keeping with the political process that this country is based on. And this Court, should there be an attack on that process, would vigorously defend those persons who have been involved with that process, because they have followed exactly what democracy urges. As a matter of fact, at every election, what you hear is the voters, "Get

involved. Go to your caucuses. Vote." That's exactly what they have done. There's nothing suspect about that.[27]

In Judge Bayless's opinion, supporters of Amendment 2 were not evil persons. They merely had their own view of what state voters should be permitted to do under Colorado's constitution. Therefore, Bayless respectfully took them into account even though the state had strategically tried to distance itself from them.

Judge Bayless also used language carefully, apparently hoping that it would not be too technical but would still reflect his allegiance to the rule of law and to Supreme Court precedent. He undertook to explain how constitutional interpretation works. He tried to make clear to his audience that constitutional meaning is not fixed for all time but can evolve (or be redeemed) as people become enlightened:

> What is the state of the law in this Court's view regarding [the] consti-
> tutionality of such an amendment? It has been mentioned that the law
> is not static. It has been mentioned that it evolves. It grows. It changes.
> And that is true. I'm going to borrow a few words from some Justices of
> the Supreme Court. It's not about these cases. Not about sexual orien-
> tation. It's about the law. It's about the law growing and changing,
> because I want to put this in a context. Quoting from Mr. Justice
> McKenna in a case called *Weems versus the United States* from a long
> time ago, 1910. He said, "The clause of the Constitution in the opinion
> of the learned commentators may be, therefore, progressive and is not
> fastened to the obsolete but may acquire meaning as public opinion
> becomes enlightened by a humane justice."
>
> I want to quote from Chief Justice Earl Warren in a 1958 case called
> *Trop versus Dulles*. He was discussing the 8th Amendment, that's cruel
> and unusual punishment. It says, "The words of the 8th Amendment
> are not precise and their scope is not static. The Amendment must draw
> its meaning from the evolving standards of decency that mark the
> progress of a maturing society."
>
> What is the law on discrimination? What has it been? As I men-
> tioned, it started with the 14th Amendment which was for former
> slaves. It related to blacks. It related to race. It has been largely domi-
> nated by racial cases.[28]

Judge Bayless then discussed the evolution of the meaning of equality under the U.S. Constitution. His opinion transparently struggled to resolve the Amendment 2 dispute in light of the limited reach of prior decisions.

Judge Bayless ultimately concluded that the plaintiffs who challenged Amendment 2 had "a reasonable probability of proving...Amendment 2...

unconstitutional beyond a reasonable doubt" because it treated a class of persons unequally based on a status.[29] Because he determined that Amendment 2 treated homosexuals unequally because of their "status, not conduct,"[30] Judge Bayless did not feel bound by the Supreme Court's decision in *Bowers v. Hardwick*, which dealt with homosexual conduct. Instead, he concluded that the relevant precedent was *Robinson v. California*:

> That case is a Supreme Court case. That case said you can't make a status a crime even though the conduct is a crime. It had to do with drugs. Can you prevent—can you say it's a crime to possess drugs? Yeah. Sell them? Yeah. Can you say it's a crime to be addicted to drugs? That's the status. And they said no.[31]

Judge Bayless's opinion may not have done everything that might be done to properly acknowledge the harms suffered by constitutional losers, to honor their constitutional stature, and to ameliorate the harm inherent in loss. However, it certainly differs from the usual published appellate opinion. Judge Bayless made a special effort to address all citizen stakeholders in the case. He carefully and patiently explained just what each party had argued. He refused to ignore important stakeholders even when the state wished to disavow them. He honored the intense commitment of both sides of the debate through both his tone and his words. He recognized that one party would see itself as a winner and that the other would see itself as a loser as a result of his decision. He refused to disrespect the losing voters of Colorado. He acknowledged that constitutional meaning evolves and that it is difficult to speak in absolutist terms about the correct answer to a given rights dispute. He refused to let technical aspects of precedent stand in the way of seeing what was at stake for homosexuals. He put himself and judgments about the legitimacy of his decision at the mercy of his audience.

There might be explanations for a state court judge's issuing an opinion of this sort, where Supreme Court justices would not so readily do so. As a state trial judge, for example, Judge Bayless was undoubtedly acutely aware of the potentially community-fracturing implications of the choice he was required to make. Unlike Supreme Court justices, he was physically part of the community that would be affected by his decision. More immediately, he might have anticipated an especially urgent need to control potentially disruptive behavior in a courtroom that would be packed with passionate advocates on both sides of the Amendment 2 controversy. Perhaps he simply had a greater incentive to properly acknowledge harm because his opinion was to be announced orally, from the bench, to an audience that was not restricted to attorneys and other judges. Then again, his words may have been linked to the fact that he had been asked to issue a preliminary injunction against a constitutional amendment approved by a majority of voters. Whatever Judge Bayless's reasons, his opinion has a number of remarkable features. He gave us a concrete example of how justices of the Supreme Court might render decisions that honor losers' constitutional stature and properly acknowledge the harm inherent in losing a rights dispute.

Notes

1. Romer v. Evans, 517 U.S. 620 (1996).
2. Kevin M. Stack, *The Practice of Dissent in the Supreme Court*, 105 YALE L.J. 2235, 2257 (1996).
3. Plessy v. Ferguson, 163 U.S. 537, 552–64 (1896) (Harlan, J., dissenting).
4. See Brown v. Bd. of Educ., 347 U.S. 483 (1954). Readers should note that *Brown* did not explicitly rely on Justice Harlan's *Plessy* dissent.
5. ALAN BARTH, PROPHETS WITH HONOR: GREAT DISSENTS AND GREAT DISSENTERS IN THE SUPREME COURT 5 (1974).
6. Benjamin N. CARDOZO, LAW AND LITERATURE 34 (1931).
7. See, e.g., Bradley v. Ohio, 497 U.S. 1011, 1011 (1990) (Brennan, J. dissenting); Watkins v. Murray, 493 U.S. 907, 907 (1989) (Brennan, J., dissenting).
8. William H. Simon, *The Ideology of Advocacy: Procedural Justice and Professional Ethics*, 1978 WIS. L. REV. 29, 119 (arguing that ideologies provide a façade of universality for group privileges and interests, rationalize widely felt tensions, anesthetize painful social choices, preserve the status quo, and blunt efforts at social change).
9. See WILLIAM H. SIMON, THE PRACTICE OF JUSTICE: A THEORY OF LAWYERS' ETHICS 138–69 (1998) (analyzing the contextual view to deciding questions regarding legal ethics and justice).
10. Texas v. Johnson, 491 U.S. 397 (1989).
11. *Id.* at 420 (Kennedy, J., concurring).
12. *Id.* at 421.
13. *Id.*
14. *Id.* at 420–21 (emphasis added).
15. ALASDAIR MACINTYRE, WHOSE JUSTICE? WHICH RATIONALITY? 176 (1988).
16. RICHARD A. POSNER, HOW JUDGES THINK 62 (2008) ("There is a parallel between the utility function of judges and that of serious artists....Artists combine craftsmanship with creativity. But so do judges displaying craftsmanship in the legalist phase of decision making.").
17. Simon, *supra* note 8, at 113–18.
18. Evans v. Romer, No. 92 CV 7223, 1993 WL 19678 (D. Colo. Jan. 15, 1993).
19. COLO. CONST. art. II, § 30(b). The text of the amendment is included at note 35, Chapter 3, *supra*.
20. *Evans*, 1993 WL 19678 at *4.
21. Reply Brief of Petitioners at 15–17, Romer v. Evans, 517 U.S. 620 (1996) (No. 94-1039).
22. Brief for the American Center for Law & Justice Family Life Project as Amicus Curiae in Support of Petitioners at 3, *Romer*, 517 U.S. 620 (No. 94-1039).
23. *Evans*, 1993 WL 19678 at *1.
24. *Id.*
25. *Id.*
26. *Id.* at *6.
27. *Id.* at *6–7.
28. *Id.* at *8–9.
29. *Id.* at *7.
30. *Id.* at *12.
31. *Id.* at *12.

Chapter 7

Harm and Regret in Abortion Disputes

When people discuss what Supreme Court justices should do when asked to resolve passionately contested rights disputes, the topic of abortion inevitably surfaces. Given the intractability of the abortion dispute, some have concluded that justices might best remove themselves altogether from the controversy. Pro-life activists, so the argument goes, are unlikely to give up their view that abortion is murder; pro-choice advocates are unlikely to be persuaded that women should be required to relinquish control of their reproductive capacity or be forced into a traditional motherhood role. It is feared that justices will only jeopardize the legitimacy of the Supreme Court if they take on the impossible task of trying to reconcile these competing views.

The characterization of participants in the abortion debate as single-minded to the extreme is oversimplified, as are predictions of how justices are likely to behave as new reproductive issues unfold. There are many differences of opinion within the pro-life movement and among pro-choice advocates. Although women secured recognition of a constitutional right to an abortion in *Roe v. Wade*,[1] for example, some women might have objected that justices seemed to give physicians' interests more attention than women's interests. As to the significant restriction on abortion upheld in *Gonzales v. Carhart*,[2] some supporters of the pro-life movement might have objected that the decision "saves not a single fetus...for it rejects only a *method* of performing abortion."[3] Moreover, justices are unlikely to take themselves out of the business of hearing challenges to government policies addressing reproductive rights, whether those policies pertain to minors, population growth, or new technologies and medical knowledge.

The important question is whether it is possible for justices to render a win–loss abortion decision that does not attack constitutional stature and therefore satisfies the harm-avoidance obligation and that also honors constitutional stature and therefore ameliorates the harm inherent in defeat. Outraged reactions to *Roe* and to *Carhart* suggest that justices have not yet achieved this goal, at least not in those particular opinions. Given what we now know about justices' obligations to the stakeholders in rights disputes, we should take a second look at *Roe* and *Carhart*. In what respects does outrage over the decisions stem from justices' indifference to their obligations to constitutional losers?

First, consider *Roe v. Wade*. In *Roe*, justices decided that a Texas statute criminalizing abortions violated women's constitutional rights. At the time the Texas statute was challenged, legal access to abortion was quite limited and women needing an abortion would often seek out illegal and unsafe abortion services. Consequently, even though today it is common to think about abortion as an individual rights issue, at the time of *Roe*, debate about abortion tended to focus on public health issues rather than on the individual rights perspective ultimately taken by *Roe* justices.

Conventional criticisms of *Roe* are probably familiar to you, but a brief summary of voices coming from within the legal profession is warranted. Some persons assert, for example, that *Roe* gave pro-choice advocates a win that wrongfully ostracized and disrespected views of abortion opponents, and that it attempted to suppress further political conversation about abortion. The community, it is argued, no longer had a meaningful ability to engage in legislative debate about important competing moral values.[4] Critics claim that, in order to deliver an absolute win to pro-choice advocates, justices engaged in a "subterfuge" or lie: they treated the fetus as nonexistent and nonhuman.[5] Others, refraining from allegations of lying, assert that justices gave women's rights an absolute priority over values associated with the fetus, especially pre-viability. Indeed, they claim, *Roe* put the fetus at the mercy of the "convenience, whim or caprice of the putative mother."[6] Furthermore, according to critics, justices adopted an individual-rights framework that did not make room for discussion of the community's collective interests in, for example, sending appropriate messages to society about respect for life. Some complain, from both sides of the abortion debate, that justices should have addressed abortion as an issue of equality for women. Finally, critics say, in failing to truthfully confront the interests at stake, justices did not acknowledge the tragic nature of their choice.[7]

These are serious criticisms. If valid, they are relevant both to the argument that justices must avoid unnecessary harm to constitutional losers and to the argument that justices should ameliorate harms inherent in their tragic choices. Some criticisms of *Roe*, however, are overblown. Contrary to popular wisdom, for example, *Roe* rather carefully took account of values and interests at stake in the abortion dispute. The most important failing of *Roe* is not that it paid insufficient attention to abstract interests and values but that it did not adequately honor the constitutional stature of the people who are key citizen stakeholders in the abortion dispute.

If you have never read or have only a vague memory of the opinion in *Roe* and have listened only to conventional debate, you will perhaps be surprised by what Justice Blackmun actually said in his majority opinion. Blackmun opened the discussion in *Roe* with an acknowledgment of "the sensitive and emotional nature of the abortion controversy, of the vigorous opposing views, even among physicians, and of the deep and seemingly absolute convictions that the subject inspires." He continued:

> One's philosophy, one's experiences, one's exposure to the raw edges of human existence, one's religious training, one's attitudes toward life and family and their values, and the moral standards one establishes and seeks to observe, are all likely to influence and to color one's thinking and conclusions about abortion.... In addition, population growth, pollution, poverty, and racial overtones tend to complicate and not to simplify the problem.[8]

In keeping with his acknowledgment, Blackmun made an effort to show respect throughout his opinion for different views of abortion and for persons on opposite sides of the debate. Although *Roe* rejected both the argument that women should be entitled to abortion on demand under any and all circumstances *and* the argument that the fetus is entitled to be treated as a person under the Constitution, for example, it did not condemn proponents of either view. Advocates of the fetus-as-person argument were not accused of wishing to subjugate women or of being fanatically intent on imposing a single religious view on everyone else. Advocates of an unqualified right of choice were not accused of being capricious murderers-in-waiting.

Moreover, rather than assuming that only absolutist positions existed, Blackmun spoke to more complicated views. Consider, for example, his discussion of the fetus, a discussion that was not one-sided. Blackmun recognized the lack of a consensus on the status of the fetus within the common law, in religious doctrine, and under the medical profession's ethical rules.[9] He reviewed the Constitution's use of the word "person" and determined that the word consistently references only individuals who have been born.[10] He considered the mixed status of abortion laws when the Constitution was ratified and when the Fourteenth Amendment was adopted.[11] He noted the adverse effect that recognition of fetal personhood might have on traditional laws concerning inheritance, personal injury, or homicide.[12] It should be emphasized that even dissenting justices did not debate the portion of Blackmun's opinion denying constitutional personhood to the fetus.

Regarding state interests in prohibiting abortion, Justice Blackmun reviewed the likelihood that the Texas statute might discourage illicit sexual activity (although Texas itself did not rely on this argument), and he identified health and safety interests that might warrant state limitations on abortion.[13] He emphasized the importance of the state's interest in potential life, which exists, he said, *throughout* a pregnancy.[14] Indeed, *Roe* concluded that the state's interest in potential life might prevail over a woman's right at viability, when a fetus is capable of life outside the mother.[15] Blackmun understandably rejected the state's theory of life as a valid justification for the Texas statute, because it was in direct conflict with *Roe*'s constitutional determination that fetuses are not persons.[16]

Blackmun also carefully reviewed the interests of physicians targeted by the Texas criminal statute. He described the medical profession's debate about whether performing an abortion is consistent with a physician's ethical responsibilities.[17] He noted that "responsible" physicians make efforts to practice medicine in accordance with medical standards, to consult with the women they are treating regarding medical issues,[18] and do not merely to yield to women's demands.[19] His discussion acknowledged that physicians themselves can choose not to perform abortions.

As for women's interests, Blackmun understood that women, not only men, are protected by Supreme Court decisions recognizing liberty and privacy rights.[20] Making an effort to better understand women and to describe the reality of their lives, he noted:

> The detriment that the State would impose upon the pregnant woman by denying [reproductive choice] altogether is apparent. Specific and direct harm medically diagnosable even in early pregnancy may be involved. Maternity, or additional offspring, may force upon the woman a distressful life and future. Psychological harm may be imminent. Mental and physical health may be taxed by child care. There is also the distress, for all concerned, associated with the unwanted child, and there is the problem of bringing a child into a family already unable, psychologically and otherwise, to care for it. In other cases, as in this one, the additional difficulties and continuing stigma of unwed motherhood may be involved.[21]

Although Blackmun did not expressly state, as Justice Stewart did, that the Texas statute risked "a broad abridgment of [women's] personal liberty,"[22] his opinion clearly attested that criminalization of abortion at all stages of pregnancy affects more than mere social and economic interests.[23]

This summary of Blackmun's opinion makes it difficult to credit accusations that *Roe* permitted one view to absolutely dominate all others and shut down future conversation. Indeed, *Roe* invited further judicial and legislative debate. In a spate of rights disputes arising subsequent to *Roe*, justices permitted state legislatures to deny public financial aid to abortion providers[24] and to women seeking even medically necessary abortions.[25] States were allowed to restrict the circumstances under which minors might obtain an abortion.[26] *Roe* thus kept open a constitutional conversation about pro-life and pro-choice values, although certainly not on terms that abortion opponents liked. In contrast, as noted by Blackmun, had justices prematurely constitutionalized the personhood of the fetus,[27] pro-choice arguments would almost certainly have been entirely nullified.[28]

Furthermore, *Roe* did not, as some critics have claimed, treat losing values and interests untruthfully or with disrespect. For example, much criticism of *Roe* focuses on justices' supposed neglect of the moral and religious interests and values held by members of the pro-life community. Blackmun, however, did not ignore moral and religious values relevant to the abortion dispute. He took note of the views of "those trained in the respective disciplines of medicine, philosophy, and theology," and he discussed beliefs held by Stoics, members of the Jewish faith, Roman Catholics, and the Protestant community.[29] Regarding fetal interests, he explicitly acknowledged differences of opinion respecting the status of the fetus in law, theology, philosophy, and science.[30] Despite denying the fetus constitutional personhood, he recognized valid state interests in health, safety, and potential life throughout pregnancy.[31] In light of his understanding of all that was at stake in *Roe*, he ultimately concluded that women's right of choice would not be absolute.[32]

Blackmun's treatment of competing interests and values in the abortion debate was not perfect. He might, for example, have said more about the family in relation to women. He might have reminded legislators that there is no reason states should not make every effort to alleviate the social and economic conditions that often lead to abortions, and he might have issued a direct appeal for such measures. Despite its imperfections, however, his opinion did a rather good and evenhanded job of reviewing interests and values on all sides of the debate.

From the standpoint of *Losing Twice*, *Roe*'s major flaw is that a relentless focus on abstract interests and values caused justices to be insufficiently attentive to a specific group of citizen stakeholders, real people committed to moral and spiritual values either as abstract principle or as applied in their own lives. Justices' inattention affected both pro-choice women and pro-life abortion opponents, but its most immediate and direct effect was on the losing pro-life stakeholders.

In *Roe*, justices essentially rendered those people committed to pro-life values invisible, and, you will recall, a disappearance is not merely a failure to honor constitutional stature; it directly inflicts harm on constitutional stature. Pro-life advocates, for example, appear only obliquely or briefly, through references to institutions such as the Catholic Church or in

Blackmun's introductory paragraph briefly noting that some individuals have strong religious beliefs about abortion.[33] Persons whose deeply held religious and moral beliefs were at odds with *Roe's* interpretation of the Constitution might therefore have reasonably accused justices of ignoring them, despite their central role in the abortion controversy. Demonstrations at abortion clinics and outside physician offices may be orchestrated by coalitions of religious organizations, but there will be no demonstrations unless real people show up. Pharmacists and doctors reluctant to provide services to women seeking an abortion are also real people struggling with personal religious belief and right of conscience, not mere paragraphs in policy pronouncements of groups such as the American Medical Association. Even if one were to conclude that *Roe* justices did not entirely ignore these citizen stakeholders, one must admit that these losing stakeholders were not given a presence proportionate to their central role in the abortion controversy or, more important, a presence sufficient to ensure that justices would respond appropriately to the central tragic choice of *Roe*.

The conventional way of thinking about *Roe* juxtaposes women's health and life against the life of the unborn child. Even those who do not concede constitutional personhood to the fetus can probably see the tragedy of this choice. *Roe*, however, also involved a tragic choice between citizen stakeholders offering competing views of constitutional meaning based on opposing moral and religious beliefs. Members of the pro-life community, whose moral or religious beliefs categorically or strongly equate fetal life with other human life, hoped to persuade justices to incorporate their beliefs into the Constitution; if limits were placed on government's power to prohibit abortions, constitutional meaning would be at odds with their moral world. Members of the pro-choice community, whose moral and religious compass is less categorically fixed and who thus give greater weight to an individual's moral autonomy, hoped justices would prefer their beliefs; were government allowed to criminalize all abortions, constitutional meaning would be at odds with their moral world. *Roe* involved a tragic choice because its outcome would inflict a harmful loss on the innocent inhabitants of one of these moral worlds.

Justices' failure to recognize that they were making this tragic choice did not result solely from their neglect of pro-life constitutional losers. A tragic choice involves at least two competing stakeholders, and justices were as indifferent to the constitutional stature of women claiming a right of choice as they were to constitutional losers' efforts to bear witness to their religious or moral beliefs. *Roe* failed to recognize that difficult moral and spiritual debates enter into and influence the decisions of women who exercise their right to choose an abortion just as they do women who choose to carry a pregnancy to term.

The full range of moral and religious perspectives that women might bring to bear on their choice is reflected in an amicus brief filed in *Webster v. Reproductive Health Services*[34] an abortion dispute that arose subsequent to *Roe*. The women filing the amicus brief stated that pregnancy raised difficult questions of moral and spiritual responsibility for them. In making their decisions, they said, they took into account their responsibility not only to the fetus but also to the child that might be born, to members of their family, and to others, and considered their ability to fulfill these responsibilities. They assessed the demands of rearing living children, the presence (or absence) of a supportive father, their financial situation, their work life needs, the stability of their marriage, their access to prenatal care, the health of the fetus, and adoption options. Hardly capricious decision makers, these women clearly valued life. Indeed, their amicus brief expressed an understanding that "potential life is a part of [a woman] from the moment of conception until birth," a "salient fact" more significant than mere abstractions about whether life begins at viability, at the moment of conception, or at some other point during pregnancy.[35] They were not fearful of referring to the fetus as an "unborn child," but they also invoked the "moral independence of women,"[36] which they described as rightfully beyond the reach of government or others who might want to impose on women a particular religious view.[37] They thought of the pre-*Roe* world as evil, presumably in its imposition of laws that could not prevent abortion but only drove women to seek life-threatening, underground medical attention.[38] In *Roe*, however, Blackmun reduced women's complicated moral and personal struggle to a list of nonmoral "factors the woman and her responsible physician necessarily will consider in consultation."[39] He replaced an account of religious, moral, and spiritual decision making with a science-based, trimester framework for evaluating abortion rights. Blackmun deferred less to women than to physicians. His opinion appeared to have been written to reassure others that *Roe* would not have "sweeping consequences" given that "the vast majority of physicians observe the standards of their profession, and act only on the basis of carefully deliberated medical judgments relating to health."[40]

Indifferent to the tragic choice at the heart of *Roe*, justices did not take affirmative steps to honor the constitutional stature of pro-life losers. *Roe* did not, for example, offer assurance to pro-life stakeholders that arguments framed in moral or religious terms would be included in future constitutional debates, or even that the consent of pro-life stakeholders equally matters to constitutional legitimacy. It did an inadequate job of reassuring pro-life stakeholders that their values could find a secure haven in laws that do not directly conflict with women's autonomy of choice, such as a law imposing appropriate civil or criminal penalties on someone taking the life of even a pre-viability fetus against the

wishes of a woman. Certainly, *Roe's* discussions of abstract or institutional religious values were no substitute for language that would truly honor the constitutional stature of real *people* holding moral and religious views opposing
abortion. *Roe's* omissions might thus reasonably have been read as a message to
pro-life losers that, although justices would permit continued conversation
about abortion, meaningful participation in that conversation would be limited
to those persons willing to divorce their religious or spiritual identity from their
constitutional leadership. In other words, *Roe* justices failed to ameliorate the
harms inherent in the loss, fueled the losers' outrage, and inflicted a second loss
on the constitutional losers.

As a companion to *Roe*, now consider *Gonzales v. Carhart*. Readers will recall
that justices in *Carhart* rejected a challenge to a federal ban on an "intact" D&E
abortion procedure. Although the federal statute did not include an exception to
protect the health of pregnant women, justices decided that the statute should
remain in effect until someone could legitimately make what is known as an "as-
applied" constitutional challenge.[41]

Carhart is an example of a rather comprehensive attack on women's constitutional stature, but chapter 3's discussion of that attack will not be revisited here.
Instead, the current inquiry parallels the narrower, preceding analysis of *Roe*.
The question is whether *Carhart* ameliorated harms by honoring the stature of
the constitutional losers, women who are constitutional leaders and moral
agents whose decisions about pregnancy are influenced by moral or religious
values.

Carhart justices expanded the analytical framework employed in *Roe*. They
did not, for example, discuss moral or religious attitudes with reference only to
the institutional interests of medical associations or the national legislature.[42]
Nor did justices consider only general societal interests of moral import, such as
the concern that permissiveness regarding abortions might lead to a moral coars-
ening regarding the value of human life.[43] Justices recognized that women contemplating a decision about pregnancy face "a painful moral decision,"[44] and
they also referenced women's need for accurate information in making that
decision.

On the other hand, *Carhart* endorsed the validity of propositions that deny
women—as a class and in all settings—moral and political agency. Here is the
relevant portion of Justice Kennedy's opinion in *Carhart*. As you read it and consider its import, keep in mind, by way of contrast, the opinion Justice Kennedy
joined in *Planned Parenthood v. Casey*,[45] which portrayed women as free persons
of conscience making significant choices about spiritual imperatives, personhood, and destiny. The *Carhart* Kennedy stepped back from the views expressed
in *Planned Parenthood* and offered the following reason for his decision to uphold
the Partial-Birth Abortion Ban Act:

Respect for human life finds an ultimate expression in the bond of love the mother has for her child.... Whether to have an abortion requires a difficult and painful moral decision. While we find no reliable data to measure the phenomenon, it seems unexceptionable to conclude some women come to regret their choice to abort the infant life they once created and sustained. Severe depression and loss of esteem can follow.

In a decision so fraught with emotional consequence some doctors may prefer not to disclose precise details of the means that will be used [to perform an abortion]....

... The State has an interest in ensuring so grave a choice is well informed. It is self-evident that a mother who comes to regret her choice to abort must struggle with grief more anguished and sorrow more profound when she learns, only after the event, what she once did not know [about details of the intact D&E procedure].[46]

Consider what Kennedy and justices joining his opinion asserted (and failed to assert) in this passage. First, they did not affirm a presumption that women facing an abortion have the capacity to make responsible decisions. Second, as Justice Ginsburg pointed out, concerns about women's informed consent were not coupled with a right-to-know analysis that would support the deliberations of a capable moral agent. Neither did their concerns lead justices to condemn the federal Partial-Birth Abortion Ban Act for failing to require that women be given information about a particular abortion procedure. Rather, concerns about women's decision making were unquestioningly accepted as a valid justification for a statutory ban on an abortion procedure that is often needed to protect a pregnant woman's health. The *Carhart* analysis was premised on an assumption that women are vulnerable decision makers requiring the protection of the State against bad choices.

Justices acknowledged that they had no reliable studies supporting the view that many, or even some, women would experience regret after having an abortion.[47] Nonetheless, they accepted what Justice Ginsburg termed a "shibboleth"[48] as unexceptionable fact. As significant, *Carhart* justices characterized regret only in psychological terms related to depression and self-esteem rather than as a phenomenon associated with moral decision making. Difficult moral decisions, to be sure, can leave a bruise on the soul, but they do not necessarily or even commonly adversely affect mental health. If they did, we could expect to encounter many psychologically damaged persons in our lives, given the frequency with which we make difficult moral decisions. Indeed, regret is an emotion that one might expect to be associated with a difficult moral choice; it may even be a positive indicator of moral agency and emotional health. If someone making a tragic choice were to tell us that she would do so without giving any thought to possible future regret, for example, we might worry about that person. Most of us hope that once we make a decision we will not be plagued with second thoughts. Someone who can make a tragic choice without even imagining the possibility of regret, however, will seem cold-hearted and even, perhaps, inhuman.

In *Carhart*, however, the emotion of regret was not taken as evidence that women are moral agents equal to others facing similarly difficult choices, such as whether to donate a life-saving kidney to a family member or to move an aging and beloved family member from home to an institutional setting. Instead, regret was used as a justification for a paternalistic law intended to protect lesser, fragile beings from the psychological consequences of their choices. Regret was equated with weakness or vulnerability.

Carhart's attitude toward regret operates as a constitutional pronouncement. The possibility that women will experience regret seems to have been accepted as a legitimate state interest supporting the regulation of abortion and, conceivably, of other choices affecting the fetus. Perhaps legislators might wish to enact a variety of laws ostensibly protecting women from, for example, emotional regret associated with the choice to smoke or drink or use drugs during pregnancy. Some legislative efforts might be so extreme as to effectively impose second-class citizenship status on women.[49]

Carhart's constitutional pronouncement on the subject of emotional regret may have even more immediate and insidious consequences insofar as it pressures women to deny the experience of a human emotion properly associated with moral agency. Women wishing to be accorded full constitutional stature may believe that they must deny the possibility of regret, lest pro-life advocates pounce on what should be seen as a valuable aspect of moral decision making and use it as a justification for ever more paternalist legislation respecting women. Yet, if women deny experiencing the regret that accompanies moral decision making, they confirm they are not proper moral agents. *Carhart* thus creates a catch-22 for women and a self-fulfilling prophecy as to constitutional stature. In this respect, *Carhart* is similar to *Roe*. Just as pro-life advocates might feel pressured by *Roe* to relinquish their moral or religious orientation and identity as the price of participating in debates about constitutional meaning, so women might believe, after *Carhart*, that they will secure constitutional protections only if they persuade others that they do not experience a unique human emotion associated with moral agency.

Carhart and *Roe* are cut from the same piece of cloth. They each fall short of fulfilling justices' harm-avoidance and harm-amelioration obligations to constitutional losers. Moreover, taken together and as bellwethers in a line of cases exploring the scope of women's autonomy in matters of reproduction, they embody a single lesson: a failure to take proper account of the constitutional stature of *any* rights stakeholder, even a winner, may deprive justices of understandings that will help them ameliorate harms to constitutional losers.

Recall that, in *Roe*, the failure of justices to recognize the tragic choice between citizens with competing moral and spiritual views resulted not only from their neglect of losing pro-life advocates but also in their neglect of the moral and spiritual orientation of winning pro-choice advocates. *Roe*'s health-oriented, scientific discussion of abortion diverted attention from a truthful account of moral and religious questions important to persons on both sides of the abortion debate. *Roe*'s analysis most immediately harmed pro-life advocates. The justices' failure to discuss and endorse the moral agency and constitutional stature of *all* stakeholders, however, set us on the problematic path that has culminated in the *Carhart* decision that seems to deny the moral agency of women.

Although it might be situationally convenient for justices to avoid talking openly about the citizens whose moral and spiritual views are at odds in the abortion debate, a more truthful account would better serve citizens themselves, in the long run. Guido Calabresi has asserted that any given individual typically respects all competing values in a rights disputes and struggles to reconcile those competing values within herself.[50] His claim rests on an assumption that each of us possesses the moral and political agency of a person of full constitutional stature. If Calabresi is right, and I believe he is, justices have little reason to fear open engagement with intractable rights disputes that implicate opposing moral and religious views. If justices will only fully acknowledge the moral agency of both constitutional winners and constitutional losers, they will be better prepared to properly honor the constitutional stature of losers and ameliorate the harms inherent in their defeat.

Imagine, for example, how *Roe* might have been written had justices talked openly about women's presumptively equal moral agency and incorporated a description, such as that offered by women who came forward in *Webster v. Reproductive Health Services*, of how women make decisions about a pregnancy. A better account of pro-choice women's moral struggles might have given *Roe* justices a more truthful way of framing the tragic choice between persons holding competing views of the moral and spiritual issues at the heart of abortion disputes. Justices might have used the accounts of women who value life highly in making a decision about abortion to signal respect for all persons who bring that value to the decision. They might have linked this signal of respect to their discussion of physician ethics, as reassurance to constitutional losers of respect for life values, and to emphasize their expectation that women will not abuse liberty rights, even within *Roe*'s understanding of the Constitution. They could have offered meaningful assurances that pro-life constitutional leaders and their spiritually informed arguments about constitutional meaning would not be rejected in future debates or in other forums. Finally, they might have used women's accounts to help political actors identify economic and other factors that are frequently dispositive in a woman's decision, and thereby encouraged the political community to address and eliminate circumstances that tend to lead to abortion decisions.

Of course, at the time *Roe* was decided, abortion had been criminalized for many years and it would have been difficult to persuade a group of women such as those who came forward in *Webster v. Reproductive Health Services* to be open about their moral and spiritual struggles with the abortion decision. The point is nonetheless valid. More truthfulness about the moral and spiritual dimensions of the abortion decision for all women might have resulted in an opinion that more forthrightly acknowledged and ameliorated the harmful consequences of *Roe*'s tragic choice for pro-life citizen stakeholders.

Honoring rather than attacking the constitutional stature of all parties is perhaps the best way that justices can ensure that the Constitution has meaning for "people of fundamentally different views."[51] It will require justices, however, to be willing to take some risks in their opinions. Justices may need, for example, to confront more honestly and directly the sensitive topic of our pluralistic moralities and religious views in relation to our Constitution and constitutional stature. Moreover, justices will need to accept that their written opinions will have a slightly different import and feel than those to which we have become accustomed. The next chapter argues that these and other changes wrought by the embrace of harm-avoidance and harm-amelioration obligations will inure to the benefit of the Supreme Court.

Notes

1. Roe v. Wade, 410 U.S. 113 (1973).
2. Gonzales v. Carhart, 550 U.S. 124 (2007) (upholding against constitutional attack the federal Partial-Birth Abortion Ban Act of 2003, which prohibits physicians from using the D&E intact procedure for performing late-term abortions).
3. Ironically, this language comes from Justice Ginsburg's dissent. *Id.* at 181 (Ginsburg, J., dissenting) (citing Stenberg v. Carhart, 530 U.S. 914, 930 (2000)).
4. MARY ANN GLENDON, ABORTION AND DIVORCE IN WESTERN LAW 34 (1987) ("*Roe v. Wade*...virtually closed down the state legislative process with respect to abortions prior to viability. Legislative attempts to provide for more information, deliberation, and counseling, more participation by others in the woman's decision-making process,...have regularly been struck down.").
5. See GUIDO CALABRESI, IDEALS, BELIEFS, ATTITUDES AND THE LAW: PRIVATE LAW PERSPECTIVES ON A PUBLIC LAW PROBLEM 92–93 (1985).
6. Doe v. Bolton, 410 U.S. 179, 221 (1973) (White, J., dissenting).
7. *See* GUIDO CALABRESI & PHILP BOBBITT, TRAGIC CHOICES 133–43 (1978) (discussing tragic choices as they relate to life-validating decisions).
8. *Roe,* 410 U.S. at 116.

9. *Id.* at 129–47.
10. *Id.* at 156–59.
11. See *id.* at 129–47, 156–62.
12. See *id.* at 161–62.
13. See *id.* at 148–50.
14. See *id.* at 163.
15. *Id.* at 163 ("With respect to the State's important and legitimate interest in potential life, the 'compelling' point is at viability...because the fetus then presumably has the capability of meaningful life outside the mother's womb.").
16. See *id.* at 164.
17. See *id.* at 141–46.
18. *Id.* at 153.
19. See *id.* at 143–44.
20. See *id.* at 152–54.
21. *Id.* at 153.
22. *Id.* at 170–71 (Stewart, J., concurring) (noting, however, that a State might regulate abortion as a medical procedure and even prohibit late-term abortions).
23. But see *id.* at 173 (Rehnquist, J., dissenting) (concluding that the Texas abortion statute should be evaluated under a rational-basis standard like other social and economic legislation).
24. Rust v. Sullivan, 500 U.S. 173 (1991).
25. Harris v. McRae, 448 U.S. 297 (1980).
26. Ohio v. Akron Ctr. for Reprod. Health, 497 U.S. 502 (1990).
27. Cf. GLENDON, *supra* note 4, at 45 (applying the phrase to criticize the recognition of women's liberty interest).
28. See *Roe*, 410 U.S. at 156–57.
29. *Id.* at 159–61.
30. See generally *id.* at 129–48.
31. *Id.* at 182 ("We repeat...the State does have an important and legitimate interest in....protecting the potentiality of human life.").
32. *Id.* at 155 ("The right [to the abortion decision]...is not absolute and is subject to some limitations.").
33. See *id.* at 116.
34. Brief for the Amici Curiae Women Who Have Had Abortions and Friends of Amici Curiae in Support of Appellees, Webster v. Reprod. Health Serv., 492 U.S. 490 (1989) (No. 88–605).
35. *Id.* at 51–52.
36. *Id.* at 7 n.4 (quoting John Hart Ely, *The Wages of Crying Wolf: A Comment on* Roe v. Wade, 82 YALE L.J. 920, 927 (1973)).
37. See *id.* at 5–10.
38. See *id.* at 3–4.
39. *Roe*, 410 U.S. at 153.
40. *Roe*, 410 U.S. at 208 (Burger, J., concurring).
41. *Carhart*, 550 U.S. at 167–68.
42. See *id.* at 141 ("Congress found...that '[a] moral, medical, and ethical consensus exists that the practice of performing a partial-birth abortion...is a gruesome and inhumane procedure.'").
43. See *id.* at 157.
44. *Id.* at 159.
45. *Planned Parenthood*, 505 U.S. 833.
46. *Carhart*, 550 U.S. at 159–60 (internal citations omitted).
47. *Id.* at 159.

48. *Id.* at 183 (Ginsburg, J., dissenting).
49. Cf. Colorado Proposition 48, placed on the 2008 general election ballot and defining life as beginning at the moment of conception, without regard to the effects such a proposition might have on the lives of women.
50. See CALABRESI, *supra* note 5, at 100–03 ("There are purists on both sides of the [abortion] issue—those who hold that a fetus is nothing at all, and those who would ban first-month abortions even when pregnancy endangers a woman's life. But there are enough indications...that most people in our pluralistic society would like to have it both ways.").
51. *Roe,* 410 U.S. at 117.

Chapter 8

Valuing Precedent Differently

Harm-amelioration practices clearly keep the courthouse door open for constitutional losers to redeem constitutional meaning in different times and contexts and make it difficult for us to deny the "never-say-never" features of rights adjudication.[1] Never-say-never terrain may seem dangerous to some, for it arguably gives us insufficiently authoritative statements of constitutional meaning, is susceptible to arbitrary judicial action, and puts judicial legitimacy on shaky ground. In particular, some may be concerned that it threatens our system of precedent, in which prior decisions are seen as final resolutions of rights disputes that control what justices do in subsequent controversies. These fears are illusory. Nothing in harm-amelioration practices compromises either precedent, which is central to our system of judicial review,[2] or appropriate finality in Supreme Court decisions. As you will see in this chapter, harm-amelioration practices only help us learn to value precedent and finality differently. There are very good reasons to welcome the types of contingencies and opportunities for enhancing judicial legitimacy that result from harm-amelioration practices. Indeed, such practices can help us ground judicial legitimacy in new understandings of the inherently democratic character of the Supreme Court.

First, consider the values we conventionally assign to precedent and the balance justices have struck between finality and contingency in the resolution of rights disputes. Advocates and justices reportedly rely more on precedent in legal briefs and written opinions than on other sources of constitutional meaning, including text, structure, or original intent.[3] According to one study, for example, precedent-based analyses were prominent features of every one of the constitutional rights opinions written over the first two terms of the Roberts Court.[4] That precedent mechanistically *controls* outcomes, however, is belied by what actually happens when precedent is invoked in a rights dispute.

For one thing, justices frequently disagree about what a prior decision means. Precedent may be thought controlling, for example, only by those whose preferred interpretation of a prior decision prevails; dissenters, on the other hand, will believe that majority justices have not been faithful to precedent. The Roberts Court is currently under attack because it is perceived by some as doggedly going about the business of effectively overturning precedent without admitting to the public that it is doing so[5] and "gradual[ly] extinguish[ing]...unloved precedents."[6] In 1968, for example, *Flast v. Cohen* authorized taxpayers to challenge the use of public funds to support religious activities.[7] In *Hein v. Freedom from Religion Foundation*, however, Roberts Court justices told taxpayers that they could not challenge President Bush's discretionary expenditures of public money to support faith-based programs.[8] *Flast* did not control, Justice Alito said, because *Flast* dealt with specific appropriations for legislative programs while *Hein* involved general appropriations of discretionary funds to the executive.[9] Justice Scalia—who concurred with Alito only in the judgment—accused Alito of pretending to respect precedent while "hid[ing] the ball."[10] According to Scalia, "honoring [precedent] requires more than beating [it] to a pulp and then sending it out to the lower courts weakened, denigrated, more incomprehensible than ever, and yet somehow technically alive."[11]

Did Justice Alito treat *Flast* and other relevant precedent appropriately? Justice Scalia's accusation that Alito relied on "meaningless and disingenuous distinctions" is valid if one believes that *Flast* gave taxpayers a way of challenging any government support of religion.[12] On the other hand, *Hein* is, as Alito claimed, factually distinguishable from *Flast*. Moreover, as Michael Gerhardt notes, *Hein* is also faithful to a number of Supreme Court decisions that limit taxpayer and citizen lawsuits in order to preserve the separation of powers between judiciary and executive.[13] There is simply no black-and-white answer to whether precedent was properly respected. What is clear is only that *Flast*, which recognized taxpayer standing to challenge government expenditures in support of religion, did not control the outcome of a subsequent taxpayer suit.

Other Supreme Court decisions confirm that the controlling effect of a prior case depends on how the Court chooses to interpret its precedents. In *Planned Parenthood v. Casey*, for example, some justices asserted that *Roe v. Wade*[14] was a proper extension of prior decisions protecting a liberty right to make intimate personal choices, while dissenters countered that the joint opinion in *Roe* had selectively and opportunistically relied on prior judicial statements to support a predetermined outcome.[15] Accusations of selective reliance on precedent were also voiced by dissenters in *Hill v. Colorado*, the decision upholding Colorado's Bubble Bill.[16] Justices debated both the meaning of a prior decision bearing on the interpretation of the Second Amendment and the proper test for determining when a prior decision should control a subsequent dispute in *District of Columbia v. Heller*.[17] In *Crawford v. Marion County Election Board*, justices disagreed on how to interpret prior voting-rights precedent.[18] The meaning of

Brown v. Board of Education[19] was contested in *Parents Involved in Community Schools v. Seattle School District No. 1*.[20] In one statutory rights dispute, Justice Alito implied that no relevant precedent supported the plaintiff's claim on the disputed statute of limitations issue, then accused the plaintiff of asking for a "deviat[ion] from...prior decisions," and finally concluded that he would resolve the dispute by applying "established precedent in a slightly different context."[21] Readers may try to draw their own conclusions about whether precedent was respected in the latter controversy.

Further attesting to the fact that precedent is not a controlling, "inexorable command," justices have asserted various justifications for ignoring or reconsidering prior decisions.[22] For some, the power to reconsider a prior decision stems from a need to "bring...opinions into agreement with experience and with facts newly ascertained,"[23] a need to take account of facts that have "come to be seen...differently,"[24] or a need to ensure that constitutional meaning is "workable over time."[25] Justice Kennedy asserted in *Lawrence v. Texas*,[26] for example, that the founders knew that "times can blind us to certain truths and later generations can see that laws once thought necessary and proper in fact serve only to oppress."[27] He argued that precedent should not stand in the way of a "Constitution [that] endures, [as] persons in every generation...invoke its principles in their own search for greater freedom."[28] Other justices might argue that their power to reject prior decisions is necessary because otherwise dysfunctional constitutional interpretations could not be undone except through the cumbersome—even practically unrealistic—constitutional amendment process. Justice Kennedy also has asserted the existence of a "tradition—to be invoked...in rare instances—that permits [justices] to maintain [their] own positions [on constitutional meaning] in the face of [precedent] when fundamental points of doctrine are at stake."[29]

By virtue of doctrines justifying departures from prior cases and justices' disagreements about how prior cases should be interpreted, constitutional precedent is anything but rigidly controlling. Nonetheless, justices do not overrule or ignore prior decisions willy-nilly. Although Court membership has recently and consistently moved to the more conservative end of the spectrum of thought, for example, Judge Richard Posner points out that no wholesale overruling of Warren Court decisions has occurred.[30]

We all understand that judicial respect for prior decisions has important benefits. A system of precedent brings a degree of certainty and finality to constitutional interpretation, which helps ensure that under-resourced courts need not perpetually reconsider their views and also enables parties to confidently rely on what the judiciary says. Moreover, it is surely not a bad thing for justices to consider the opinions of others who have confronted similar disputes. Finally, if justices must explain their actions with reference to prior decisions, their discretion is limited. As Justice Scalia might proclaim, respect for precedent is an antidote to an otherwise illegitimate "keep-what-you-want-and-throw-away-the-rest" jurisprudence.[31] Agreeing, justices in *Planned Parenthood* endorsed the understanding that precedent protects against arbitrariness, ensures liberty, and supports the rule of law.[32]

In contrast to what some might argue, however, the considerable benefits of respect for prior decisions do not need to be embraced to the exclusion of benefits resulting from harm-amelioration practices. As previous chapters illustrate, for example, harm-amelioration practices help ensure that judicial untruthfulness does not result in an unstable, meaningless consent by citizens. Less than absolute finality in constitutional meaning gives losing stakeholders hope for future recoupment of losses in other arenas and in other contexts, which also enhances legitimacy. Indeterminacy flowing from harm-ameliorating practices may also give justices needed interpretational room to deviate from earlier decisions without arbitrary or technical distinctions that can cause citizens to doubt the integrity of judicial review.

In any case, as a practical matter, harm-amelioration practices will not radically upset the balance struck between finality and contingency in our existing system of precedent. There is already much contingency in constitutional meaning. Even the Roberts Court doctrine of judicial minimalism that cautions justices to resolve rights disputes one case at a time, for example, results in a contingency that is informed by the understanding that stability and judicial legitimacy can be enhanced rather than put at risk by less than absolute finality in constitutional meaning. And, of course, there will continue to be a fair degree of finality as long as justices remain in control of what prior decisions mean and cautiously wait for lower courts to explore constitutional meaning before intervening to resolve important rights disputes.

Indeed, harm-amelioration practices will actually give us an enriched understanding of the precedential force of prior decisions. Rather than mistakenly believing that only the few words stating a narrow holding of a case have precedential force—to the exclusion of the many other words constituting an opinion—we will clearly see *all* of the ways in which a given decision is taken into account in future disputes. Decisions have broad precedential impact, for example, in affirming (or debasing) constitutional stature, in the messages they send about who owns a decision, and in their acknowledgment (or rejection) of the importance of citizen consent to judicial review.

First, recall how prior decisions affirm or undermine constitutional stature. *Bowers v. Hardwick* did not merely deny homosexuals a constitutional right of consensual sexual privacy.[33] It also embraced a view of homosexuals as diminished persons. The narrow holding of *Bowers* did not result in the adoption of a wave of criminal sodomy statutes. Rather, its precedential force stemmed more from its message about the constitutional stature of homosexuals. That aspect of *Bowers*, for example, arguably set the stage for Colorado's infamous Amendment 2, an effort to consign homosexuals to secondary citizenship status. In other words, the precedential force of Bowers rested not in its narrow holding but in its message about constitutional stature. Similarly, *Gonzales v. Carhart*[34] belongs in a discussion of precedent not merely because its narrow holding seems to be at odds with *Stenburg v. Carhart*,[35] or *City of Boerne v. Flores*,[36] or *Planned Parenthood v. Casey*,[37] but because it promoted both a diminished constitutional stature for women and an enhanced status for the fetus, albeit without recognizing the fetus as a constitutional "person." *Gonzales v. Carhart*'s precedential force is thus grounded not only in a narrow holding but in assertions about stature that may, in future, be invoked to the detriment of women.

A rights decision also has precedential force in the messages it sends about who owns the decision and about prior cases on which that decision relies. Although decisions are part of the res publica, justices sometimes act as if their written opinions were resources for only lawyers and judges to deploy in argument or, even worse, as if justices were the sole owners of decisions by virtue of their power to interpret them as precedent. In *Parents Involved in Community Schools v. Seattle School District No. 1*,[38] for example, plurality justices interpreted *Brown v. Board of Education*[39] to stand for a formalist equality principle at odds with the ownership claims of citizens who had participated in *Brown*'s creation, who had relied on *Brown* as a resource, and who had endowed *Brown* with meaning through their daily actions. More will be said in chapter 9 about this aspect of *Parents Involved*. For now, simply note that *Parents Involved* belongs in a discussion of precedent not because the plurality opinion did—or did not— adhere to prior decisions concerning voluntary public school desegregation but because its interpretation of *Brown* sends a disturbing message that may exclude African Americans from making traditional ownership claims to *Brown*.

Finally, consider a third point about the precedential value of decisions: their import for the issue of citizen consent. The joint opinion in *Planned Parenthood v. Casey* argued that some decisions, such as *Brown* or *Roe*,[40] embody interpretations of the Constitution that call for "the contending sides of a national controversy to end their national division by accepting a common [liberty or equality] mandate rooted in the Constitution."[41] In other words, some decisions have the broad, primary goal of securing citizen consent and sustaining national unity despite potentially divisive issues. The precedential force of such a decision will reside both in that call and in its narrower holding, even if the call does not have the desired effect.

Decisions that ignore the importance of citizen consent also have precedential import. The plurality's analysis in *Parents Involved*, for example, sent a message that citizen consent and ownership of even groundbreaking decisional law such as *Brown* matter less than a formalist, technical analysis of the issues. Justice Breyer recognized this aspect of the *Parents Involved* plurality opinion. He complained, in dissent, that:

> Law is not an exercise in mathematical logic. And statements of a legal rule set forth in a judicial opinion [such as *Brown* and other decisions] do not always divide neatly into "holdings" and "dicta." ... The constitutional principle enunciated in [important judicial decisions]... and relied upon over many years, provides, and has widely been thought to provide, authoritative legal guidance. And if the plurality now chooses to reject that principle, it cannot adequately justify its retreat simply by affixing the label "dicta" [i.e., advisory rather than controlling portions of an opinion] to reasoning with which it disagrees. Rather, it must explain to the courts and to the Nation *why* it would abandon guidance set forth many years before, guidance that countless others have built upon over time, and which the law has continuously embodied.[42]

Implicit in Breyer's complaint is the understanding that the plurality justices of *Parents Involved* had ignored citizen consent and ownership of constitutional meaning. That, along with its endorsement of a colorblindness equality principle, is a precedential effect of the plurality opinion.

A Supreme Court decision can thus have precedential effect in its message that citizen consent does (or does not) matter, in its recognition that citizens are (or are not) equal owners of the body of decisional law, and in its honoring of (or disrespect for) constitutional stature. It is when we acknowledge justices' obligations regarding harms to constitutional losers that we become fully cognizant of the precedential forces of a decision, beyond its narrow holding. And when we have a better understanding of all of the precedential effects of a rights decision, we are better able to make informed judgments about the legitimacy of what justices do in particular cases.

Judicial legitimacy is a central concern of *Losing Twice*. Although it is well beyond the scope of this book to make a complete argument about the Supreme Court's institutional legitimacy, a few words of reassurance are nonetheless offered to those who might fear that justices' fulfilling their obligations to ameliorate harm will compromise their legitimacy.

The Court's institutional role is conventionally defined with reference to one or both of two arguments set forth in the 1803 decision that defended the legitimacy of judicial review: *Marbury v. Madison*.[43] In *Marbury*, Chief Justice John Marshall explained that the Court exists to decide cases and to provide remedies for individual wrongs, in the common-law tradition.[44] The Court also holds forth definitively on the meaning of the Constitution and laws as a matter of principle[45] and thus functions as an oracle. There may be disagreement about the proper limit and mix of these two institutional roles, but most accept that both roles are in play when the Court engages in judicial review. As justices announce constitutional principles and apply those principles to specific controversies, relationships among citizens and government change or, I would say, are renegotiated.

Although not always described in terms of a renegotiation, the transactional function of the Court is discernibly important to scholars who explore democratic constitutionalism, democratic experimentalism, judicial pragmatism, law as discourse, or law as an invitation to problem solving. In the work of these scholars, there is a shared understanding of the Supreme Court's transactional function that may be either overlooked or considered a suspect feature of rights disputing.

Most of us have probably been taught to think of the Supreme Court and its unelected justices as a necessary anomaly within the otherwise democratic institutional framework established by the Constitution. Democracy, we assume, consists of a process of tallying votes to determine a majority preference. We have been encouraged to believe that the job of courts is only to facilitate such democratic interactions in other branches of government and to ensure that elected officials do not run amok.

There is, however, an alternative to a majority-vote, aggregative view of democracy and the commonplace belief that an institution will qualify as democratic only if its members are elected. Democracy might also consist of any process that ensures self-government by people presumed to be equal moral and political agents. This view of democracy is expressed, for example, in the political theory of Jürgen Habermas.[46] At the risk of oversimplifying Habermas's theory, let me offer a brief summary of key aspects of his work, which suggest that we would be justified in describing as democratic the judicial role that would emerge from harm-amelioration practices.

Habermas worried that citizen political sovereignty was threatened because institutions that supported self-government were on the verge of breaking down. According to Habermas, the market—one means of self-regulation and social integration—is distorted, administrative bureaucracies undermine citizen control of government, moral authorities such as the church or concepts of natural law no longer have the power they once had, and modern, pluralistic societies lack a background consensus that supports self-government. Motivated by these concerns, Habermas attempted to envision institutions that would enable diverse citizens to reach mutual understandings about rules for living together.[47] If we want institutions of government to secure self-government, he said, we should give them the traits that sustain any discourse intended to resolve conflict. He went so far as to suggest that we define democracy as a discourse transaction.

Habermas identified four characteristics of institutions that would qualify as democratic in their ability to sustain self-governance. First, he argued, democratic institutions accord participants in debate a presumed equal status and capacity.[48] Second, a democratic institution will be structured so that participants must base their arguments on reasons that can be accepted by all persons who, now and in the future, might be affected by its decisions.[49] Third, Habermas asserted that democratic institutions are legitimate if they respectfully "regulate expectations and conflicts in the equal interest of all."[50] Finally, democratic legitimacy also depends on interaction between law-making institutions and ordinary citizens. Habermas opposed a law-making institution that would evaluate its legitimacy according only to its own criteria.[51] A legitimate law-making institution, he said, pays attention to the judgments of ordinary citizens acting outside the institutional framework and keeps "one foot in the medium of ordinary language."[52] Only through the interplay between institutions and "informal opinion-formation"[53] will citizens be both authors and subjects of law[54] and therefore truly self-governing.

Although judicial constitutional review is often described as undemocratic, Habermas gives us reason to understand that justices who properly acknowledge the harms of constitutional losers will also act as legitimate "custodian[s] of deliberative democracy."[55] To the extent that justices treat constitutional losers in accordance with practices based on equality and consent, they are faithful to the important foundational requirements of a self-governance theory of democracy. If they make an effort to base their legitimacy on constitutional reasons that can be accepted by all those potentially affected, they also implicitly affirm this conception of democracy. If they insist that the communion of interests applies to courts, they make a similar affirmation. If they pay attention to citizens' own view of their constitutional stature—a factor outside the control of the Court—they will avoid becoming antidemocratic custodians of a closed constitutional system that privileges legal professionals and is cut off from ordinary people. Through harm-amelioration practices, in other words, justices will satisfy important criteria of *democratic* legitimacy.

Please do not misunderstand the argument. It is not a top-down effort to persuade anyone that justices *should* adopt the goal of transforming the Court into a democratic forum. It is a simple request that we take bottom-up note of the correspondence between the characteristics of legitimate democratic institutions under Habermas's theory and of judicial harm-amelioration practices. The harm-amelioration obligation arises primarily from ethical principles rather than from grand theory. Once the obligation is both recognized and realized through judicial practice, however, we will see more clearly the democratic, transactional role the Court already has.

It has been argued that the ability of individuals to have constitutional disputes heard by the Court may be more important to democracy than the right to vote.[56] You do not need to endorse this view in order to insist on harm-amelioration practices that reassure us of the Court's democratic legitimacy. Rights disputes, in which constitutional leaders offer views of constitutional meaning that repeatedly test the legitimacy of existing political structures and distributions of power, cry out for a democratic conception of the Court. The alternative, which begrudgingly endorses judicial review as an antidemocratic element of our government, can lead to excessive judicial deference to decisions of political majorities that too often emerge from dysfunctional legislative processes. We need every governmental institution at our disposal as we seek to retain our sovereignty and secure respect for the constitutional stature of all citizens. Disregarding justices' ability to assist us in this regard, through their implementation of harm-amelioration practices, makes little sense.

Notes

1. Vieth v. Jubelirer, 541 U.S. 267, 303 (2004) (arguing that Justice Kennedy's approach, leaving the door open to future political gerrymandering claims, will result in a never-say-never approach to rights disputes).
2. RICHARD A. POSNER, HOW JUDGES THINK 175–76 (2008) (describing the interpretation of precedent as central to "legalist" theories).
3. Michael J. Gerhardt, *The Irrepressibility of Precedent*, 86 N.C. L. REV. 1279, 1284 (2008). See also MICHAEL J. GERHARDT, THE POWER OF PRECEDENT (2008).
4. Gerhardt, *Irrepressibility*, *supra* note 3, at 1283.
5. RONALD DWORKIN, THE SUPREME COURT PHALANX: THE COURT'S NEW RIGHT-WING BLOC, at xii (2008).
6. POSNER, *supra* note 2, at 277 (2008).
7. Flast v. Cohen, 392 U.S. 83 (1968).
8. Hein v. Freedom from Religion Found., 551 U.S. 587, 127 S. Ct. 2553, 2559 (2007).
9. *Id.* at 2568.
10. *Id.* at 2578 (Scalia, J., concurring in the judgment).
11. *Id.* at 2584.
12. *Id.* at 2582.
13. Gerhardt, *Irrepressibility*, *supra* note 3, at 1287.
14. Roe v. Wade, 410 U.S. 113 (1973).
15. Planned Parenthood of Se. Pa. v. Casey, 505 U.S. 833 (1992).
16. Hill v. Colorado, 530 U.S. 703 (2000).
17. Dist. of Columbia v. Heller, 554 U.S. 570, 128 S. Ct. 1610 (2008).
18. Crawford v. Marion County Election Bd., 553 U.S. 181 (2008).
19. Brown v. Bd. of Educ., 347 U.S. 483 (1954).
20. Parents Involved in Cmty. Sch. v. Seattle Sch. Dist. No. 1, 551 U.S. 701 (2007).
21. Ledbetter v. The Goodyear Tire & Rubber Co., 550 U.S. 618, 633-640 (2007).
22. *Planned Parenthood*, 505 U.S. at 854.
23. *Heller*, 128 S. Ct. at 2824 n.4 (Stevens, J., dissenting) (quoting Vasquez v. Hillery, 474 U.S. 254, 265–66 (1986)).
24. *Planned Parenthood*, 505 U.S. at 855.
25. *Parents Involved*, 127 S. Ct. at 2831 (Breyer, J., dissenting). In the same opinion, Breyer lamented the majority's handling of precedent: "What has happened to stare decisis?" *Id.* at 2835.

26. Lawrence v. Texas, 539 U.S. 558 (2003).

27. *Id.* at 579.

28. *Id.*

29. *Parents Involved*, 551 U.S. at 792 (Kennedy, J., concurring in part and concurring in the judgment) (citing Fed. Mar. Comm'n v. S.C. Ports Auth., 535 U.S. 743, 770 (2002)).

30. POSNER, *supra* note 2, at 55–56.

31. *Planned Parenthood*, 505 U.S. at 993 (Scalia, J., dissenting).

32. See *id.* at 844, 869–70 (plurality opinion).

33. Bowers v. Hardwick, 478 U.S. 186 (1986).

34. Gonzales v. Carhart, 550 U.S. 124 (2007).

35. Stenberg v. Carhart, 530 U.S. 914, 922 (2000) (invalidating a state statute similar to the Partial-Birth Abortion Ban Act of 2003). The only explanation Justice Ginsburg could discern for the different outcomes in the two cases was that "the Court [is] differently composed than it was" when *Stenberg* was decided. *Gonzales*, 550 U.S. at 191 (Ginsburg, J., dissenting).

36. City of Boerne v. Flores, 521 U.S. 507, 519 (1997) (holding that Congress cannot redefine the terms of the Constitution by adopting a statute).

37. *Planned Parenthood*, 505 U.S. at 883–84 (deferring to medical judgment because of conflicting medical opinion and preserving an arena of choice for people with different moral views). Regarding this point, see DWORKIN, *supra* note 5, at 37–49.

38. *Parents Involved*, 551 U.S. at 748 ("The way to stop discrimination on the basis of race is to stop discriminating on the basis of race.").

39. *Brown*, 347 U.S. 483.

40. *Id.*; *Roe*, 410 U.S. 113.

41. *Planned Parenthood*, 505 U.S. at 867.

42. *Parents Involved*, 551 U.S. at 831 (Breyer, J., dissenting) (emphasis in original); see generally *id.* at 823-28 (describing the precedents that the *Parents Involved* plurality was declining to follow).

43. Marbury v. Madison, 5 U.S. (1 Cranch) 137 (1803).

44. *Id.* at 163–73.

45. *Id.* at 176–78. See also City of Boerne, 521 U.S. at 516.

46. JÜRGEN HABERMAS, BETWEEN FACTS AND NORMS: CONTRIBUTIONS TO A DISCOURSE THEORY OF LAW AND DEMOCRACY (William Rehg trans., 1996).

47. *Id.* at 83–84.

48. *Id.* at 110 (describing how citizens engage each other as equals); *id.* at 111 ("[Citizens are] free and equal consociates *under law.*") (emphasis in original); *id.* at 127 ("[Citizens must have] equal chances to exercise the communicative freedom to take a position on criticizable validity claims.").

49. *Id.* at 102–4, 107.

50. *Id.* at 98, 102 (the common good is "what lies equally in the interest of each"). See also *id.* at 99 (arguing that legal institutions that do not base their legitimacy on these ideas will produce cognitive dissonance with ordinarily accepted moral precepts).

51. *Id.* at 130–31 ("[Institutions] must draw on sources of legitimation that are not at [their] disposal.").

52. *Id.* at 81.

53. *Id.* at 308.

54. *Id.* at 126, 130.

55. *Id.* at 275.

56. PAUL W. KAHN, THE REIGN OF LAW: MARBURY V. MADISON AND THE CONSTRUCTION OF AMERICA 204 (1997).

Chapter 9

Losing Twice: The Lottery

The indifference of justices both to the harm they inflict on constitutional stature and to the opportunities they have to enhance their legitimacy by honoring stature can run deep. This chapter analyzes troubling features of Chief Justice Roberts's plurality opinion in *Parents Involved in Community Schools v. Seattle School District No. 1*[1] and the majority opinion in *Citizens United v. Federal Election Commission.*[2] The *Parents Involved* plurality opinion repeats previously discussed failures to satisfy the harm-avoidance obligation which are evident in earlier decisions such as *Bowers v. Hardwick.*[3] The plurality opinion also reveals an indifference to harm-amelioration obligations. The adamant refusal in *Citizens United* to acknowledge important differences between corporations and citizens is disquieting confirmation of arguments in *Losing Twice* that some justices may not highly value the constitutional stature of citizens.

The *Parents Involved* plurality opinion and the *Citizens United* majority opinion were written by justices typically described as conservative. Readers should recall, however, that indifference to harm-avoidance and harm-amelioration obligations transcends conservative or liberal judicial philosophy. It is of no particular importance that the opinions under scrutiny in this chapter were endorsed by conservative justices. Indeed, it is possible that the very justices who wrote the opinions in *Parents Involved* and *Citizens United* will discover—perhaps in their favored doctrine of minimalist judicial review—a reason to pay better attention to the shared understandings on which citizens' constitutional stature is based. What the opinions reveal is not a basis for indicting a particular wing of the Court but only a reason to believe that constitutional losers remain at unpredictable risk of losing twice in rights disputes.[4]

First, consider the disquieting portents of the plurality opinion in *Parents Involved,* which arose as a constitutional challenge to policies of two school districts that used race as a tiebreaker in making student school assignments. Each

school district claimed it had adopted its policy as a means of securing the benefits of integrated schools, and each used its demographic composition as a benchmark for determining whether schools were sufficiently integrated. Relying on a
"binary conception of race," one district classified students as "white" or "non-
white" and the other classified students as "black" or "other."[5]

Parents Involved was essentially an educational affirmative action dispute like
Grutter v. Bollinger.[6] The plaintiffs challenging the tiebreaking policies had done
nothing wrong; they simply wanted their children to attend their preferred
school. Persons benefiting from the tie-breaking policies were also innocent;
they also wanted their children to attend a good school. Moreover, the plaintiffs,
school districts, and supporters of the tie-breaking policies acted as constitutional leaders in making reasonable constitutional arguments.

Parents Involved thus presented justices with a dispute necessitating a tragic choice.
As a result, stakeholder equality and consent expectations would have been high, as
was the potential for harm to the losers' constitutional stature inflicted by justices
indifferent to their obligations. Sadly, rather than acknowledging the tragic choice
and their responsibility for inflicting harm on an innocent party, plurality justices
engaged in a self-forgiving, regret-free, doctrine-made-me-do-it analysis. They
depicted the constitutional losers as blameworthy. They were indifferent to the truth
of what was at stake for the constitutional losers. Finally, in a curious epilogue to their
opinion,[7] they treated the decision in Brown v. Board of Education[8] as if it were their
own and appropriated it to the exclusive use of the Parents Involved constitutional
winners.

What is the evidence that plurality justices evaded responsibility for making
a tragic choice? First, justices set the stage for denying the innocence of the
school districts and their supporting stakeholders by categorically denouncing
every conceivable justification the districts offered for using race as a tiebreaker
in making school assignments. As a matter of constitutional doctrine, they
insisted that, with only minor exceptions, the Constitution requires government
to be absolutely colorblind. In addition, they accused districts of engaging in
racial balancing, which they deemed to be always and under any circumstances
pernicious and unconstitutional.[9] They insisted, in effect, that the districts'
understanding of the Constitution had no plausible merit; they encouraged us
to think of the districts as wrongdoers rather than as respected constitutional
leaders.

As further encouragement to think of districts as wrongdoers, plurality justices attacked the good character and truthfulness of the school districts and
their supporters. They refused to credit the truth of the districts' arguments that
racial balancing itself was not an ultimate objective and that tiebreakers were
intended to preserve the important educational benefits of racial integration.
Instead, plurality justices asserted, "The plans are directed only to racial balance,

pure and simple,"[10] and they charged the districts with employing "extreme measures" to attain a racial balance.[11] In addition, they equated the school districts with the defenders of *de jure* racial segregation in *Brown v. Board of Education*[12] and *Plessy v. Ferguson.*[13]

Sharpening the characterization of the eventual constitutional losers as wrongdoers, plurality justices impugned the character of the Seattle school district because of a web site it had once maintained.[14] Justice Thomas's concurring opinion, for example, chastised the district for its web site statement that "individualism as opposed to a more collective ideology" is a form of "cultural racism," and it also asserted that the district had wrongfully rejected Thomas's view that the Constitution requires absolute colorblindness.[15] According to Thomas:

> The Seattle school district's website formerly contained the following definition of "cultural racism": "Those aspects of society that overtly and covertly attribute value and normality to white people and whiteness, and devalue, stereotype, and label people of color as 'other,' different, less than, or render them invisible. Examples of these norms include... emphasizing individualism as opposed to a more collective ideology [and] defining one form of English as standard...." More recently, the school district sent a delegation of high school students to a "White Privilege Conference." One conference participant described "white privilege" as "an invisible package of unearned assets which I can count on cashing in each day, but about which I was meant to remain oblivious."[16]

Justice Thomas's criticism of the Seattle district's web site is not a curious footnote having no direct relevance to the constitutional issues in *Parents Involved*. Rather, it is a partisan rebuke of anyone who might object to having our Constitution interpreted to require absolute colorblindness. Ignoring respected scholarship confirming the deleterious effects of racial stereotypes, questioning the ideology of racial colorblindness, and noting the link between individual and group discrimination, the footnote was structured to support the message that the districts should not be viewed as respected constitutional leaders but as entities acting completely outside the boundaries of acceptable constitutional meaning.

In addition to characterizing the districts as wrongdoers and thereby denying a tragic choice, the *Parents Involved* plurality opinion neglected truths important to the constitutional losers. The realities of rights litigation might excuse some shortcomings in the truthfulness of the opinion. For example, more than one hundred amicus curiae briefs were filed in the Supreme Court. Such a wealth of information would make it difficult for any justice to tell the entire truth about the dispute. Moreover, governmental entities were the named defendants, which ensured that facts pertaining to citizen stakeholders and beneficiaries of the school districts' policies were not at the forefront of constitutional analysis. These typical features of rights litigation, however, do not explain the opinion's failure to properly acknowledge the truth of the situation as understood by the constitutional losers. For a sense of what plurality justices omitted from their opinion, simply read Justice Kennedy's concurring account of the constitutional losers' dilemmas, his description of how society and law interact so as to re-segregate public schools, his recognition of the difficulty of separating *de facto* from *de jure* racial discrimination, and his acknowledgment of the legitimacy and value to our nation of the diversity interest accepted in the Court's higher education decisions.[17] An *a priori* ideological commitment to a principle of colorblindness made this information irrelevant to plurality justices and resulted in an opinion that was untruthful about citizens attempting to do their best to live with the social realities of race.

Plurality justices' failure to truthfully discuss what was at stake for constitutional losers was coupled with their assignment of atypical evidentiary burdens to losers and winners. As government entities, the districts were properly given a heavy burden of justification for their use of race, but plurality justices further tipped the evidentiary scales against the districts. For example, they did not require the plaintiffs to offer factual support for many allegations. They accepted as true what they described as the undeniable costs of the districts' policies.[18] They repeated unsubstantiated assertions that all racial distinctions promote racial inferiority and racial hostility.[19] They took for granted that racial distinctions divide the nation into racial blocs and demean a person's dignity by ignoring "his or her own merit and essential qualities."[20] Although justices usually require plaintiffs to identify and suffer more than generalized societal harms as a prerequisite to a challenge to government policies, plurality justices described the *Parents Involved* plaintiffs' interests largely with reference to just such generalized costs. That justices would rely on such unsubstantiated assumptions and generalizations is no small matter. The persons who challenged racial school segregation in *Brown v. Board of Education* and who secured judicial support for voluntary desegregation efforts had prevailed only because the National Association for the Advancement of Colored People (NAACP) and others spent years documenting the harms of segregation.[21] No comparable documentation was required of the *Parents Involved* plaintiffs. Moreover, despite a voluminous record of evidence attesting to the *benefits* of the challenged school district policies, plurality justices asserted that "the need for...racial classifications" was "unclear."[22]

While denying a tragic choice, ascribing wrongful conduct to constitutional losers, and failing to provide a truthful account of the values and interests held by constitutional losers are disturbing features of the plurality opinion, the most significant breach of justices' obligations may have resulted from their appropriation of the decision in *Brown v. Board of Education* to serve their ideological commitments. *Brown* involved a challenge to racially segregated public schools. In their acknowledgment that racial segregation was rooted in a system of slavery and eighty years of enforcement of Jim Crow laws, *Brown* justices rejected a formalist conception of constitutional equality. *Brown* refused to permit government to maintain racially separate schools even if those schools were equally funded and treated equally in other ways. Because justices did not give government the option of treating different races as formal equals, we have rightly come to see *Brown* as embodying an anti-subordination conception of constitutional equality.[23] Plurality justices in *Parents Involved*, however, invoked *Brown* to support a purely formalist rule for what school districts can do to avoid the racial segregation of public schools. School districts, plurality justices said, must always be colorblind even though the world is not. They must not differentiate among students by race for any purpose other than remedying their own prior discrimination. They must ignore the likelihood that race routinely affects people's decisions, a fact that might explain housing patterns and other obstacles to racially integrated public schools. In the simplistic view of plurality justices, if school districts want to stop discrimination on the basis of race, they should just "stop discriminating on the basis of race."[24] As Justice Stevens noted in his dissent, the plurality's colorblindness principle holds that equality is satisfied by a statute "[forbidding] rich and poor alike to sleep under bridges, to beg in the streets, and to steal their bread."[25]

Justice Stevens charged that plurality justices' transformation of *Brown*'s constitutional meaning constituted a "cruel irony,"[26] and Justice Breyer accused plurality justices of engaging in a "cruel distortion"[27] of history. The first definition of "cruel" in my dictionary is "deliberately seeking to inflict pain and suffering; enjoying others' suffering; without mercy or pity."[28] Given other aspects of the *Parents Involved* plurality opinion, constitutional losers might reasonably view the mischaracterization of *Brown* as an intentional, merciless, or even gleeful reminder of justices' power to ignore them.

These are strong words, so let me elaborate, taking into account Justice Thomas's concurring opinion in *Parents Involved*, which flatly stated that "[the] Court does not sit to 'create a society that includes all Americans.'"[29] Whatever arguments might be made about plurality justices' interpretation or use of *Brown* as precedent,[30] their treatment of *Brown* was certainly not inclusive of constitutional losers. By associating *Brown* with only a principle of formal equality, plurality justices threatened to remove *Brown* from a body of decisional law available to the constitutional losers as a symbol and as a working anti-subordination principle. Moreover, plurality justices failed to respect the constitutional stature of citizens who have relied on the anti-subordination meaning of *Brown*.[31] They minimized the significance of the struggle of persons who have fought for racial integration of public schools,[32] and they made a gift of *Brown* to persons willing to be indifferent to our history of racial subordination, the old snake that Frederick Douglass cautioned would ever find new skins to wear.

The exclusionary effect of the plurality's handling of *Brown* might well prompt constitutional losers to ask, along with Justice Breyer, but "what of the hope and promise of *Brown*?"[33] Breyer's query is more than an anguished rhetorical flourish. It goes to the heart of plurality justices' indifference to harm. There were, after all, alternatives to what the plurality justices did.[34] The plurality justices, by following Justice Kennedy's lead, could have decided that the school districts had acted unconstitutionally, accepting the school districts' interests as sincerely held, yet still strictly scrutinizing and rejecting district policies as too crude and inherently stigmatizing to satisfy the Constitution.[35] Instead of insisting on absolute colorblindness, they might have entertained the possibility that merely race conscious policies are different from invidious discrimination because they do not necessarily lead to different treatment based on a classification that tells each student he or she is to be defined by race.[36] Their opinion could have avoided erecting an ideological barrier to continuing conversations about legitimate and illegitimate uses of race, if they had taken seriously the admonition that one should interpret the Constitution "as a practical document that . . . transmit[s] its basic values to future generations through principles that remain workable over time."[37] They might have done more to recognize the efforts of school districts to act as constitutional leaders in sustaining public school integration.

Instead, plurality justices went out of their way to rewrite *Brown*'s history and meaning. They did not rely on *Brown* in the main body of their opinion, surely recognizing that the systemic, *de jure* discrimination challenged in *Brown* was significantly different from the quite limited use of race to avoid re-segregation challenged in *Parents Involved*.[38] They simply appended a short epilogue to their analysis in which they chose to associate *Brown* with a constitutional command of absolute colorblindness.

By refusing to truthfully acknowledge the constitutional losers' stakes in *Parents Involved* and by using *Brown* to serve an ideological end at odds with a central aspect of *Brown*'s history, plurality justices acted as if they were the sole owners of an important part of the res publica. Their opinion thus became vulnerable to the serious charge that plurality justices think of themselves not as trustees for citizens of full constitutional stature but as ideological victors who have a right to treat the Court's body of decisional law as the spoils of war.

Just as the *Parents Involved* plurality opinion might have been written differently, so might the majority's recent campaign-finance opinion, *Citizens United v. Federal Election Commission*. The *Citizens United* opinion has been the object of much criticism that is not directly relevant to justices' harm-avoidance and harm-amelioration obligations. From the perspective of *Losing Twice*, for example, there is no reason to complain that justices accorded *Citizens United* a right to broadcast a film criticizing Hillary Clinton immediately before a primary election. Nor is *Citizens United* objectionable because justices held that corporate speech should be protected under the First Amendment. Even dissenting justices accepted the proposition that there is no legitimate argument that speech falls outside the protection of the First Amendment simply because it emanates from a corporation.[39]

The difficulty with *Citizens United* is that, in establishing constitutional meaning, justices "almost completely elide[d]" important differences between citizens and artificial corporate structures.[40] Consequently, justices failed to truthfully acknowledge what was at stake for citizens of full constitutional stature.

To be fair, majority justices did mention some differences between corporations and citizens. They acknowledged in passing, for example, that corporations enjoy limited liability for their owners and managers, have perpetual life, and enjoy a legal status that offers advantages in accumulating and distributing assets.[41] Moreover, they also occasionally spoke of corporations as merely a means to an end, as democratic institutions[42] and "forms" or "forums" for the expression of ideas that "citizens must be free to use."[43]

These references, however, were offset by assertions that seemed to accord true rather than merely figurative personhood to corporations. While avoiding any explicit assertion that corporations are just like living human beings, majority justices nonetheless designated the corporation as a speaker. Discussing speaker identity,[44] they compared corporations to speakers who are living beings: public school children, prisoners, military personnel, and federal employees. They worried that government restrictions on corporations might interfere with "the right to use speech to strive to establish worth, standing, and respect for the speaker's voice,"[45] without explaining why this concern—which has obvious meaning for natural beings, especially citizens and constitutional leaders—is relevant to a nonliving, artificial entity.

Their analysis also failed to come to terms with the less than straightforward relationship between human beings associated with corporations and corporate-funded speech. As dissenting justices observed, when a business corporation endorses or attacks a particular candidate, it does not speak on behalf of customers or employees, who "typically have no say in such matters."[46] In addition, shareholders also "tend to be far removed from the day-to-day decisions of the firm," and their "political preferences may be opaque to management."[47] Moreover, it is mistaken to imagine that corporations permit shareholders to make decisions about speech through a shareholder vote or through suits enforcing fiduciary duties for, as "many corporate lawyers will tell you... 'these rights are so limited as to be almost nonexistent.' "[48] As for officers or directors of a corporation, "their fiduciary duties generally prohibit them from using corporate funds for personal ends."[49]

Dissenting justices sensibly asked how restricting a corporation's ability to use general treasury funds for electioneering speech can infringe an individual's autonomy, dignity, or political equality. Majority justices, however, preferred to downplay differences between corporations and individuals that are relevant to constitutional stature. They did not acknowledge that corporations do not have presumptively equal moral or political agency. They did not accord significance to the fact that corporations do not have a right to vote and "are not themselves members of 'We the People' by whom and for whom our Constitution was established";[50] that corporations can be foreign controlled;[51] or that corporations have "no consciences, no beliefs, no feelings, no thoughts, no desires."[52] Only dissenting justices took note of these matters.

Not surprisingly, political commentary and letters to newspaper editors have reacted with outrage to the failure of *Citizens United* to differentiate between human beings and corporations. Were justices to declare that there is no constitutional difference between a bullhorn and the antiwar activist who uses it, or between HAL (the renegade computer in *2001: A Space Odyssey*) and the human astronauts HAL was intended to serve, I suspect that citizens would be similarly concerned.

The comparison of corporate entity to human being will be particularly disturbing to citizens who believe justices are not paying adequate attention to their obligations to constitutional losers. One might reasonably fear that if justices are unable to see that the differences between corporations and citizens are relevant to the integrity of our democratic system, as was the case in *Citizens United*, justices will also have an impoverished view of citizens' unique capacities for moral and political agency. And in such a case, how can justices be persuaded of the importance of satisfying obligations derived from citizens' unique capacities? And why should justices feel compelled to speak truthfully about what is at stake for constitutional losers?

Indeed, in *Citizens United* majority justices did fail to give a truthful account of what was at stake for constitutional losers. Dissenting justices, acting as the voice of the constitutional losers, described those stakes and argued that corporations able to fund electioneering campaigns through general treasury funds have the power to unduly influence the judgment of elected officials. Because the merits of an issue or the desires of political constituencies will be subordinated to that influence, political accountability and the willingness of citizens to participate in elections will be adversely affected, and "the fundamental demands of a democratic society"[53] will be compromised.

Readers will probably recognize the similarity of the interests of the constitutional losers in *Citizens United* to the interests at the heart of the rights dispute in *Shaw v. Reno*,[54] in which voters asserted that political boundaries drawn on the basis of race would significantly interfere with important representational interests. In *Shaw*, justices acted to protect voters from artificial structures that gave a racial group a controlling voice in elections and increased the likelihood that government officials would hold themselves accountable to only a segment of their constituency rather than to voters as a whole. In *Citizens United*, however, justices did not truthfully credit these same interests. They ignored the voluminous record that Congress had compiled when it adopted corporate campaign-finance restrictions,[55] and disregarded the conclusions of "Congress and half the state legislatures...that core functions of administering elections and passing legislation cannot operate effectively without some narrow restrictions on corporate electioneering paid for by general treasury funds."[56] Dissenting justices accused the majority of declaring "by fiat that the appearance of undue influence by high-spending corporations '[would] not cause the electorate to lose faith in democracy'...[although the] electorate itself [had] consistently indicated otherwise, both in opinion polls, and in the laws its representatives [had] passed."[57]

The difficulty with *Citizens United* is thus not that majority justices entirely ignored voters in *Citizens United*. Indeed, they repeatedly asserted that they wished to protect the electorate's access to all opinions and voters' ability to make informed choices among candidates. Nor is the difficulty that majority justices' description of citizens' interests was based on an ideological proposition that more speech is always better for the political process. The problem is that justices concluded that corporate expenditures would not interfere with governmental functions but would further the democratic process,[58] without first properly and truthfully acknowledging the representational interests at stake for constitutional losers.[59] As dissenting justices admonished, when some speakers are not real people and a First Amendment argument rests on the importance of voters being able to listen to all opinions, "it becomes necessary to consider how listeners [say that their interests] will actually be affected."[60]

The perspective of majority justices in *Citizens United* and of plurality justices in *Parents Involved* will be of concern to constitutional losers who believe they should not be subjected to losing twice in any given rights decision. It bodes ills for arguments made in *Losing Twice*. On the other hand, you will recall that the internal housekeeping traditions linked to professional role obligations can have a strong influence on justices, as noted in the Introduction to this book. Moreover, the doctrine of judicial minimalism to which both liberal and conservative justices profess adherence in one form or another, may offer an opportunity to persuade justices to pay better attention to their obligations to constitutional losers.

Judicial minimalism is said to be especially suited to a pluralistic society sharing only "thin" understandings about substantive constitutional principles.[61] In such a society, minimalism posits, it is difficult if not impossible for justices to reconcile substantive views on intractable issues such as abortion or race-based decision-making. It is therefore wise for justices to write both narrowly, with reference only to the facts of a specific dispute (the narrow-ground tenet), and also shallowly, at a high degree of abstraction (the shallow-ground tenet).

Important aspects of judicial minimalism obviously tend to work against recognition of the harm-amelioration and harm-avoidance obligations discussed in *Losing Twice*. For example, the doctrine assumes that courts are not inherently democratic in nature but instead exist to facilitate democratic processes of the elected branches of government. The view that democracy consists only of aggregate, vote-counting processes associated with the political branches of government might easily prevent justices from recognizing institutional values served by fulfilling their obligations, most notably the value of enhancing the legitimacy of the Court's inherently democratic functions. Moreover, although the narrow-ground tenet of minimalism has the potential to support ongoing constitutional debate and recognition of constitutional losers' values and interests in different times or contexts, the tenet might be interpreted to forbid justices from expressing opinions about constitutional losers' values and interests or signaling that even rejected constitutional values are worthy of attention. The narrow-ground tenet might also prevent justices from realizing that expanding the pie of interests relevant to a rights dispute can sometimes lead to explanations for a decision that constitutional losers can accept. In abortion disputes, for example, silence regarding difficult questions of religious freedom and rights of conscience might have comported with narrow-ground judicial minimalism, but it also contributed to justices' failure to honor the full constitutional stature and moral agency of losers. The shallow-ground tenet of judicial minimalism is especially problematic, insofar as it may cause justices to unquestioningly assume that rights disputes involve only "thin" constitutional understandings.

If no more could be said about judicial minimalism, constitutional losers would face a dispiriting future. We know, however, that rights disputes are not only about substantive principle but also frequently involve debates about constitutional stature, and *Losing Twice* argues that constitutional stature is not based on thin understandings. As Michael Walzer notes, procedural theories of justice often make thick assumptions about people and proper rules of engagement that are based on shared understandings within a given culture.[62] The assumptions underlying citizens' constitutional stature (e.g., that each of us is equal in constitutionally relevant ways and therefore that our consent matters equally to the legitimacy of government) are of a thick, procedural ilk. They are embodied in long-standing interpretations of foundational documents and in our political

discourse. These thick understandings of constitutional stature are a potent coun-
terweight to judicial conventions and practices that inflict second losses on constitutional losers.

It is to be hoped that justices schooled to take note of pluralistic, thin understandings of substantive constitutional principle are also prepared to recognize a
thick understanding when they see it. If citizens share thick understandings
about constitutional stature, surely justices will find it worthwhile to respect
those understandings in judicial opinions that resolve our most contentious
rights disputes. By refusing to harm and instead honoring constitutional stature,
justices will help proponents of opposing constitutional meanings march
together in spirit without relinquishing their own parade.[63]

Ultimately, however, recognition of the obligations discussed in *Losing Twice*
depends on whether citizens like you and I firmly insist on proper recognition of
and respect for our constitutional stature. That stature, which gives rise to harm-
avoidance and harm-amelioration obligations, is more than a matter of abstract,
academic theory. It is the key to maintaining a proper relationship between justices and citizens with significant stakes in what the Constitution means.

What can we do to claim our constitutional stature? For one thing, especially
as older justices are replaced by new ones, we can refuse to let ourselves become
complicit in fomenting the red-herring issue of judicial activism. Concerns about
judicial activism typically surface in Senate confirmation hearings for Supreme
Court nominees. Senators ask questions about judicial activism, and nominees
give responses intended to reassure us that they are not activists. No one ever
defines what is meant by activism, of course, but the implication is that judicial
activists improperly make law as they interpret the Constitution. As we know,
however, judicial law-making is a natural and inevitable attribute of judicial
review. The most obvious law-making by justices is the creation of doctrines that
implement constitutional principle. The Constitution does not say that some
forms of discrimination ought to be subjected to strict scrutiny while other
discrimination is permissible even if supported only by a rational justification.
Rather, justices have crafted and applied strict scrutiny and rational-basis doctrines to give meaning to the Constitution's equality guarantee. Moreover, justices make law in other ways. In *District of Columbia v. Heller*, for example, justices
extended Second Amendment protection to possession of firearms not in
existence in the eighteenth century; said that the amendment's drafting history
offered questionable interpretational guidance to justices; and imported a new
and malleable right of self-defense into the Constitution.[64] As Justice Steven
observed, *Heller* gives the judiciary an "active . . . role in making vitally important
national policy decisions" about gun regulation, using "the common-law process
of case-by-case judicial lawmaking to define the contours of acceptable gun
policy."[65]

Because some degree of judicial lawmaking goes hand in hand with judicial review, we must not let a *faux* debate about judicial activism drown out discussion of other issues. In particular, we should be asking whether constitutional interpretation and judicial review—by sitting or new justices, conservative or liberal—are pursued by justices with due regard to their harm-avoidance and harm-amelioration obligations. We should ask that justices remember that they are deciding cases that affect real people, not merely debating among themselves about abstract principles of law.[66]

Finding effective words for voicing our expectations of justices and for challenging judicial indifference to harm will not be easy, but the alternative is unacceptable. We rightfully expect justices to recognize our full constitutional stature and to protect us against a judicial lottery in which arbitrary and sporadic indifference puts us at risk of losing twice in rights disputes.

Notes

1. Parents Involved in Cmty. Schs. v. Seattle Sch. Dist. No. 1, 551 U.S. 701 (2007).
2. Citizens United v. Federal Election Commission, 130 S. Ct. 876 (2010).
3. Bowers v. Hardwick, 478 U.S. 186 (1986).
4. As this book goes to press, justices have arguably issued another opinion reflecting indifference to harm-avoidance and harm-amelioration obligations. In Christian Legal Soc'y Chapter of the Univ. of Cal. v. Martinez, 130 S. Ct. 2971 (2010), Justice Ginsburg's majority opinion does not directly undermine the constitutional stature of the losing party, but its description of what is at stake for the constitutional loser can reasonably be accused of untruthfulness in understating the importance of belief to religious groups and the burdens imposed on student groups denied law school recognition. The opinion also does not pursue the argument that the constitutional loser was allegedly a target of discrimination or that the law school's admit-all-comers policy allegedly served as a pretext for discrimination. These shortcomings may result from the majority's decision to interpret a joint stipulation as narrowing the parties' dispute to a disagreement about the scope of the First Amendment's limited public forum doctrine. Even if the majority properly interpreted the stipulation, an opinion intended to ameliorate harm might have included a more comprehensive and clearer account of these matters.
5. *Parents Involved*, 551 U.S. at 710.
6. Grutter v. Bollinger, 539 U.S. 982 (2003).
7. *Parents Involved*, 551 U.S. at 745–48. See, Emily Calhoun, "Beyond the Pale: Supreme Court Opinions in Rights Disputes," *English Language Notes* (forthcoming 2010).
8. Brown v. Bd. of Educ., 347 U.S. 483 (1954).
9. *Parents Involved*, 551 U.S. at 729–33.
10. *Id.* at 726.
11. *Id.* at 728.
12. See *id.* at 745–46.
13. *Parents Involved*, 551 U.S. 772–81 (Thomas, J., concurring).
14. *Parents Involved*, 551 U.S. at 730 n.14 (plurality opinion); *id.* at 781 n.30 (Thomas, J., concurring).
15. *Parents Involved*, 551 U.S. at 781 n.30 (Thomas, J., concurring).
16. *Id.* (internal citations omitted).
17. *Parents Involved*, 551 U.S. at 793–98 (Kennedy, J., concurring).
18. See *Parents Involved*, 551 U.S. at 745.

19. See *id.* at 745 (quoting Richmond v. Croson Co., 488 U.S. 469, 493 (1989)).
20. *Id.*
21. See Brown v. Bd. of Educ., 347 U.S. 483 (1954).
22. *Parents Involved,* 551 U.S. at 745–46.
23. Cf. Shaw v. Reno, 509 U.S. 630 (1993) (invalidating the creation of a race-based electoral district by relying on a community-of-interests conception of equality).
24. *Parents Involved,* 551 U.S. at 748.
25. *Parents Involved,* 551 U.S. at 799 (Stevens, J., dissenting) (quoting ANATOLE FRANCE, THE RED LILY 95 (W. Stevens trans., 6th ed. 1922)).
26. *Id.* at 798.
27. *Parents Involved,* 551 U.S. at 867 (Breyer, J., dissenting).
28. WEBSTER'S NEW WORLD DICTIONARY OF THE AMERICAN LANGUAGE (2d ed. 1980).
29. *Parents Involved,* 551 U.S. at 766 n.14 (Thomas, J., concurring).
30. Dissenting justices argued that the plurality's principle of absolute constitutional colorblindness was not a reasonable interpretation of precedent. It was neither "loyal" nor "faithful" to prior decisions. See *Parents Involved,* 551 U.S. at 803 (Stevens, J., dissenting); and see also *id.* at 863-65 (Breyer, J., dissenting). See also RONALD DWORKIN, THE SUPREME COURT PHALANX: THE COURT'S NEW RIGHT-WING BLOC 49–58(2008) (discussing *Parents Involved* in relation to Grutter v. Bollinger, 539 U.S. 306 (2003), which considered affirmative action in the context of university admissions).
31. Cf. Rebecca L. Brown, *Liberty, the New Equality,* 77 N.Y.U. L. REV. 1491, 1539 (2002) ("To ask another to accept a position without a justification that is open to reasoned debate is to fail in the obligation to respect the equality of others.").
32. Cf. PAUL W. KAHN, THE REIGN OF LAW: *MARBURY V. MADISON* AND THE CONSTRUCTION OF AMERICA 89 (1997) (arguing that the rule of law embraces an obligation "not to forget and so make as nothing the significance of the lives and deaths of our predecessors").
33. *Parents Involved,* 551 U.S. at 867 (Breyer, J., dissenting).
34. Cf. *Parents Involved,* 551 U.S. at 735 (plurality opinion) (criticizing the school districts for failing to consider methods "other than the [exlplicit] racial classifications" to achieve their goal of achieving a racially balanced student body).
35. See *Parents Involved,* 551 U.S. at 798 (Kennedy, J., concurring).
36. *Id.* at 787–98.
37. *Parents Involved,* 551 U.S. at 858 (Breyer, J., dissenting). Cf. Planned Parenthood of Se. Pa. v. Casey, 503 U.S. 933 (1992).
38. Plurality justices cited Brown v. Bd. of Educ., 349 U.S. 294 (1955) (*Brown II*), for the limited proposition that equal protection rights are individual not group rights, but Brown v. Bd. of Educ., 347 U.S. 483 (1954) (*Brown I*), was cited only in the epilogue, with reference only to arguments made by parties in the *Brown* lawsuits, not to the opinions themselves.
39. Citizens United v. Federal Election Comm'n, 130 S.Ct. 876, 960 (2010) (Stevens, J., concurring in part and dissenting in part).
40. *Id.* at 971.
41. *Citizens United,* 130 S. Ct. at 905–06.
42. *Id.* at 913–16 (discussing disclosure requirements).
43. *Id.* at 917.
44. *Id.* at 904–05.
45. *Id.* at 899.
46. *Citizens United,* 130 S.Ct. at 972 (Stevens, J., concurring in part and dissenting in part).
47. *Id.*
48. *Id.* at 978.
49. *Id.* at 972.
50. *Id.*
51. *Id.* at 971.
52. *Id.* at 972.

53. *Id.* at 974–76.

54. Shaw v. Reno, 509 U.S. 630 (1993).

55. *Citizens United*, 130 S. Ct. at 968–69 (Stevens, J., concurring in part and dissenting in part).

56. *Id.* at 946 n.46.

57. *Id.* at 963 n.64.

58. *Citizens United*, 130 S. Ct. 876 (majority opinion).

59. See, e.g., *id.* at 898 ("speech is an essential mechanism of democracy, for it is the means to hold officials accountable to the people"); *id.* at 898–99, 907 (expressing concern that the electorate will be deprived of information); *id.* at 911 (noting a concern about whether elected officials will surrender their best judgment and put expediency before principle); but the cure is more speech, not less. *Id.* at 911.

60. *Citizens United*, 130 S. Ct. at 974, 976 (Stevens, J., concurring in part and dissenting in part).

61. MICHAEL WALZER, THICK AND THIN: MORAL ARGUMENT AT HOME AND ABROAD 8 (1994).

62. *See* WALZER, *supra* note 57, at 11–15.

63. *Id.* at 6–9.

64. District of Columbia v. Heller, 554 U.S. 570, 128 S. Ct. 2783 (2008).

65. *Id.* at 2847 (Stevens, J., dissenting).

66. Cf. *Christian Legal Soc'y Chapter*, 130 S. Ct. 2971, in which some of the shortcomings of the majority opinion may be attributed to the fact that the petition for certiorari was, apparently, granted to resolve a pure question of constitutional law, on the assumption that no material facts were in dispute.

BIBLIOGRAPHIC ESSAYS

Introduction: Losing Twice in Constitutional Rights Disputes

Standard approaches to judicial legitimacy start with top-down theory. They include, for example, the methods of constitutional interpretation presented in ANTONIN SCALIA, A MATTER OF INTERPRETATION: FEDERAL COURTS AND THE LAW (Amy Gutmann ed., 1997), and in STEPHEN BREYER, ACTIVE LIBERTY (2008); and the method of judicial decision-making described in CASS R. SUNSTEIN, A CONSTITUTION OF MANY MINDS: WHY THE FOUNDING DOCUMENT DOESN'T MEAN WHAT IT MEANT BEFORE (2009); CASS R. SUNSTEIN, RADICALS IN ROBES: WHY EXTREME RIGHT-WING COURTS ARE WRONG FOR AMERICA (2005); and CASS R. SUNSTEIN, ONE CASE AT A TIME: JUDICIAL MINIMALISM ON THE SUPREME COURT (1999). In contrast, LOSING TWICE follows the lead of Owen M. Fiss, who observed in *Free Speech and Social Structure*, 71 IOWA L. REV. 1405, 1421 (1986), that an exploration of case-by-case harms and injustices is frequently the better path to take.

In exploring unjust harms suffered by constitutional losers, I have benefited tremendously from a large body of literature. It includes highly philosophical work, such as the essays included in INJUSTICE AND RECTIFICATION (Rodney C. Roberts ed., 2002), and STEPHEN K. WHITE, POLITICAL THEORY AND POSTMODERNISM (1991); elegantly poetic treatments, such as JUDITH N. SHKLAR, THE FACES OF INJUSTICE (1990); influential and powerful theoretical analyses of law such as EDMOND N. CAHN, THE SENSE OF INJUSTICE (1949), Robert M. Cover, *Violence and the Word*, 95 YALE L.J. 1601 (1986); the essays collected in LAW'S VIOLENCE (Austin Sarat & Thomas R. Kearns eds., 1995); and social science perspectives such as that of KRISTIN BUMILLER, THE CIVIL RIGHTS SOCIETY: THE SOCIAL CONSTRUCTION OF VICTIMS (1988), or GLENN C. LOURY, THE ANATOMY OF RACIAL INEQUALITY (2002). See also COSTAS DOUZINAS & RONNIE WARRINGTON, JUSTICE MISCARRIED: ETHICS AND AESTHETICS IN LAW (1994).

LOSING TWICE links the topics of injustice and judicial legitimacy through a study of judicial role obligations. Cf. Richard H. Fallon Jr., *Judicially Manageable Standards and Constitutional Meaning*, 119 HARV. L. REV. 1274, 1317 (2006) (suggesting the usefulness of this approach). As David Luban has said, the resulting scholarship is an exploration of a "personalize[d] jurisprudence." DAVID LUBAN, LEGAL ETHICS AND HUMAN DIGNITY 105 (2007).

I have benefited greatly from Luban's work, which also includes LAWYERS AND JUSTICE: AN ETHICAL STUDY (1988) and LEGAL ETHICS AND HUMAN DIGNITY. In the latter, Luban argues that if attorneys ignore their obligation to avoid harm, otherwise legitimate acts are transformed into exercises of raw power. Moreover, Luban refuses to accept the way things have always been done in the adversary system as a justification for attorney-inflicted harm. *The Adversary System Excuse*, in THE GOOD LAWYER: LAWYERS' ROLES AND LAWYERS' ETHICS (David Luban ed., 1983). He also recognizes that the harmful effects of attorney acts are not limited to specific clients but can have much broader effects. For example, he writes, "Repetitions and reiterations of the same action-type create norms, by the familiar processes through which precedents and customs become law. When a repeated pattern of behavior has been elevated to the status of a formal or quasi-formal norm[,] the world has become qualitatively different [for us all]." David Luban, *The Social Responsibility of Lawyers: A Green Perspective*, 63 GEO. WASH. L. REV. 955, 961 (1995). These arguments about attorney obligations are equally applicable to the realm of judging and to the unique harms that justices can inflict on constitutional losers.

I also recommend WILLIAM H. SIMON, THE PRACTICE OF JUSTICE: A THEORY OF LAWYERS' ETHICS (1998). Simon offers a number of examples—among them the "Innocent Convict"—of what he labels the "moral anxiety" of attorneys confronted with choices that risk harm to innocent third persons. *Id.* at 4–7. He rejects the idea that we need to accept "deliberate injustice in the here-and-now" in order to secure a more abstract, future, and greater good. *Id.* at 3. He is an advocate of a contextual rather than a categorical approach to ethical questions pertaining to role obligations, although he understands the difficulty of institutionalizing a contextual ethics. Finally, he recognizes that "the key issues of legal ethics are jurisprudential, that is, they implicate questions of the nature and purpose of law and the legal system." *Id.* at 13. See also William H. Simon, *Solving Problems vs. Claiming Rights: The Pragmatist Challenge to Legal Liberalism*, 46 WM. AND MARY L. REV. 127, 132 (2004) (recognizing "the implicit jurisprudence of practicing lawyers").

One other interesting argument about attorney role obligations that makes points applicable to the realm of judging is W. Bradley Wendel, *Professionalism as Interpretation*, 99 NW. U. L. REV. 1167 (2005). Wendel asserts that transactional attorneys must not ignore harms that they can inflict on law and its purposes. According to Wendel, the obligation is fiduciary-based. This book endorses a fiduciary-based obligation owed by justices, whose resolution of constitutional rights disputes has a transactional character.

I am indebted to many who have explored judicial ethos and ethics, and their bearing on the legitimacy of judicial review. In particular, I acknowledge Lawrence B. Solum, *Judicial Selection: Ideology versus Character*, 26 CARDOZO L. REV. 659, 681–85 (2005); Lawrence B. Solum, *Public Legal Reason*, 92 VA. L. REV. 1449 (2006); and Lawrence B. Solum, *Virtue Jurisprudence: An Aretaic Theory of Law*, Address at the University of Colorado School of Law (September 12, 2006). Solum explores the idea that justices should be "virtuous agents" possessed of dispositions such as sobriety, impartiality (evenhanded sympathy for all parties), and wisdom (situation sense) that permit them to reason well in deciding cases. Lawrence B. Solum, *Natural Justice*, 51 AM. J. JURIS. 65 (2006).

Sarah M. R. Cravens, *Judges as Trustees: A Duty to Account and an Opportunity for Virtue*, 62 WASH. & LEE L. REV. 1637 (2005), has linked virtue ethics theory to a concept of judicial trustee-ship. Cravens notes that an ethical system becomes especially important for judges working within a system of law that has indeterminacy. *Id.* at 1641–42 (attributing the idea to Aristotle). Chapter 1 also employs a trusteeship metaphor as a device to aid a discussion of judicial obligation, and it characterizes the resolution of rights disputes as indeterminate. Indeterminacy is also explored in Chapter 8.

Also relevant to the argument of this book is Penelope Pether, *Militant Judgment?: Judicial Ontology, Constitutional Poetics, and "The Long War,"* 29 CARDOZO L. REV. 2279, 2300 (2008), who recommends an ethics of judging based on "egalitarian relations between state and citizen...and citizen and other, and...the egalitarian address of the militant judge to those he judges," in the context of challenges to executive detention. David McGowan, *Judicial Writing and the Ethics of the Judicial Office*, 14 GEO. J. LEGAL ETHICS 509 (2001), has proposed a party-centered model of judging compatible with the recommendations made in this book.

Neil S. Siegel, *The Virtue of Judicial Statesmanship*, 86 TEX. L. REV. 959 (2008), offers an argument that in some respects overlaps the argument I make. Siegel searches for a concept of judicial responsibility suitable to significant constitutional rights disputes and capable of legiti-mating law. He rejects the view that the work of justices is purely interpretational. He explores the relevance of judicial statesmanship to rights disputes in which personal and collective identities are at stake. He argues that the rule of law is "sustained by a particular relationship between those who make and apply the law and those whom the law purports to govern," *id.* at 966, and that judicial statesmanship may require a justice to show that he or she understands what defeat means for all stakeholders in a controversy. *Id.* at 1009.

I would be remiss if I did not note the correspondence between the reflections of RICHARD A. POSNER, HOW JUDGES THINK (2008), and some arguments made in this book. Like David Luban, who rejects an adversary excuse for inflicting harm, Posner wants to remove the mask of legalism employed to obscure judicially inflicted cruelties and to deflect blame from judges. POSNER, *supra* at 252. According to Posner, comprehensive constitutional theories have been an "embarrassing failure," *id.* at 375; as an alternative, he would focus on the consequences of judicial decisions and pay attention to judicial role. When Posner asserts that judges are constrained by the rules of the game, he is not referring to formalist legal rules. Rather, he emphasizes that he is speaking about judicial rules of articulation, awareness of boundaries and role, process values, and professional culture.

The role-obligation perspective of this book is not limited to a rule-based, regulatory system applicable to judicial behavior. Although justices of the Supreme Court are constrained by some specific ethical rules, and I am indebted to Debra Lyn Bassett, *Recusal and the Supreme Court*, 56 HASTINGS L.J. 657 (2005), for her discussion of those rules, an ethos rests on much more than a set of rules. An ethos constitutes a way of living in a unique professional world, and it always focuses special attention on role obligations within that world. See, e.g., Robert Cover, *The Supreme Court, 1982 Term—Foreword: Nomos and Narrative*, 97 HARV. L. REV. 4, 6 (1983) (to be part of a normative community, one must "know how to live in it"); and Emily M. Calhoun, *Academic Freedom: Disciplinary Lessons from Hogwarts*, 77 U. COLO. L. REV. 843 (2006) (analogizing a professional ethos to the use of magic in the Harry Potter novels: if persons conform to role obligations and use magic properly, they live within the discipline; if not, they are culpable, even if they have brilliantly and effectively made use of a complicated body of theoretical knowledge). HOWARD GARDNER, FIVE MINDS FOR THE FUTURE 129–31 (2008), offers an elegant presentation of what an ethos entails. See also WILLIAM H. SIMON, THE PRACTICE OF JUSTICE: A THEORY OF LAWYERS' ETHICS (1998). Readers may also be interested in the discussion of inculcating ethical attitudes in attorneys in WILLIAM M. SULLIVAN ET AL., EDUCATING LAWYERS: PREPARATION FOR THE PROFESSION OF LAW (2007). I gratefully acknowledge Stephen Odendahl, my former student, for bringing to my attention the relevance of the justices' oath of office to questions of judicial ethos.

I was first introduced to the issue of professional role obligations by Richard Wasserstrom. Wasserstrom's discussion in *Roles and Morality*, in THE GOOD LAWYER: LAWYERS' ROLES AND LAWYERS' ETHICS 25 (David Luban ed., 1983) is relevant to the text's observations regarding ethical prohibitions on inflicting harm, how professional ethical systems sometimes relieve persons of usual moral obligations, and the necessity of strictly testing the validity of ethical systems that do so. I also come to the issue by way of the field of rhetoric, which addresses the role obligations of speaker to audience. Readers will note the rhetorical perspective that is reflected throughout LOSING TWICE and that draws on ideas advanced by, among others, WAYNE C. BOOTH, MODERN DOGMA AND THE RHETORIC OF ASSENT (1974); FRANCIS J. MOOTZ III, RHETORICAL KNOWLEDGE IN LEGAL PRACTICE AND CRITICAL LEGAL THEORY (2006); and James Boyd White, *Law as Rhetoric, Rhetoric as Law: The Arts of Cultural and Communal Life*, 52 U. CHI. L. REV. 684 (1985). See also the sources referenced in the bibliographic essays to chapters 4, 5, and 6.

Scholars working from a role-obligation perspective attest that the analysis is self-referential (or internal) to the profession. They usually emphasize the conservative nature of the analysis, although, as noted by ROBERTO MANGABEIRA UNGER, WHAT SHOULD LEGAL ANALYSIS BECOME? (1996), if one works within existing jurisprudential and discursive frameworks, one can nonetheless identify new practices that have the potential to become institutionally transformative. For a discussion of the internal character of the role-obligation perspective in law, I recommend WILLIAM H. SIMON, THE PRACTICE OF JUSTICE: A THEORY OF LAWYERS' ETHICS (1998). See also W. Bradley Wendel, *Legal Ethics as "Political Moralism" or the Morality of Politics*, 93 CORNELL L. REV. 1413 (2008) (describing the perspective as Aristotelian and noting its centrality to the political philosophy of John Rawls). That justices might be receptive to an internal role-obligation perspective is suggested by the Court's decision in *Boumediene v. Bush*, 128 S. Ct. 2229 (2008), which closely tracks an argument made in Emily Calhoun, *The Accounting: Habeas Corpus and Enemy Combatants*, 79 U. COLO. L. REV. 77 (2008) (applying the internal perspective to the habeas writ). See also Caperton v. A. T. Massey Coal Co., 129 S. Ct. 2252 (2009) (discussing the obligation of judicial recusal). I concur, however, with DAVID LUBAN, LEGAL ETHICS AND HUMAN DIGNITY 139 (2007), that a substantial number of both citizens and justices must adopt an effectively internal point of view toward law if we are to have a legitimate legal system.

Contemporary debate regarding attorney role obligations has frequently focused on post–September 11 dilemmas. See, e.g., Mary M. Cheh, *Should Lawyers Participate in Rigged Systems?: The Case of the Military Commissions*, 1 J. NAT'L SEC. L. & POL'Y (2005); and Jesselyn Radack, *Tortured Legal Ethics: The Role of the Government Advisor in the War on Terrorism*, 77 U. COLO. L. REV. 1 (2006). To appreciate the importance of the internal, role-obligation perspective to professions other than law, I recommend reading ATUL GAWANDE, BETTER: A SURGEON'S NOTES ON PERFORMANCE (2007) (discussing physicians who are asked to assist in the administration of the death penalty); CHARLES L. BOSK, FORGIVE AND REMEMBER: MANAGING MEDICAL FAILURE (1981) (distinguishing between technical errors and errors regarding breaches of a professional ethos, and the relative importance of the latter); and Emily M. Calhoun, *Academic Freedom: Disciplinary Lessons from Hogwarts*, 77 U. COLO. L. REV. 843 (2006) (recounting the resistance of Dr. Howard Levy to demands that he train military personnel who might later use what was learned in improper interrogation techniques).

The role-obligation dimensions of the Loring controversy are discussed in, e.g., Paul Finkelman, *Legal Ethics and Fugitive Slaves: The Anthony Burns Case, Judge Loring, and Abolitionist Attorneys*, 17 CARDOZO L. REV. 1793 (1996); Owen M. Fiss, *Can a Lawyer Ever Do Right?*, 17 CARDOZO L. REV. 1859 (1996); Sanford Levinson, *Allocating Honor and Acting Honorably: Some Reflections Provoked by the Cardozo Conference on Slavery*, 17 CARDOZO L. REV. 1969 (1996); and Ruth Wedgwood, *Ethics under Slavery's Constitution: Edward Loring and William Wetmore Story*, 17 CARDOZO L. REV. 1865 (1996).

The text asserts that little has been written about whether judges are justified in inflicting harm, and the absence of discussion is especially striking as it relates to harms inflicted on the parties who lose constitutional rights disputes. There are, of course, notable exceptions.

GUIDO CALABRESI, IDEALS, BELIEFS, ATTITUDES, AND THE LAW: PRIVATE LAW PERSPECTIVES ON A PUBLIC LAW PROBLEM (1985), for example, has argued that we owe respect to constitutional losers and that denying them respect can add significantly to their loss. ROBERT A. BURT, THE CONSTITUTION IN CONFLICT (1992), has objected to "authoritarian" judicial practices that designate people as absolute constitutional losers and give them a slavelike status. Others tend to focus on judicial obligations to minority groups only. See, e.g., Richard Delgado & Jean Stefancic, *Norms and Narratives: Can Judges Avoid Serious Moral Error?*, 69 TEX. L. REV. 1929, 1958 (1991); Richard Delgado, *Norms and Normal Science: Toward a Critique of Normativity in Legal Thought*, 139 U. PA. L. REV. 933, 942–44 (1991); and Toni M. Massaro, *Empathy, Legal Storytelling, and the Rule of Law: New Words, Old Wounds?*, 87 MICH. L. REV. 2099, 2123–24 (1989). More recently, Dan M. Kahan, *The Cognitively Illiberal State*, 60 STAN. L. REV. 115, 153 (2007), has taken a cognitive perspective on the meaning of losing and the losers' experience of autonomy. See also Dan M. Kahan et al., *Whose Eyes Are You Going to Believe? Scott v. Harris and the Perils of Cognitive Illiberalism*, 122 HARV. L. REV. 837 (2009) (exploring ways in which justices' personal values influence their view of empirical fact and how neglect of this phenomenon can result in harm to constitutional losers). As in this book, Kahan et al. approach the discussion of losers with reference to concepts of equality and consent. In addition, they view judicial legitimacy not only in terms of outcomes but also according to how constitutional losers are treated as judges arrive at or justify a decision. Compare Cass R. Sunstein, *If People Would Be Outraged by Their Rulings, Should Judges Care?*, 60 STAN. L. REV. 155 (2007) (linking conclusions about whether justices ought to care that they have provoked outrage to theories of constitutional interpretation rather than to obligations to avoid harm).

Recently, Lani Guinier, *The Supreme Court 2007 Term—Foreword: Demosprudence through Dissent*, 122 HARV. L. REV. 4 (2008), has explored how dissenting opinions might be used by Supreme Court justices to respond to the plight of constitutional losers. Guinier is engaged in what she sees as a broad effort "to reimagine the 'roles' of institutional players in a democracy." *Id.* at n.213. She finds value for constitutional losers in dissenting opinions that, if properly delivered, inspire losers to seek change through means other than litigation. *Id.* at 95. My argument, in contrast, emphasizes neglected opportunities to treat losers properly in majority opinions.

LINDA RADZIK, MAKING AMENDS: ATONEMENT IN MORALITY, LAW, AND POLITICS (2009), does not address justices' obligations to redress harm to constitutional losers, but she does explore the obligation of persons and institutions who inflict harm on relationships to atone for their conduct. Her arguments about atonement are particularly relevant to chapters 5 and 6 of this book.

The text asserts that citizens become outraged when justices fail to satisfy their obligations to constitutional losers. Outrage is frequently expressed in accusations of judicial activism. I recommend the following as excellent summaries of contemporary attacks on judicial review and federal courts: OWEN M. FISS, THE LAW AS IT COULD BE (2003); MARK KOZLOWSKI, THE MYTH OF THE IMPERIAL JUDICIARY: WHY THE RIGHT IS WRONG ABOUT THE COURTS (2003); and LARRY D. KRAMER, THE PEOPLE THEMSELVES: POPULAR CONSTITUTIONALISM AND JUDICIAL REVIEW (2004). As do I, these scholars question the validity of premises underlying politically motivated trashing of the courts, attempt to think somewhat outside the box about the Supreme Court and constitutional rights disputes, and call for a renewed commitment to the federal judiciary as an important institution. Their analysis and recommendations, however, differ substantially from mine. KRAMER, *supra*, as well as JEFFREY ROSEN, THE MOST DEMOCRATIC BRANCH: HOW THE COURTS SERVE AMERICA (2006), and MARK TUSHNET, TAKING THE CONSTITUTION AWAY FROM THE COURTS (1999), for example, argue that the People, acting legislatively, deserve a more prominent role than do the courts in constitutional interpretation. LOSING TWICE argues instead for finding new ways to engage citizens in judicial proceedings through which constitutional meaning is formed. As discussed in Emily Zackin, *Popular Constitutionalism's Hard When You're Not Very Popular: Why the ACLU Turned to Courts*, 42 LAW & SOC'Y REV. 367 (2008), political activity is not always an adequate substitute for judicial review.

Other assessments of judicial review and the Supreme Court include RONALD DWORKIN, THE SUPREME COURT PHALANX: THE COURT'S NEW RIGHT-WING BLOC (2008); JEFFREY ROSEN, THE SUPREME COURT: THE PERSONALITIES AND RIVALRIES THAT DEFINED AMERICA (2007); JEFFREY TOOBIN, THE NINE: INSIDE THE SECRET WORLD OF THE SUPREME COURT (2007). Readers interested in basic information about the internal workings of the Supreme Court might profitably consult BERNARD SCHWARTZ, DECISION: HOW THE SUPREME COURT DECIDES CASES (1996). Also relevant is the debate between GERALD N. ROSENBERG, THE HOLLOW HOPE: CAN COURTS BRING ABOUT SOCIAL CHANGE? (1991) (arguing that the effect of federal court decisions on our lives is overstated, even negligible), and BRADLEY C. CANON & CHARLES A. JOHNSON, JUDICIAL POLICIES: IMPLEMENTATION AND IMPACT 209–16 (2d ed. 1999) (critiquing Rosenberg's argument and concluding that "[American courts], and particularly the Supreme Court, have had a primary role in achieving social reforms"). Similarly, readers may be interested in the proposition that less assertive practices of judicial review might result in more extensive legislative protection of rights. See, e.g., MARK TUSHNET, WEAK COURTS, STRONG RIGHTS: JUDICIAL REVIEW AND SOCIAL WELFARE RIGHTS IN COMPARATIVE CONSTITUTIONAL LAW (2008). Compare Ruth Colker & James J. Brudney, *Dissing Congress*, 100 MICH. L. REV. 80 (2001); Robert C. Post & Reva B. Siegel, *Equal Protection by Law: Federal Antidiscrimination Legislation after Morrison and Kimel*, 110 YALE L.J. 441 (2000); and Jed Rubenfeld, *The Anti-Antidiscrimination Agenda*, 111 YALE L.J. 1141 (2002) (each detailing the Court's tendency to invalidate civil rights legislation).

Recent congressional efforts to abrogate judicial review are recounted in Supreme Court decisions concerning the Detainee Treatment Act of 2005 and the Military Commissions Act of 2006. See, e.g., *Boumediene v. Bush*, 128 S. Ct. 2229 (2008); *Hamdan v. Rumsfeld*, 548 U.S.

557 (2006). These efforts were unsuccessful, but Congress has succeeded in substantially cur-
tailing judicial review in a number of other areas. See, e.g., John H. Blume, *AEDPA: The "Hype"
and the "Bite,"* 91 CORNELL L. REV. 259 (2006) (general discussion of provisions of the
Antiterrorism and Effective Death Penalty Act); James E. Robertson, *The Jurisprudence of the
PLRA: Inmates as "Outsiders" and the Countermajoritarian Difficulty,* 92 J. CRIM. L. &
CRIMINOLOGY 187 (2002) (overview of the Prison Litigation Reform Act). In general,
although justices may assert that the Supreme Court acts illegitimately when it undertakes
constitutional review, see, e.g., *Hamdan v. Rumsfeld,* 548 U.S. 557, 678 (2006) (Thomas, J.,
dissenting); *Hamdi v. Rumsfeld,* 542 U.S. 507, 582–90 (2004) (Thomas, J., dissenting); *Lewis
v. Casey,* 518 U.S. 343, 385–88 (1996) (Thomas, J., concurring); and *Missouri v. Jenkins,* 515
U.S. 70, 124–36 (1995) (Thomas, J., concurring), the Court has typically rejected extreme
attacks on the power of judicial review and has preserved the Court as an institution capable of
sustaining separated-powers government, even during times of national exigency. See Emily
Calhoun, *The Accounting: Habeas Corpus and Enemy Combatants,* 79 U. COLO. L. REV. 77
(2008). For a general discussion of Court-made, discretionary doctrines limiting judicial
review, however, see RICHARD H. FALLON JR. ET AL., HART AND WECHSLER'S THE FEDERAL
COURTS AND THE FEDERAL SYSTEM 100–248 (6th ed. 2009); and RICHARD H. FALLON JR.,
IMPLEMENTING THE CONSTITUTION (2001).

To understand the variety and number of stakeholders in a rights dispute, see Tomiko Brown-
Nagin, *Race as Identity Caricature: A Local Legal History Lesson in the Salience of Intraracial Conflict,*
151 U. PA. L. REV. 1913 (2003) (describing the conflicting interests of stakeholders in the Atlanta
school desegregation litigation), and Emily M. Calhoun, *Workplace Mediation: The First-Phase,
Private Caucus in Individual Discrimination Disputes,* 9 HARV. NEGOT. L. REV. 187 (2004) (discussing the intrinsic group nature of workplace discrimination). Chapter 4 contains a more complete
discussion of this topic.

The text's caution that readers should not trivialize harms inflicted on constitutional losers is
prompted by Justice Scalia's opinion in *Hein v. Freedom from Religion Foundation,* 551 U.S. 587
(2007) (Scalia, J., concurring) (labeling harms to freedom of conscience as a mere "psychic
injury"). Readers should resist thinking of harms to constitutional losers as intangible emotional
harms. LINDA RADZIK, MAKING AMENDS: ATONEMENT IN MORALITY, LAW, AND POLITICS
76–78 (2009), offers an explanation of the significance of the harms of moral wrongdoing that
echoes the argument of this book. Such harms signal that a victim is not valued or is a lesser being,
and they also encourage or permit more of the same treatment by others.

I and others in my field often wonder how much attention ordinary citizens pay to Supreme
Court decisions. Some insights can be gleaned from studies of the impact of the Court's abortion
decisions on legislatures and public opinion. See, e.g., Samantha Luks & Michael Salamone,
Abortion, in PUBLIC OPINION AND CONSTITUTIONAL CONTROVERSY, 80, 80–107 (Nathaniel
Persily, Jack Citrin, & Patrick J. Egan eds., 2008) (discussing the impact of both court decisions
and media coverage on public opinion); and Mary Ziegler, *The Framing of a Right to Choose*: Roe v.
Wade *and the Changing Debate on Abortion Law,* 27 L. HIST. R. 281 (2009) (discussing the way in
which judicial decisions can change political dialogue). See also Barry Friedman, *Mediated Popular
Constitutionalism,* 101 MICH. L. REV. 2596, 2620–23 (2003) (linking public knowledge about
Supreme Court decisions to the amount of media coverage a decision receives). VALERIE J.
HOEKSTRA, PUBLIC REACTION TO SUPREME COURT DECISIONS (2003), surveys research that has
been done on how people learn about Supreme Court decisions and what effect those decisions
have on attitudes toward the Court.

I agree with Neil S. Siegel, *The Virtue of Judicial Statesmanship,* 86 TEX. L. REV. 959 (2008),
who concludes:

> It is not necessary to assume that the public parses Supreme Court opinions. It is
> necessary to assume only that how the Court speaks is relevant to the actual effects of
> its holding and that the meaning of Court opinions is conveyed to the public in com-
> plex, highly mediated ways.

Id. at n.348. Moreover, as Lani Guinier, *The Supreme Court 2007 Term—Foreword: Demosprudence through Dissent*, 122 HARV. L. REV. 4, 53–54 (2008), recognizes, there are many new technological tools that enable the Court to reach out to new listeners and that help all of us gain more access to the Court, whether justices reach out or not. An important strain of scholarship relevant to this debate is found in the work of those who study the relationship between cultural and social change and judicial activity. I recommend especially JAMES BOYD WHITE, ACTS OF HOPE: CREATING AUTHORITY IN LITERATURE, LAW, AND POLITICS 179 (1994) (premising his work on the view that "law is a process of culture that works across time"); Robert Cover, *The Supreme Court, 1982 Term—Foreword: Nomos and Narrative*, 97 HARV. L. REV. 4 (1983) (discussing the importance of interpretive communities and their relationship to a Supreme Court that may assert a monopolistic power to tell us what the law is); and Robert C. Post, *The Supreme Court, 2002 Term—Foreword: Fashioning the Legal Constitution: Culture, Courts, and Law*, 117 HARV. L. REV. 4 (2003) (concluding that although culture and the behavior of individuals influence how the Court decides cases, the Court also plays a significant role in obstructing or encouraging cultural trends).

Chapter 1: Constitutional Stature in Rights Disputes

Constitutional stature is always important in rights debates. Readers will find an excellent introduction to the issue of constitutional stature, as it pertains to African Americans, in David A. J. Richards, *Public Reason and Abolitionist Dissent*, 69 CHI.-KENT L. REV. 787 (1994). Martin Luther King Jr.'s appeal to traditional constitutional principle and new constitutional stature is recounted in TAYLOR BRANCH, PARTING THE WATERS: AMERICA IN THE KING YEARS 1954–63 (1988).

Women have also made constitutional stature central to their arguments for equal rights. In the nineteenth century, Angelina Grimke compared the position of women to that of slaves insofar as they had both been "robbed . . . of essential rights, the right to think and speak and act on all great moral questions." Richards, *supra*, at 817 (quoting Angelina E. Grimke, *Letters to Catherine E. Beecher*, in THE PUBLIC YEARS OF SARAH AND ANGELINA GRIMKE: SELECTED WRITINGS 1835–1839 195 (Larry Ceplair ed., 1989)). An early feminist complained that men "worshipped [woman's] ideal through the age of chivalry as though she were a goddess, but he . . . governed her as though she were an idiot." Carrie Chapmen Catt, *Prejudice against Women*, in THE AMERICAN READER: WORDS THAT MOVED A NATION 213 (Diane Ravitch ed., 1990). The discussion of constitutional stature in the abortion cases is a modified and updated version of the argument in Emily Calhoun, *The Breadth of Context and the Depth of Myth: Completing the Feminist Paradigm*, 4 HASTINGS WOMEN'S L.J. 87 (1993). For other commentary on the Supreme Court and abortion controversies, see Reva B. Siegel, *The New Politics of Abortion: An Equality Analysis of Women-Protective Abortion Restrictions*, 2007 U. ILL. L. REV. 991 (2007); and Reva B. Siegel, *The Right's Reasons: Constitutional Conflict and the Spread of Woman-Protective Antiabortion Argument*, 57 DUKE L. J. 1641 (2008). Rebecca E. Ivey, *Destabilizing Discourses: Blocking and Exploiting a New Discourse at Work in Gonzales v. Carhart*, 94 VA. L. REV. 1451 (2008), takes note of the effect of medical discourses on the analysis of women's rights in the abortion decisions. Cf., Peter M. Ladwein, *Discerning the Meaning of Gonzales v. Carhart: The End of the Physician Veto and the Resulting Change in Abortion Jurisprudence*, 83 NOTRE DAME L. REV. 1847 (2008). Chapters 3 and 7 will return to a discussion of abortion rights disputes.

Constitutional stature is also important for homosexuals. See, e.g., Anthony V. Alfieri, *(Un)Coverering Identity in Civil Rights and Poverty Law*, 121 HARV. L. REV. 805 (2008) (illustrating the importance of status and identity to homosexuals as stakeholders in litigation). Chapter 3's discussion of *Bowers v. Hardwick*, 478 U.S. 186 (1986), will illustrate the point.

The text argues that constitutional stature embodies widely shared understandings about citizens. MICHAEL WALZER, THICK AND THIN: MORAL ARGUMENT AT HOME AND ABROAD (1994), would probably label these understandings "thick," *id.* at 49, and as proceeding "from within a tradition," *id.* at 50. This is why they are so potent. See, e.g., VACLAV HAVEL, *The Power of the Powerless*, in THE POWER OF THE POWERLESS 23, 30–31 (John Keane ed., 1985) (explaining that rights arguments based on constitutional stature can be particularly effective because they threaten to expose the hypocrisy of people who oppose the extension of rights to all individuals). Walzer would remind us that assertions about constitutional stature are particular to a given society; they do not reflect universal values. Nonetheless, where they exist, thick understandings underlying constitutional stature may trump traditions that are widely shared and revered. In *United States v. Virginia,* 518 U.S. 515, 556 (1996), for example, Justice Scalia insisted that the Virginia Military Institute's refusal to admit women should be upheld as part of "the history of our people," but the majority rejected the appeal to tradition because tradition's "people" excluded women as equals. See also *J.E.B. v. Alabama ex rel. T.B.,* 511 U.S. 127 (1994) (O'Connor, S., and Kennedy, J., concurring) (rejecting a tradition embodying a diminished constitutional stature respecting women). Readers should note that tradition itself is not necessarily static. JÜRGEN HABERMAS, BETWEEN FACTS AND NORMS: CONTRIBUTIONS TO A DISCOURSE THEORY OF LAW AND DEMOCRACY 182, 499 (1996). See also *Washington v. Glucksberg,* 521 U.S. 702, 770, 786–87 (1997) (Souter, J., concurring) (constitutional change is itself a tradition that must be respected, as it is the means by which the Court secures the consent of contemporary citizens when time has overtaken past factual assumptions and understandings); and compare *Romer v. Evans,* 517 U.S. 620, 647 (1996) (Scalia, J., dissenting) (arguing that the judiciary must respect the "most democratic" of electoral processes, the direct citizen initiative, used to give legal approval to traditional societal views of homosexuals).

The text discusses constitutional stature from several perspectives. Liberal philosophers typically employ some version of the counterfactual presumption of each individual's capacity to function as a moral and political agent. See, e.g., JÜRGEN HABERMAS, BETWEEN FACTS AND NORMS (1996) (assuming that all persons have an equal capacity to engage in moral dialogue); JERRY MASHAW, DUE PROCESS IN THE ADMINISTRATIVE STATE 160–62 (1985) (discussing the claim of all citizens to be worthy political agents); JOHN RAWLS, POLITICAL LIBERALISM 216–25 (1993) (stating that arguments against government coercion rest on the premise that all citizens have faculties of individual agency and are equally capable of reasoning about the public good); LON FULLER, THE MORALITY OF LAW (1977) (arguing that a lawmaker must act as if each citizen is a responsible moral agent and a member of a common interpretive community). In EXPLAINING AMERICA: THE FEDERALIST (1981), Garry Wills argues that a presumption that all individuals equally possess a moral sensibility that guides them to act communally and benevolently toward others is embedded in our founding political documents. Some legal scholars have linked the presumption of equal moral and political agency to individual dignity. See, e.g., DAVID LUBAN, LEGAL ETHICS AND HUMAN DIGNITY (2007); W. Bradley Wendel, *Legal Ethics as "Political Moralism" or the Morality of Politics,* 93 CORNELL L. REV. 1413 (2008) (each exploring the link between a "political conception of human dignity" based on a presumed equal moral agency of citizens and professional ethics and the rule of law). Readers interested in discussions of dignity interests embedded in substantive constitutional rights might wish to consult Reva B. Siegel, *Dignity and the Politics of Protection: Abortion Restrictions Under* Casey/Carhart, 117 YALE L. J. 1694 (2008); Toni M. Massaro, *Empathy, Legal Storytelling and the Rule of Law: New Words, Old Wounds?,* 87 MICH. L. REV. 2099 (1989); Martha C. Nussbaum, *The Supreme Court 2006 Term—Foreword: Constitutions and Capabilities: "Perception" against Lofty Formalism,* 121 HARV. L. REV. 4 (2007).

A trust metaphor also informs the concept of constitutional stature. The text draws heavily on PETER CHARLES HOFFER, THE LAW'S CONSCIENCE: EQUITABLE CONSTITUTIONALISM IN AMERICA (1990), which asserts that Locke invoked the trust concept far more frequently than an ordinary contract metaphor to explore the legitimacy of government. *Id.* at 73. See JOHN LOCKE, TWO TREATISES OF GOVERNMENT 413 (Peter Laslett ed., Cambridge Univ. Press 1988) (1960) (stating that government acts as a trustee to ensure a variety of ends related to the "publick Good"). THOMAS E. CRONIN, DIRECT DEMOCRACY: THE POLITICS OF INITIATIVE, REFERENDUM, AND RECALL (1989), echoes Hoffer's assessment of the importance of the trust metaphor in the founding documents of the United States, especially the Declaration of Independence. Both

Hoffer and Cronin note the presence of the trust concept in state law. Hoffer also argues that the trust concept informed the establishment of the Freedmen's Bureau and other post–Civil War laws affirming the right of all citizens to share equally in the benefits of society.

I mention only a few of the many other scholars who have explored aspects of the trust metaphor. They include BRUCE ACKERMAN, WE THE PEOPLE: FOUNDATIONS 3–7 (1991); JUDITH SHKLAR, THE FACES OF INJUSTICE (1990); Cynthia R. Farina, *Conceiving Due Process,* 3 YALE J.L. & FEMINISM 189 (1991); Steven L. Winter, *The Meaning of "Under Color of"* Law, 91 MICH. L. REV. 323, 399 (1992); and others referenced in the bibliographical essay for the Introduction. Compare RICHARD A. POSNER, HOW JUDGES THINK (2008) (maintaining that judges are agents of government); Akhil R. Amar, *Of Sovereignty and Federalism,* 96 YALE L.J. 1425, 1432–37 (1987) (asserting that the concept of government as agent of the people is influenced by the development of corporate charters).

The trust metaphor is most clearly relevant to the stature of citizens, by far the largest group of stakeholders in constitutional rights disputes. As Frank Michelman, *Law's Republic,* 97 YALE L.J. 1493, 1518 (1988), notes, citizenship is the status that provides freedom for "constant redetermination by the people for themselves of the terms on which they live together." If my arguments are persuasive, however, judicial conventions in rights disputes will be altered in ways that will also benefit noncitizens. Neal Katyal, *Equality in the War on Terror,* 59 STAN. L. REV. 1365 (2007), draws on the history of the Fourteenth Amendment to argue that citizens and noncitizens should be treated equally in matters other than immigration and government benefits; and dignity-based theories of rights, referenced above, might also recognize harm-avoidance and harm-amelioration obligations respecting noncitizens. For further reading relevant to the status of noncitizens under the Constitution, I recommend Bruce Ackerman, *The Citizenship Agenda,* in THE CONSTITUTION IN 2020, at 109 (Jack M. Balkin & Reva B. Siegel eds., 2009) (noting the Court's failure to have given meaning to the Constitution's Citizenship Clauses and expressing a need to revive citizenship-based institutions such as the citizen army, the jury, and the public school); Rachel F. Moran, *Terms of Belonging,* in THE CONSTITUTION IN 2020, *supra* at 133 (arguing that the American Dream is bigger than citizenship and that citizenship-based rights will exclude many persons); and David Cole, *"Strategies of the Weak": Thinking Globally and Acting Locally Toward a Progressive Constitutional Vision,* in THE CONSTITUTION IN 2020, *supra* at 298 (arguing that foreign nationals deserve constitutional protection).

The idea that each party to a rights dispute should be thought of as a constitutional leader is not necessarily dependent on a trust metaphor. In thinking about constitutional leadership, I am indebted to DAVID A. J. RICHARDS, CONSCIENCE AND THE CONSTITUTION: HISTORY, THEORY, AND THE LAW OF THE RECONSTRUCTION AMENDMENTS 257 (1993) (contending that those who test the legitimacy of status quo arrangements illuminate what our Constitution and society are really about); and PAUL W. KAHN, THE REIGN OF LAW: *MARBURY V. MADISON* AND THE CONSTRUCTION OF AMERICA 204 (1997) (insisting that all citizens should be considered constitutional leaders in that they each have reason to assert that they are the true representatives of the Constitution's meaning). See also James E. Pfander, *Sovereign Immunity and the Right to Petition: Toward a First Amendment Right to Pursue Judicial Claims Against the Government,* 91 Nw. U. L. REV. 899, 937–53 (1997).

For a discussion of the presumptive innocence of constitutional leaders, see David Chang, *Discriminatory Impact, Affirmative Action, and Innocent Victims: Judicial Conservatism or Conservative Justices?,* 91 COLUM. L. REV. 790 (1991). I am indebted to his thoughts on the issue in the context of affirmative action disputes.

There are, of course, many rights disputes similar to garden-variety personal injury lawsuits, in which a court might legitimately focus on party blameworthiness. See, for example, *Scott v. Harris,* 550 U.S. 372 (2007), in which Victor Harris sued a police officer to recover damages for injuries he received when his car rolled over during a police chase. Harris argued that the pursuing officer used excessive force to stop his flight. Culpability was relevant to the Court's analysis of reasonable force and police officer immunity. A party's culpability may also influence outcomes in other ways. In *Hill v. Colorado,* 530 U.S. 703 (2000), for example, Justice Scalia sympathetically described antiabortion plaintiffs as persons who hoped "to forge, in the last moments before another of her sex is to have an abortion, a bond of concern and intimacy that might enable her to persuade the woman to change her mind and heart." He added:

> The counselor may wish to walk alongside and to say, sympathetically and as softly as the circumstances allow, something like: 'My dear, I know what you are going through. I've been through it myself. You're not alone and you do not have to do this. There are other alternatives. Will you let me help you? May I show you a picture of what your child looks like at this stage of her human development?'

Id. at 757 (Scalia, J., dissenting). Although hypothetical, this conversation accurately reflected the absence of any evidence that the *Hill* antiabortion activists had resorted to violent tactics against women or abortion providers. Nonetheless, some stakeholders in the antiabortion movement have used violence against women, physicians, and abortion clinics. Although the *Hill* plaintiffs could properly be described as innocent "sidewalk counselors" who simply wanted to "persuade women contemplating abortion that what they are doing is wrong," *id.* at 742, other, violent anti-abortion stakeholders would not necessarily be seen as innocent. Recognition of the behavior of some violent antiabortion activists may have influenced justices to sustain against constitutional attack Colorado's Bubble Bill, which prohibited protesters from coming within eight feet of persons entering medical facilities.

The innocence of corporate entities who are parties to constitutional disputes is a complex issue. Indeed, it is challenging even to imagine how to apply the concept of constitutional stature to an artificial entity. Cf. Reuven S. Avi-Yona, "To Be or Not to Be? Citizens United and the Corporate Form" (February 2010), *University of Michigan Legal Working Paper Series, Empirical Legal Studies Center*, Working Paper 4, available at http://law.bepress.com/umichlwps/empirical/art4. Chapter 9 will return to the topic of corporate entities as it surfaced in *Citizens United v. Federal Election Commission*, 2010 U.S. LEXIS 766 (January 21, 2010). For now, simply note that, as anyone who has been involved in a bankruptcy proceeding or has attempted to refinance a home mortgage is well aware, it can be difficult to identify a tangible thing that constitutes a corporate entity. Moreover, any given entity will be composed of many individuals and units with competing interests. See, e.g., Nathaniel B. Edmonds, *Associational Standing for Organizations with Internal Conflicts of Interest*, 69 U. CHI. L. REV. 351 (2002). Readers may be interested in the discussions of corporate liability explored in the context of slave reparations cases, in which plaintiffs seek compensation from contemporary defendants who have personally benefited from slavery, e.g., Eric A. Posner & Adrian Vermeule, *Reparations for Slavery and Other Historical Injustices*, 103 COLUM. L. REV. 689 (2003), and in human rights litigation against multinational corporations, e.g., Beth Stephens, *The Amorality of Profit: Transnational Corporations and Human Rights*, 20 BERKELEY J. INT'L L. 45 (2002), and Jordan J. Paust, *Human Rights Responsibilities of Private Corporations*, 35 VAND. J. TRANSNAT'L L. 801 (2002). See also LINDA RADZIK, MAKING AMENDS: ATONEMENT IN MORALITY, LAW, AND POLITICS 175–197 (2009) (addressing the issue of collective atonement for institutional wrongs).

That rights disputes recur and are resolved differently in different times and contexts is undeniable. Contingency in constitutional meaning is not a consequence merely of changes in the membership of the Court. It is true that justices will retire and be replaced, a fact that has driven fears (or raised expectations) about the possibility that a decision such as *Roe v. Wade* will ultimately be overruled. Some undoubtedly believe that the recent decision in *Citizens United v. Federal Election Commission*, 2010 U.S. LEXIS 766 (January 21, 2010), can be explained only with reference to a change in membership on the Supreme Court. It is also true that a justice may, on occasion, change his or her mind about constitutional doctrine or principle. Perhaps the simple act of putting an argument on paper or responding to opposing arguments will alter a justice's views. See, e.g., Patricia M. Wald, *The Rhetoric of Results and the Results of Rhetoric: Judicial Writings*, 62 U. CHI. L. REV. 1371, 1374–75 (1995). The papers of the late Justice Blackmun contain an account of how views changed in *Roe v. Wade*. *See* LINDA GREENHOUSE, BECOMING JUSTICE

BLACKMUN: HARRY BLACKMUN'S SUPREME COURT JOURNEY 88–95 (2005). Cf. ANTHONY G. AMSTERDAM & JEROME BRUNER, MINDING THE LAW 283–84 (2000) (discussing justices' "dialectical" role when choosing between canonical or traditional doctrine and the "imaginatively possible" claims made in rights disputes).

As Chapter 8 will argue, however, contingency in constitutional meaning is largely inherent in judicial decision-making. The Supreme Court selects cases for review through its certiorari jurisdiction under criteria set forth in SUPREME COURT RULE 10. See Edward A. Hartnett, *Questioning Certiorari: Some Reflections Seventy-Five Years after the Judges' Bill*, 100 COLUM. L. REV. 1643 (2000). Selection criteria emphasize the importance of having the Court available to resolve significant conflicts in constitutional meaning and to decide important public issues. See Sullivan v. Little Hunting Park, 396 U.S. 229, 250 (1969) (Harlan, J., dissenting).

Notwithstanding certiorari rules, justices do not fully and finally resolve constitutional conflicts. They leave interpretational gaps in their decisions. See Daniel A. Farber, *The Rule of Law and the Law of Precedents*, 90 MINN. L. REV. 1173, 1200–2 (2006). Some gaps are created because of the fact-intensive nature of rights disputing. Justices may occasionally complain that "fact-intensive analysis" permits the Court to decide whatever it wants in any given case, *Planned Parenthood of Se. Pa. v. Casey*, 505 U.S. 833, 991 (1992) (Scalia, J., concurring in part and dissenting in part), but they also recognize the need for context-appropriate responses in constitutional doctrine. See, e.g., *Kyllo v. United States*, 533 U.S. 27 (2001) (interpreting the Constitution's Fourth Amendment to require a warrant for the use of thermal-imaging equipment intended to register heat emanating from a house). In many rights controversies, justices refuse to answer general questions until presented in a proper factual context. See, e.g., *Crawford v. Marion County Election Bd.*, 128 S. Ct. 1610, 1622–23 (2008); *Wash. State Grange v. Wash. State Republican Party*, 128 S. Ct. 1184, 1195 (2008). For interesting discussions of the fact-based character of constitutional rights disputes, I recommend Timothy Zick, *Constitutional Empiricism: Quasi-Neutral Principles and Constitutional Truths*, 82 N.C. L. REV. 115 (2003); David L. Faigman, "*Normative Constitutional Fact-Finding*": *Exploring the Empirical Component of Constitutional Interpretation*, 139 U. PA. L. REV. 541 (1991); and Rachel N. Pine, *Speculation and Reality: The Role of Facts in Judicial Protection of Fundamental Rights*, 136 U. PA. L. REV. 655, 712–13, 720–21 (1988). Even disputes that at first glance involve only abstract principles, such as the constitutional status of homosexuals, generate fact-intensive litigation. See, e.g., Sharon E. Debbage Alexander, *Romer v. Evans and The Amendment 2 Controversy: The Rhetoric and Reality of Sexual Orientation Discrimination*, 6 TEX. F. ON C.L. & C.R. 261 (2002).

In any event, readers should note that the meaning of a Supreme Court decision is contingent on what *future* justices will say about it. See, e.g., PAUL W. KAHN, THE CULTURAL STUDY OF LAW 51–72 (1999); Richard B. Cappalli, *The Common Law's Case Against Non-Precedential Opinions*, 76 S. CAL. L. REV. 755 (2003). As disputes recur, in different times and contexts, there is every reason to expect that constitutional meaning will change. Chapter 8 explores change in constitutional meaning through a discussion of judicial precedent.

For readers interested in how public discourse and culture influence constitutional meaning, I recommend THE CONSTITUTION IN 2020 (Jack M. Balkin & Reva B. Siegel eds., 2009); Reva B. Siegel, *Constitutional Culture, Social Movement Conflict and Constitutional Change: The Case of the De Facto ERA*, 94 CAL. L. REV. 1323 (2006); or Reva B. Siegel, *Text in Contest: Gender and the Constitution from a Social Movement Perspective*, 150 U. PA. L. REV. 297 (2001), and scholars referenced in the bibliographical essay to the Introduction. For additional discussions of how law is built from the ground up, readers should consult Michael C. Dorf & Charles F. Sabel, *A Constitution of Democratic Experimentalism*, 98 COLUM. L. REV. 267 (1998); Rosa Ehrenreich Brooks, *The New Imperialism: Violence, Norms, and the "Rule of Law*," 101 MICH. L. REV. 2275 (2003); William N. Eskridge Jr., *Some Effects of Identity-Based Social Movements on Constitutional Law in the Twentieth Century*, 100 MICH. L. REV. 2062 (2002); and John O. McGinnis, *Reviving Tocqueville's America: The Rehnquist Court's Jurisprudence of Social Discovery*, 90 CAL. L. REV. 485 (2002). I also recommend Lani Guinier, *The Supreme Court, 2007 Term—Foreword: Demosprudence through Dissent*, 122 HARV. L. REV. 4 (2008) (arguing that citizens are constitutional norm entrepreneurs who build law from the ground up and that oral dissents remind ordinary people that they can make law). For analyses of how disadvantaged groups find new ways to "name" their situations and thereby affect law, see, for example, SALLY ENGLE MERRY, GETTING JUSTICE AND GETTING EVEN: LEGAL CONSCIOUSNESS AMONG WORKING-CLASS AMERICANS (1990); and KRISTIN BUMILLER, THE CIVIL RIGHTS SOCIETY: THE SOCIAL CONSTRUCTION OF VICTIMS (1988). The work of scholars who discuss storytelling may also be of interest. See, e.g., ROBIN WEST, NARRATIVE, AUTHORITY, AND LAW (1993); Lynne N. Henderson, *Legality and Empathy*, 85 MICH. L. REV. 1574 (1987); Martha Minow, *The Supreme Court 1986 Term—Foreword: Justice Engendered*, 101 HARV. L. REV. 10 (1987); Kim Lane Scheppele, *Foreword: Telling Stories*, 87 MICH. L. REV. 2073 (1989).

Evolution is the conventional term used to characterize the development of constitutional meaning over time. I like to think that constitutional meaning is redeemed, as suggested by WILLIAM H. SIMON, THE PRACTICE OF JUSTICE: A THEORY OF LAWYERS' ETHICS (1998). Simon takes note of how Frederick Douglass reconciled abolition of slavery with a Constitution that expressly permitted it. Douglass reportedly came to see that evolution in constitutional meaning regarding slavery might more accurately be viewed as redemption of fundamental constitutional values. According to Simon, Douglass saw that novel rights claims are not "a fight against the constitutional order…[but] a struggle to redeem it." *Id.* at 102. See also THE CONSTITUTION IN 2020, at 2–3 (Jack M. Balkin & Reva B. Siegel eds., 2009) (addressing the need to redeem the Constitution and developing a concept of "redemptive constitutionalism").

The legitimacy of evolution in constitutional meaning generates much debate and commentary. See, e.g., SANFORD LEVINSON, CONSTITUTIONAL FAITH (1988) (discussing the Living Constitution); JAMES R. STONER JR., COMMON-LAW LIBERTY: RETHINKING AMERICAN CONSTITUTIONALISM (2003) (explaining common-law constitutionalism); ATONIN SCALIA, A MATTER OF INTERPRETATION: FEDERAL COURTS AND THE LAW (1997) (adamantly opposing an evolutionary perspective on constitutional rights disputes); STEPHEN BREYER, ACTIVE LIBERTY (2005) (accepting evolution in constitutional meaning). In *Planned Parenthood v. Casey*, 505 U.S. 833, 940 (1992) (Blackmun, J., concurring in part and dissenting in part), Justice Blackmun noted the existence of two different worlds of constitutional interpretation, one of evolution and one "stunted" with liberties defined only in terms of history or tradition.

Regarding the argument that few constitutional principles are absolutely and finally set in stone, readers might wish to consult the discussion in AMY GUTMANN & DENNIS THOMPSON, DEMOCRACY AND DISAGREEMENT: WHY MORAL CONFLICT CANNOT BE AVOIDED IN POLITICS, AND WHAT SHOULD BE DONE ABOUT IT 76–79 (1996). Readers should note that broad constitutional principles are given meaning through judge-made doctrines that may shift over time. Readers interested in the difference between constitutional principle (e.g., "no state shall…deny to any person…the equal protection of the laws," U.S. CONST. AMEND. XIV, § 1) and judge-made doctrine (which tells us whether, for example, race-based differences alleged to deny equal protection will be absolutely prohibited, strictly scrutinized, or accepted when justified by merely rational explanations), should consult RICHARD H. FALLON JR., IMPLEMENTING THE CONSTITUTION (2001).

Excellent discussions of the evolving, redemptive story of equality include MILNER S. BALL, THE WORD AND THE LAW (1993); Jack M. Balkin & Reva B. Siegel, *Remembering How to Do Equality*, in THE CONSTITUTION IN 2020, at 93 (Jack M. Balkin & Reva B. Siegel eds., 2009); David Breshears, *One Step Forward, Two Steps Back: The Meaning of Equality and the Cultural Politics of Memory* in Regents of the University of California v. Bakke, 3 J.L. SOC'Y 67 (2002); and Robert M. Cover, *The Origins of Judicial Activism in the Protection of Minorities*, 91 YALE L.J. 1287 (1982). The evolution of the meaning of equality has spilled over into the interpretation of other constitutional principles. See, e.g., Kenneth L. Karst, *The Liberties of Equal Citizens: Groups and the Due Process Clause*, 55 UCLA L. REV. 99 (2007) (noting that egalitarian values spill over into interpretation of other rights, such as due process); Susan Sturm, *The Architecture of Inclusion: Advancing Workplace Equity in Higher Education*, 29 HARV. J.L. & GENDER 247 (2006) (asserting that when equality proves unsatisfactory in protecting against some forms of discrimination, it is necessary to turn to other constitutional principles, e.g., citizenship).

Excellent accounts of the evolution or redemption of equality concepts in voting rights disputes include Pamela S. Karlan, *Voting Rights and the Third Reconstruction, in* THE CONSTITUTION IN 2020, at 160 (Jack M. Balkin & Reva B. Siegel eds., 2009); Samuel Issacharoff, *Polarized Voting and the Political Process: The Transformation of Voting Rights Jurisprudence,* 90 MICH. L. REV. 1833 (1992). See also Samuel Issacharoff, *Gerrymandering and Political Cartels,* 116 HARV. L. REV. 593 (2002) (arguing that political competition is at stake in voting rights disputes, along with other conventionally recognized interests).

For a description of the evolution of the meaning of equality in the school desegregation context, see Reva B. Siegel, *Equality Talk: Antisubordination and Anticlassification Values in Constitutional Struggles over* Brown, 117 HARV. L. REV. 1470 (2004). During recent celebrations of the fiftieth anniversary of the *Brown* decision, the debate about separate-but-equal resurfaced and embraced the possibility that the African American community might be better served through greater allocation of resources to public schools than through more traditional ways of addressing racial integration. See, e.g., CHARLES J. OGLETREE JR., ALL DELIBERATE SPEED: REFLECTIONS ON THE FIRST HALF-CENTURY OF BROWN V. BOARD OF EDUCATION 234–35, 309–10 (2004). Regarding the separate-but-equal principle and sex segregation in public schools, readers should consult Kimberly J. Jenkins, *Constitutional Lessons for the Next Generation of Public Single-Sex Elementary and Secondary Schools,* 47 WM. & MARY L. REV. 1953 (2006); Isabelle Katz Pinzler, *Separate but Equal Education in the Context of Gender,* 49 N.Y.L. SCH. L. REV. 785 (2004–2005); and Galen Sherwin, *Single-Sex Schools and the Antisegregation Principle,* 30 N.Y.U. REV. L. & SOC. CHANGE 35 (2005).

The evolution of the constitutional meaning of equality implicates the concept of colorblindness. See, e.g., LESLIE G. CARR, "COLOR-BLIND" RACISM (1997); Christopher W. Schmidt, Brown and the *Colorblind Constitution,* 94 CORNELL L. REV. 203 (2008); and RONALD DWORKIN, THE SUPREME COURT PHALANX 56 (2008). Chapter 9 will return to this topic, through a discussion of the decision in *Parents Involved in Community Schools v. Seattle School District No. 1,* 551 U.S. 701 (2007).

Because the text explains constitutional stature through several metaphors, it is important to recall that metaphors are commonplace in discussions of constitutional meaning. In addition to the old-snake and rock-rolling metaphors associated with constitutional leadership, for example, we could add a third metaphor suggested by ROBERT GRUDIN, ON DIALOGUE: AN ESSAY IN FREE THOUGHT 191–92 (1996), where constitutional decisions represent a "playing field" for making judicial choices, *id.* at 191, and constitutional issues are constant "force fields generated by mutually empowering oppositions... [that] cannot be tamed, but reassert themselves in ever-new configurations." *Id.* at 192. Readers might also be interested in discussions of the rule-of-law metaphor in Richard H. Fallon Jr., *"The Rule of Law" as a Concept in Constitutional Discourse,* 97 COLUM. L. REV. 1 (1997); and PAUL W. KAHN, THE REIGN OF LAW: MARBURY V. MADISON AND THE CONSTRUCTION OF AMERICA (1997).

Metaphors can be powerful forces. See, e.g., MARK OSIEL, MASS ATROCITY, COLLECTIVE MEMORY, AND THE LAW (1997) (recounting how stories that are widely shared have tangible effects within society); PAUL W. KAHN, THE CULTURAL STUDY OF LAW: RECONSTRUCTING LEGAL SCHOLARSHIP 66 (1999) (effective metaphors are sufficiently general and evocative that they can work on our imaginations and we can give them our own signature). If, for example, justices approach constitutional rights disputes so as to help the country "see itself through its constitutional ideals," as was once suggested by the joint opinion in *Planned Parenthood v. Casey,* 505 U.S. 833, 868 (1992), metaphors can help individuals from very different backgrounds constitute a collective national identity. See, e.g., DAVID A. J. RICHARDS, CONSCIENCE AND THE CONSTITUTION: HISTORY, THEORY, AND LAW OF THE RECONSTRUCTION AMENDMENTS (1993) (discussing how constitutional processes work in tandem with metaphor and constitutional ideal); WAYNE C. BOOTH, MODERN DOGMA AND THE RHETORIC OF ASSENT (1974) (arguing from a rhetorical perspective that the institution of language enables us to constitute ourselves in relation to others); GARRY WILLS, LINCOLN AT GETTYSBURG: THE WORDS THAT REMADE AMERICA (1992) (stressing that abstract ideals are essential to the formation of the identity of a nation whose people are immigrants; and analyzing Lincoln's funeral oration, which includes a plea that "the living should prove worthy of the fallen," to illustrates how symbols can create political identity across time).

Of course, metaphors can be used in ways that mischaracterize, mislead, and confuse. See, e.g., Steven L. Winter, *The Metaphor of Standing and the Problem of Self-Governance*, 40 STAN. L. REV. 1371 (1998) (mapping the structure of standing law and its incoherence, through cognitive models and metaphors). See also *Citizens United v. Federal Election Commission*, 2010 U.S. LEXIS 766 (January 21, 2010) (Stevens, J., concurring in part and dissenting in part) (complaining that a marketplace metaphor applied to political speech could suggest that laws and votes are properly bought and sold); and *Paul v. Davis*, 424 U.S. 693, 700 (1976) (referencing the metaphor of "Our Federalism" and stating that the Fourteenth Amendment, ratified after the Civil War, did not alter original understandings of the proper relationship of national and state governments). Regarding the decision in *Paul*, skeptical readers might recall that the Civil War undoubtedly had a significant impact on constitutional meaning. See CHARLES L. BLACK JR., A NEW BIRTH OF FREEDOM: HUMAN RIGHTS, NAMED AND UNNAMED (1997).

This chapter's description of rights disputes takes into account the origins of the disputes and their evolution through the judicial system. Excellent discussions of how rights disputes typically arise and evolve are found in CHARLES R. EPP, THE RIGHTS REVOLUTION: LAWYERS, ACTIVISTS AND SUPREME COURTS IN COMPARATIVE PERSPECTIVE (1998); STEPHEN L. WASBY, RACE RELATIONS LITIGATION IN AN AGE OF COMPLEXITY (1995); Charles F. Sabel & William H. Simon, *Destabilization Rights: How Public Law Litigation Succeeds*, 117 HARV. L. REV. 1015 (2004); and Susan Sturm, *Lawyers at the Prison Gates: Organizational Structure and Corrections Advocacy*, 2 U. MICH. J.L. REFORM 1 (1993). The litigation model historically used to secure rights is sometimes criticized. Readers interested in this topic might consult Orly Lobel, *The Paradox of Extralegal Activism: Critical Legal Consciousness and Transformative Politics*, 120 HARV. L. REV. 937 (2007); or Susan Sturm, *The Architecture of Inclusion: Advancing Workplace Equity in Higher Education*, 29 HARV. J.L. & GENDER 247 (2006). For a compelling explanation of why individuals pursue constitutional claims that, although reasonable, are unlikely to result in a favorable judicial decision, I highly recommend JULES LOBEL, SUCCESS WITHOUT VICTORY: LOST LEGAL BATTLES AND THE LONG ROAD TO JUSTICE IN AMERICA (2003).

Chapter 2: Constitutional Stature: Equality and Consent Expectations

Concepts of equality and consent are central to many theoretical perspectives on judicial review and the institutional role of the Supreme Court. They inform, for example, discussions of deliberative democracy, civic republicanism, rhetorical justice, and public reason. Although the Court's institutional role will receive some attention in chapter 8, LOSING TWICE argues that equality and consent are also at the heart of an individual justice's obligation to avoid and ameliorate harm to the constitutional stature of constitutional losers.

As readers think about this chapter's exploration of a concept of equality suited to constitutional stature, they might recall not only the evolving substantive principles recounted in Chapter 1 but also the admonition of GLENN C. LOURY, THE ANATOMY OF RACIAL INEQUALITY 152 (2002), that, if we seriously believe we are "One Nation, Indivisible," we will try to behave so that "people languishing at the margins, even if they are strange and threatening, are to be seen, in the ways that most fundamentally count for our politics and civic life, as being essentially like us."

I am indebted to Rebecca L. Brown, *Liberty, The New Equality*, 77 N.Y.U. L. REV. 1491 (2002), for her thoughts on equality and the communion of interests. Brown explains that elected officials do not behave in accordance with the communion of interests when they enact legislation out of hostility or animosity toward some citizens, adopt we/they legislation reflecting "in" and "out" citizen status, or do not offer "good" reasons for the laws they adopt. Good reasons reflect "equal concern" for the interests of all, *id.* at 1527, are "legitimately supported by the common good," and "accord 'respect' to the burdened group as equal citizens." *Id.* at 1524. Respect entails "reciprocity," which means that citizens must "offer reasons that other similarly motivated citizens can accept, even [if] ...they share only some of one another's values." *Id.* at 1538. Thus, reasons must be "accessible" to all citizens and should "narrow" "the areas of intractable moral disagreement." *Id.* at 1538. I have also drawn on the account of the founding generation's concerns about faction and Madison's beliefs in particular in GARRY WILLS, EXPLAINING AMERICA: THE FEDERALIST 193–94 (1981).

Readers should note the link between equality and consent that emerges in Brown's discussion of the communion of interests. Randy E. Barnett, *The People or the State?*: Chisolm v. Georgia *and Popular Sovereignty*, 93 VA. L. REV. 1729 (2007), called my attention to the opinion of Justice Jay in *Chisolm v. Georgia*, 2 U.S. 419 (1793). See also ALEXIS DE TOCQUEVILLE, DEMOCRACY IN AMERICA 53–55 (Harvey C. Mansfield & Delba Winthrop eds. & trans., Univ. of Chicago Press 2000) (linking equality expectations to the founding generation's commitment to popular sovereignty).

The communion of interests should be distinguished from the common good, a term associated with theories of civic virtue and civic republicanism. Discussions of the common good tend to unrealistically assume that society is homogeneous and that citizens are public-regarding. See, e.g., Frank Michelman, *Law's Republic*, 97 YALE L.J. 1493 (1988); MARK KINGWELL, A CIVIL TONGUE: JUSTICE, DIALOGUE, AND THE POLITICS OF PLURALISM (1995); MICHAEL J. SANDEL, DEMOCRACY'S DISCONTENT: AMERICA IN SEARCH OF A PUBLIC PHILOSOPHY (1996). Although the literature of civic republicanism has been important to the development of the ideas in this book, LOSING TWICE assumes that constitutional rights litigants are self-interested and committed to diverse values.

The idea that law is a public good and part of the res publica can be traced to CICERO, ON GOVERNMENT (Michael Grant trans., Penguin Books 1993), whose influence on the Constitution's Framers is generally acknowledged. See, e.g., MARK KINGWELL, A CIVIL TONGUE: JUSTICE, DIALOGUE, AND THE POLITICS OF PLURALISM 25 (1995); JUDITH N. SHKLAR, THE FACES OF INJUSTICE 105 (1990). For commentary on adjudication as a public good, readers might consult Owen M. Fiss, *The Supreme Court 1978 Term—Foreword: The Forms of Justice*, 93 HARV. L. REV. 1 (1979); and David Luban, *Settlements and the Erosion of the Public Realm*, 83 GEO. L.J. 2619 (1995). Sarah M. R. Cravens, *Judges as Trustees: A Duty to Account and an Opportunity for Virtue*, 62 WASH. & LEE L. REV. 1637, 1639 (2005), thinks of a judicial opinion as a public good resulting from adjudication, *id.* at 1646, owned by the public, *id.* at 1639, and she argues that justices are not merely "umpires between the parties" but trustees who take an "involved role in ensuring the proper development of the law." *Id.* at 1640.

Many scholars have adverted to ownership in discussing constitutional meaning. They include MARK TUSHNET, TAKING THE CONSTITUTION AWAY FROM THE COURTS 181 (1999) (quoting Lincoln's statement in his First Inaugural Address, that "this country, with its institutions, belongs to the people who inhabit it"); Lani Guinier, *The Supreme Court 2007 Term—Foreword: Demosprudence through Dissent*, 122 HARV. L. REV. 4 (2008) (arguing that oral dissents help losing citizens secure some ownership stake in rights decisions); Dan M. Kahan et al., *Whose Eyes Are You Going to Believe?* Scott v. Harris *and the Perils of Cognitive Illiberalism*, 122 HARV. L. REV. 837, 885–87 (2009) (asserting that in order for us to see the law as ours, judges must show "due respect for [our] understanding of reality and ... identities"); Penelope Pether, *Inequitable Injunctions: The Scandal of Private Judging in the U.S. Courts*, 56 STAN L. REV. 1435, 1500 (2004) (commenting on Justices Stevens's and Blackmun's views of precedent as being something other than the property of private litigants, and criticizing the way in which low-power citizens are left out of conversations about constitutional meaning when judges selectively publish only some of their opinions); and W. Bradley Wendel, *Professionalism as Interpretation*, 99 NW. U. L. REV. 1167, 1190–92 (2005) (claiming that judges have to appeal to an interpretive community for acceptance of their decisions; therefore, "the meaning of these texts ... becomes a property of the community"). Cf. Naomi Mezey, *The Paradoxes of Cultural Property*, 107 COLUM. L. REV. 2004 (2007) (discussing the ownership of things produced through cultural interactions). I am indebted to William B. Rubenstein, *Divided We Litigate: Addressing Disputes among Group Members and Lawyers in Civil Rights Campaigns*, 106 YALE L.J. 1623 (1997), for directing my attention to George Vaughn's argument to the Supreme Court in *Shelley v. Kraemer*, 334 U.S. 1 (1948).

Ownership arising out of citizen interactions with the Constitution is a theme of the literature on democratic experimentalism. See, e.g., Michael C. Dorf & Charles F. Sabel, *A Constitution of Democratic Experimentalism*, 98 COLUM. L. REV. 267 (1998); Michael C. Dorf, *Legal Indeterminacy and Institutional Design*, 78 N.Y.U. L. REV. 875 (2003). For other commentary pursuing this theme, readers may be interested in Mark J. Osiel, *Ever Again: Legal Remembrance of Administrative Massacre*, 144 U. PA. L. REV. 463, 500 (1995), who argues that "the memory of our discursive engagements . . . establishes . . . solidarity between us," that shared memories travel through institutions, and that memory holds citizens together. According to Osiel, the "experience of disagreement . . . creates a kind of joint understanding: that we have . . . faced the issues dividing us, that we are united in caring deeply about them and about what the other thinks of them." *Id.* at 494. Through memory, "a measure of social unity is achieved, not on the mystical model of fusion, with its political romanticism, but on the legal model of the contract." *Id.* at 495.

As with equality, many scholars have written uncountable words on the topic of consent. Readers wishing a brief account of the history of the consent concept in its relationship to courts might consult MARTIN SHAPIRO, COURTS: A COMPARATIVE AND POLITICAL ANALYSIS 2–8 (1981) (noting that contemporary courts have attempted to substitute law and office for more literal forms of consent). See also MARTIN SHAPIRO, FREEDOM OF SPEECH: THE SUPREME COURT AND JUDICIAL REVIEW 28–39 (1966) (reminding us that the Court has a citizen clientele that it cannot ignore). Cf. Dan M. Kahan, *The Cognitively Illiberal State*, 60 STAN. L. REV. 115 (2007) (discussing the importance of a workable concept of consent to liberal philosophers and the practical difficulties faced in achieving such a concept, from the perspective of cognitive theory).

Consent expectations are frequently associated with a trust metaphor. Alexander Hamilton argued that it is only because courts act as agents of the People, bound by their wishes and consent, that they can be considered democratic. THE FEDERALIST NO. 78 at 100–5 (Alexander Hamilton) (Edward Gaylord Bourne ed., 1901). As BERNARD WILLIAMS, TRUTH & TRUTHFULNESS: AN ESSAY IN GENEALOGY 221 (2002), and JERRY L. MASHAW, DUE PROCESS IN THE ADMINISTRATIVE STATE (1985), remind us, when people are principals and the government is agent, consent lies at the heart of questions of governmental legitimacy. For an extended application of the trust metaphor and agency principles to courts, consult Sarah M. R. Cravens, *Judges as Trustees: A Duty to Account and an Opportunity for Virtue*, 62 WASH. & LEE L. REV. 1637 (2005). But see Theodore W. Ruger, *"A Question Which Convulses a Nation": The Early Republic's Greatest Debate about the Judicial Review Power*, 117 HARV. L. REV. 826 (2004) (arguing that agency theory and judicial review are in tension).

MICHAEL WALZER, THICK AND THIN: MORAL ARGUMENT AT HOME AND ABROAD 56–57 (1994), asserts that, in the "thick account of democratic idealism," power is legitimate only if it is exercised with the consent of *all* rather than only some of the people. Scholars who share Walzer's belief include PAUL W. KAHN, THE CULTURAL STUDY OF LAW: RECONSTRUCTING LEGAL SCHOLARSHIP 12–15 (1999) (emphasizing that everyone's consent matters); DAVID A. J. RICHARDS, CONSCIENCE AND THE CONSTITUTION: HISTORY, THEORY, AND LAW OF THE RECONSTRUCTION AMENDMENTS 134–35 (1993) (discussing Locke's notion that a requirement of institutional legitimacy is that the institution will produce outcomes that are acceptable to all); and JOHN RAWLS, POLITICAL LIBERALISM 216–25 (1993) (stating that all members of the community must be recognized in public reason because of the importance of consent to legitimacy). See also Dan M. Kahan et al., *Whose Eyes Are You Going to Believe? Scott v. Harris and the Perils of Cognitive Illiberalism*, 122 HARV. L. REV. 837, 886 (2009) (arguing that judges must be wary of facts that seem to speak for themselves but in reality reflect only the beliefs of a majority, for judges need the support of a consensus "devoid of any partial understanding of social reality the endorsement of which by the law would alienate or stigmatize an identifiable subcommunity, whose perspective has been excluded from consideration").

Arguments that courts need not worry about the consent of some citizens, however, are also made. See, e.g., AMY GUTMANN & DENNIS THOMPSON, DEMOCRACY AND DISAGREEMENT (1996) (arguing that winners must do their best to justify their win to the losers, unless losers have been trying to defend something reprehensible, such as slavery); Rachael N. Pine, *Speculation and*

Reality: The Role of Facts in Judicial Protection of Fundamental Rights, 136 U. PA. L. REV. 655 721–25 (1988) (arguing that everyone ought to be able to relitigate constitutional issues in light of changed circumstances except, perhaps, people who would like to relitigate *Brown v. Board of Education*).

Reva B. Siegel, *Equality Talk: Antisubordination and Anticlassification Values in Constitutional Struggles over Brown*, 117 HARV. L. REV. 1470 (2004), recognizes—as does this book—that justices cannot ignore even defenders of slavery. Using a somewhat softer term than consent, Siegel asserts that when the Supreme Court came under attack for its decision in *Brown v. Board of Education*, "it needed an account of the Constitution that could command the allegiance—if not the assent, then the *engaged dissent*—of those the Court's decisions had estranged." *Id*. at 1544 (emphasis added). Cf. Robert Post, *Law and Cultural Conflict*, 78 CHI.-KENT L. REV. 485, 501 (2003) (describing "constitutional adjudication [as] a kind of continuous judicial gamble whereby the Court summons the nation to *embrace* the cultural values that inform and sustain its own decisions") (emphasis added). Justices themselves speak of "acceptance." See, e.g., *Planned Parenthood of Se. Pa. v. Casey*, 505 U.S. 833, 865 (1992); *Vieth v. Jubelirer*, 541 U.S. 267, 269, 291 (2004).

Regarding the importance of the consent of current generations to constitutional meaning, Thomas Jefferson reportedly questioned how a government decision made long after the Constitution was ratified could claim to reflect the consent of current generations. David A. Strauss, *Common Law, Common Ground, and Jefferson's Principle*, 112 YALE L.J. 1717, 1718 (2003). ALEXANDER M. BICKEL, THE LEAST DANGEROUS BRANCH: THE SUPREME COURT AT THE BAR OF POLITICS 28–33 (1962) (arguing that the Court must conduct itself in a way that retains the consent of current generations to practices of judicial decision-making), and PAUL W. KAHN, THE CULTURAL STUDY OF LAW: RECONSTRUCTING LEGAL SCHOLARSHIP 69 (1999) (arguing that "law must…respect[ ] revolution—both as fact and possibility"), are relevant.

Readers who wish to know more about originalism in constitutional interpretation and its relationship to consent might consult ROY L. BROOKS, STRUCTURES OF JUDICIAL DECISION MAKING FROM LEGAL FORMALISM TO CRITICAL THEORY 61–84 (2d ed. 2005) (discussing Justice Scalia's philosophy and the problems with it); PAUL W. KAHN, THE REIGN OF LAW: MARBURY V. MADISON AND THE CONSTRUCTION OF AMERICA 87 (1997) (rejecting the idea that there is a "correct" approach to constitutional interpretation, such as originalism); Jack M. Balkin, *Fidelity to Text and Principle*, in THE CONSTITUTION IN 2020, at 11 (Jack M. Balkin & Reva B. Siegel eds., 2009) (arguing that originalists limit their interpretations to "original expected applications" of constitutional principle); Sanford Levinson, *Law as Literature*, 60 TEX. L. REV. 373 (1982) (reviewing criticisms of originalism); and Cass R. Sunstein, *Justice Scalia's Democratic Formalism*, 107 YALE L.J. 529 (1997) (pointing out that the Constitution does not prescribe any rules for its own interpretation and criticizing what he calls democratic formalism).

Many Supreme Court decisions attest that contending parties and justices can always find something in constitutional history to justify an "originalist" interpretation. See Robert Post & Reva Siegel, *Originalism as a Political Practice: The Right's Living Constitution*, 75 FORDHAM L. REV. 545 (2006). See also John B. Gates & Glenn A. Phelps, *Intentionalism in Constitutional Opinions*, 49 POL. RES. Q. 245 (1996) (concluding that there is no significant difference in the way Justices Rehnquist and Brennan use history in constitutional interpretation); and Christopher W. Schmidt, *Brown and the Colorblind Constitution*, 94 CORNELL L REV. 203 (2008) (referencing the ineptness of the Court when it attempts to incorporate history into its justifications).

Cynicism about originalism and constitutional interpretation is encouraged by decisions such as *District of Columbia v. Heller*, 128 S. Ct. 2783 (2008). After working through an arcane, linguistic analysis of the text of the Second Amendment, justices recognized a right to self defense that allegedly preexisted the Constitution. "It is dubious," justices proclaimed, "to rely on [the drafting history of the Second Amendment] to interpret a text that was widely understood to codify a pre-existing right." *Id*. at 2804. As a result, justices in the majority—many staunch advocates of originalist methods of constitutional interpretation—offered an analysis that will likely produce a body of constitutional law that cannot meaningfully be tied to the consent of the founding generation.

Constitutional avoidance doctrines partly relied on as a means of retaining citizen consent embody a paradox: they actually preclude some litigants from testing the boundaries of citizen consent to government and result in deference to laws adopted by only a subset of citizens. For a conventional view of the benefits of avoidance, however, see JEFFREY ROSEN, THE MOST DEMOCRATIC BRANCH: HOW THE COURTS SERVE AMERICA (2006) (arguing that avoidance enhances legitimacy).

Readers debating whether technical rationality might compensate for the practical impossibility of securing actual citizen consent to laws will be interested in liberal philosophy. GERALD F. GAUS, CONTEMPORARY THEORIES OF LIBERALISM 121 (2003); and BERNARD WILLIAMS, TRUTH & TRUTHFULNESS: AN ESSAY IN GENEALOGY 225 (2002), both attribute to Jürgen Habermas the idea that consent to a particular proposition should be evaluated in terms of whether all parties would agree to it if debate could continue into the future for an indefinite period of time. The notion is also implicit in John Rawls's concept of public reason. JOHN RAWLS, POLITICAL LIBERALISM (2d ed. 2005) (pointing out that public reasons are not grounded only in logic; they must be accessible to and accepted by the public at large). Many scholars accept this frame of reference. See, e.g., JUDITH JARVIS THOMSON, THE REALM OF RIGHTS 84–86 (1990) (explaining why consent cannot be achieved through technical rationality alone); MARK KINGWELL, A CIVIL TONGUE: JUSTICE, DIALOGUE, AND THE POLITICS OF PLURALISM 35–45 (1995) (positing that a benchmark for deciding whether justice is fulfilled is assessing whether a conversation about meaning has been shut down and arguing that rationality by itself is suited only to persons uninterested in forging binding political agreements); Robert Post, *The Supreme Court 2002 Term—Foreword: Fashioning the Legal Constitution: Culture, Courts, and Law*, 117 HARV. L. REV. 4 (2003) (arguing that judicial legitimacy is not pegged to a single opinion; it unfolds over time as the Court renders decisions as part of a conversation); David A. Strauss, *Common Law, Common Ground, and Jefferson's Principle*, 112 YALE L.J. 1717 (2003) (suggesting that common-law reasoning and the continuing conversation are a solution to the problem of consent).

Decisions other than *District of Columbia v. Heller*, 128 S. Ct. 2784 (2008), discussed in the text, illustrate that reason alone "is never in itself a sufficient ground for a rule." PAUL W. KAHN, THE CULTURAL STUDY OF LAW: RECONSTRUCTING LEGAL SCHOLARSHIP 14 (1999). Kahn cites *Brown v. Board of Education* and *Roe v. Wade* as judicial opinions that relied heavily on reason but were ultimately flawed in failing to appeal to justifications that might secure consent. *Id.* at 13. Reva B. Siegel, *Equality Talk: Antisubordination and Anticlassification Values in Constitutional Struggles over Brown*, 117 HARV. L. REV. 1470, 1544–46 (2004), concurs. Her account of *Brown* illustrates that, although the opinion carefully relied on social science data attesting to the harms of a separate-but-equal education, no one would claim that it reflected the consent of all of the people at the time it was written. In fact, Southern judges actually resisted *Brown* by exploiting its internal, social science logic to conclude—based on their own social science data—that the harms of integration would outweigh the harms of racial segregation. See also RICHARD A. POSNER, HOW JUDGES THINK 279 (2008) (*Brown* may be considered "right" because it is accepted, not because of its formal analytical approach). Cf. Lawrence B. Solum, *Public Legal Reason*, 92 VA. L. REV. 1449 (2006) (discussing how judges, in deciding hard cases, need something more than traditional, authoritative sources such as precedent or text); Barbara Yngvesson, *Inventing Law in Local Settings: Rethinking Popular Legal Culture*, 98 YALE L.J. 1689 (1989) (noting that logic is hierarchical and not well suited to discussing many of the conflicts that arise in constitutional rights disputes, which involve things such as betrayal or trusteeship); BERNARD WILLIAMS, TRUTH & TRUTHFULNESS: AN ESSAY IN GENEALOGY 214 (2002) (describing how arguments proceed within academia, within an "idealized [academic] market," where the worth of ideas is measured by disciplinary acceptance); LAW'S VIOLENCE (Austin Sarat & Thomas R. Kearns eds., 1992) (arguing that logic in law attempts to civilize that which is inherently violent); and THOMAS S. KUHN, THE STRUCTURE OF SCIENTIFIC REVOLUTIONS (2d ed. enlarged 1970) (illustrating why rationality is insufficient even in matters of scientific truth, when scientists are involved in paradigm debates).

On the subject of judicial rationality, I highly recommend ROBERTO MANGABEIRA UNGER, WHAT SHOULD LEGAL ANALYSIS BECOME? (1996). Unger recognizes that rationality guards against arbitrariness and can ensure equality of treatment, but he is not blind to the fact that rationality itself can also be arbitrary and indeterminate and cannot itself confer judicial legitimacy. Unger turns to the possibility that judicial decisions might be seen as legitimate were we to think of judges as facilitators of citizen decisions and of judicial activity as leading to collective self-determination. In Unger's view, decisional law should accept the "centrality and the legitimacy of [interest group politics and] conflict." *Id.* at 55. His statement that "law in a democracy can be understood as the regulation of conflict by groundrules and as the moderation of conflict by compromise," *id.*, comes close to an implicit acknowledgment of the Supreme Court's transactional role, discussed in chapter 8.

It has been asserted that justices should identify and use reasoning processes suited to their unique role, rather than appropriating a form of rationality no different from that employed by the elected branches of government. See, e.g., Owen M. Fiss, *The Other Goldberg,* in THE CONSTITUTION OF RIGHTS: HUMAN DIGNITY AND AMERICAN VALUES 229 (Michael J. Meyer & William A. Parent eds., 1992). Cf. JÜRGEN HABERMAS, BETWEEN FACTS AND NORMS: CONTRIBUTIONS TO A DISCOURSE THEORY OF LAW AND DEMOCRACY (William Rehg trans., 1996).

Readers interested in various forms of reasoning available to justices in rights disputes would find guidance in the following discussions: PHILIP BOBBITT, CONSTITUTIONAL INTERPRETATION (1991) (describing six modalities of constitutional analysis: historical, textual, doctrinal, prudential, structural, and ethical—all of which might pursue what could be called a rational structure of argumentation); GUIDO CALABRESI, IDEALS, BELIEFS, ATTITUDES, AND THE LAW: PRIVATE LAW PERSPECTIVES ON A PUBLIC LAW PROBLEM (1985) (discussing approaches to making tragic choices); Michael C. Dorf, *Legal Indeterminacy and Institutional Design,* 78 N.Y.U. L. REV. 875, 971–72 (2003) (discussing two types of moral reasoning, one of which involves people who attempt to cooperatively solve common problems, the other involving people who butt heads in adversarial argument); STUART HAMPSHIRE, INNOCENCE AND EXPERIENCE (1989) (discussing practical reasoning and moral conflict); WILLIAM H. SIMON, THE PRACTICE OF JUSTICE: A THEORY OF LAWYERS' ETHICS 21–25 (1998) (describing different types of practical reasoning); ALASDAIR MACINTYRE, WHOSE JUSTICE? WHICH RATIONALITY? (1988) (describing a view of rationality that contrasts with presuppositions of the Enlightenment and discussing how one might use traditions, empathy, and humility to solve problems); MARTHA C. NUSSBAUM, LOVE'S KNOWLEDGE: ESSAYS ON PHILOSOPHY AND LITERATURE 291–93 (1990) (stating that "emotional responses [are] valuable sources of information," which, being "intimately related to beliefs or judgments about the world" and about what is valuable and important, have a cognitive content useful in reasoning); RICHARD A. POSNER, HOW JUDGES THINK (2008) (characterizing judging as an art rather than a science, in which analogies can help judges discover but not justify results, and arguing that legalism offers only an illusion of intellectual rigor); and Cass R. Sunstein, *On Analogical Reasoning,* 106 HARV. L. REV. 741 (1993) (discussing analogical reasoning as no guarantee of agreement about constitutional meaning).

Discussions of rationality occasionally overlook the importance of framing to the rationality enterprise. Framing choices, also discussed in chapter 4, explain why justices who use the same form of reasoning will not always reach the same conclusions. Depending on how questions in a rights dispute are framed, for example, different facts will be relevant and different analogies may be drawn. In *Hein v. Freedom from Religion Foundation,* 551 U.S. 587 (2007), for example, framing affected the constitutional analysis of a challenge to White House initiatives supportive of religious, faith-based organizations. To have standing to pursue an Establishment Clause argument, the plaintiff taxpayers were required to show that they were personally harmed by the initiatives. Justice Scalia characterized their harm as merely psychic, while Justice Souter said the plaintiffs suffered a harm to individual conscience. It is no surprise that Justice Souter, who identified a significant harm, wanted the Court to hear the plaintiffs' challenge, while Justice Scalia, who recognized only a trivial psychic harm, found the challenge unworthy of judicial review. The two different descriptions of harm reflected a discretionary framing choice that was not dictated by logic.

One final word about consent is in order. Although most of us assume that consent gives legitimacy to the elected branches of government, Rebecca L. Brown, *Liberty, The New Equality*, 77 N.Y.U. L. REV. 1491 (2002), and others recognize that actual, literal consent is not attainable even in the legislative arena. See, e.g., Randy E. Barnett, *Restoring the Lost Constitution, Not the Constitution in Exile*, 75 FORDHAM L. REV. 669 (2006); Christopher J. Peters, *Persuasion: A Model of Majoritarianism as Adjudication*, 96 Nw. L. REV. 1 (2001). Peters, noting that legislative and judicial decision-making both impose legal rules on persons who disagree with those rules, presents a mirror image of some of the arguments made in this book. He seeks insights into the "majoritarian" problem of legislative legitimacy by looking at theories conventionally associated with the problem of judicial legitimacy. In the process, he presents interesting summaries of theories of judicial legitimacy in relation to losers.

Chapter 3: Harm to Constitutional Stature in *Bowers* and *Carhart*

Much has been written about *Bowers v. Hardwick*, 478 U.S. 186 (1986). See, e.g., Courtney G. Joslin, *Equal Protection and Anti-Gay Legislation: Dismantling the Legacy* of Bowers v. Hardwick, 32 HARV. C.R.-C.L. L. REV. 225 (1997); Thomas B. Stoddard, Bowers v. Hardwick: *Precedent by Personal Prediliction*, 54 U. CHI. L. REV. 648 (1987). For general comment on the dehumanization of homosexuals, readers may wish to review Evan Wolfson, *Civil Rights, Human Rights, Gay Rights: Minorities and the Humanity of the Different*, 14 HARV. J.L. & PUB. POL'Y 21 (1991). See also William N. Eskridge Jr., *A Liberal Vision of U.S. Family Law*, in THE CONSTITUTION IN 2020, at 245 (Jack M. Balkin & Reva B. Siegel eds., 2009). William B. Rubenstein, *The Myth of Superiority*, 16 CONST. COMMENT. 599 (1999), argues that state court judges, who have much more exposure to the lives of gays and lesbians, through family law and other ordinary disputes, may be more likely than federal judges to acknowledge the equal stature of homosexuals.

Regarding the immorality of lotteries as mechanisms for making decisions about fundamental human rights, see GUIDO CALABRESI & PHILIP BOBBITT, TRAGIC CHOICES 41–44, 49 (1978); and ROBERT M. COVER, JUSTICE ACCUSED: ANTISLAVERY AND THE JUDICIAL PROCESS 102–4 (1975). According to the account in JOHN T. NOONAN JR., THE ANTELOPE: THE ORDEAL OF THE RECAPTURED AFRICANS IN THE ADMINISTRATIONS OF JAMES MONROE AND JOHN QUINCY ADAMS 119 (1977), the Supreme Court's first opinion did not unambiguously approve the use of a lottery to decide the question of freedom, yet neither did the Court's opinion bar the use of a lottery. *Id.* at 116, 119. A second opinion also fell short of clarifying whether a lottery could be used, although the Court did state that slaves should be distinguished from non-slaves by "proof" to the satisfaction of the court below. *Id.* at 121. Ultimately, in a third opinion, the Court approved the designation of thirty-nine Africans as slaves. *Id.* at 127–28. Proof of ownership had been based on flimsy evidence, at best, but the Court believed that "under the peculiar and special circumstances of the case" (presumably the ambivalent attitude of society toward the personhood of Africans) the evidence was satisfactory. *Id.* at 131.

Gonzales v. Carhart, 550 U.S. 124 (2007), is a more recent opinion than *Bowers*, but much has also been written about this decision. I recommend the discussions of *Carhart* included in Rebecca E. Ivey, *Destabilizing Discourses: Blocking and Exploiting a New Discourse at Work in* Gonzales v. Carhart, 94 VA. L. REV. 1451 (2008); Martha C. Nussbaum, *The Supreme Court, 2006 Term— Foreword: Constitutions and Capabilities: "Perception" against Lofty Formalism*, 121 HARV. L. REV. 4 (2007); Robert Post & Reva Siegel, *Roe Rage: Democratic Constitutionalism and Backlash*, 42 HARV. C.R.-C.L. L. REV. 373 (2007); and Neil S. Siegel, *The Virtue of Judicial Statesmanship*, 86 TEX. L. REV. 959 (2008). In addition, Reva Siegel has written extensively about the Supreme Court's abortion decisions. See, e.g., Reva B. Siegel, *Dignity and the Politics of Protection: Abortion Restrictions under* Casey/Carhart, 117 YALE L.J. 1694 (2008); Reva B. Siegel, *The Right's Reasons: Constitutional Conflict and the Spread of Woman-Protective Antiabortion Argument*, 57 DUKE L.J. 1641 (2008); Reva B. Siegel, *The New Politics of Abortion: An Equality Analysis of Woman-Protective*

Abortion Restrictions, 2007 U. ILL. L. REV. 991 (2007). Carol Sanger, *Seeing and Believing: Mandatory Ultrasounds and the Path to a Protected Choice*, 56 UCLA L. REV. 351, 351 (2008), may be of special interest for its argument that "not only is an abortion decision itself protected, but so is the deliberative path a woman takes to reach that decision."

Hill v. Colorado, 530 U.S. 703 (2000), deserves mention in the discussion of women's constitutional stature and abortion disputes. As discussed in chapter 1, *Hill* involved a challenge to Colorado's Bubble Bill, which excluded protesters from certain physical locations around medical clinics. Majority justices deferred to a legislative judgment that women (and others approaching medical clinics) should be protected from the face-to-face speech of sidewalk counselors seeking to discourage abortions, while dissenters objected that the Bubble Bill's restrictions were not justified. The positions and language of justices in *Hill* respecting women's vulnerability should be contrasted to assumptions embodied in *Gonzales v. Carhart*, and to the joint opinion in *Planned Parenthood v. Casey*.

Readers might note that, like the harm to constitutional stature in *Bowers*, the harms inflicted by *Carhart* justices apparently derived from moral concerns with far-reaching consequences. *Gonzales v. Carhart*, 550 U.S. 124, 182 (2007) (Ginsburg, J., dissenting) ("Moral concerns... could [potentially] yield prohibitions on any abortion."). For example, although the Supreme Court has not recognized the fetus as a person within the meaning of the Constitution, *Carhart* justices expressed concern for the fetus as though it were a person. In the majority opinion "a fetus is described as an 'unborn child,' and as a 'baby.'" *Id.* at 187 (Ginsburg, J., dissenting). Justices stated that the banned D&E procedure "kills" the fetus, *Gonzales v. Carhart*, 550 U.S. 124, 139, 148 (2007), and they noted its "disturbing similarity" to infanticide. Id. at 158 (internal citations omitted). "No one would dispute," they said, "that, for many, D&E is a procedure itself laden with the power to devalue human life." *Id.* They explained that "the Act expresses respect for the dignity of human life," *id.* at 157, and the state's interest in potential life, which was undervalued after *Roe*. *Id.* The abortion decisions will be revisited in chapter 7 as part of a discussion of rights stakeholders who are committed to religious or other strong moral beliefs.

Bowers and *Carhart*, of course, only undermine and do not formally negate the constitutional stature of homosexuals and women, respectively. For examples of disputes in which constitutional doctrine formally withholds a presumption of full constitutional stature, readers might consider rights disputes involving children who, because of their age and special circumstances, are treated differently than competent adults. See, e.g., the Court's public school drug-prevention decisions in *Safford Unified School District No. 1 v. Redding*, 129 S. Ct. 2633 (2009); *Board of Education v. Earls*, 536 U.S. 822 (2002); and *Vernonia School District 473 v. Acton*, 515 U.S. 646 (1995).

Finally, readers might be interested in the Supreme Court's standing doctrine as it relates to issues of constitutional stature. As the text notes, the plaintiffs in *Gonzales v. Carhart*, 550 U.S. 124 (2007), were physicians rather than women whose constitutional rights were actually at stake in the decision. Physicians did not claim that they had a right to practice medicine as they saw fit. Cf. *Conn v. Gabbert*, 526 U.S. 286 (1999) (rejecting an attorney's claim to have a right to practice his profession). Instead, they relied on what is called third-party standing to represent women's interests. Cf., e.g., *Bush v. Gore*, 531 U.S. 98 (2000) (political candidate permitted to represent the constitutional rights of voters).

Standing doctrine, which requires a party making a constitutional claim to show that he has suffered a concrete, nonspeculative injury, can lead to debates about whether a particular litigant's interests are legitimate or visible to the Constitution. Moreover, because standing doctrines may exclude parties from court entirely, the harms flowing from a denial of standing can be significant. Parties who have no standing have absolutely no ability to participate in judicial conversations about the constitutional legitimacy of status quo relationships. In *Hein v. Freedom from Religion Foundation*, 127 S. Ct. 2553 (2007), for example, dissenting Justice Souter objected that the majority's refusal to accord standing to plaintiffs challenging the expenditure of taxpayer dollars on President Bush's faith-based initiatives treated the plaintiffs as "outsiders, not full members of the political community." *Id.* at 2588 (internal citations omitted). Decisions telling parties that they have no technical standing can also easily fall into objectionable rhetoric and analysis of the sort discussed in this chapter. For interesting and relevant discussions of standing doctrine, readers might wish to consult Richard H. Fallon Jr., *The Linkage between Justiciability and Remedies—and Their Connections to Substantive Rights*, 92 VA. L. REV. 633 (2006); and Stephen L. Winter, *The Metaphor of Standing and the Problem of Self-Governance*, 40 STAN. L. REV. 1371 (1988).

Readers should note that in *Roe v. Wade*, 410 U.S. 113 (1973), a physician was denied third-party standing to challenge a statute criminalizing abortion. The State of Texas had decided to prosecute the physician, and federal courts are prohibited by abstention doctrines from interfering with state criminal proceedings. The denial of standing in *Roe* is relevant to *Carhart's* decision not to render a definitive decision about the constitutionality of the challenged federal statute until justices were given concrete evidence of the effect of the statute on physicians and women. Abstention doctrines will limit the circumstances in which as-applied challenges based on concrete evidence can be successfully asserted against statutes criminalizing abortion. Readers interested in learning more about facial and as-applied constitutional attacks, in the context of *Carhart*, might wish to consult Laura J. Tepich, Gonzales v. Carhart: *The Partial Termination of the Right to Choose*, 63 U. MIAMI L. REV. 339 (2008) (noting that most challenges to abortion laws prior to *Carhart* involved facial attacks).

Chapter 4: Harms of Untruthfulness

This chapter and accompanying notes can only begin to explore the question posed by Stephen Ellmann, *The Rule of Law and the Achievement of Unanimity in Brown*, 49 N.Y.L. SCH. L. REV. 741, 750 (2004): conceding that a court might wish to avoid truthfulness in order to achieve consent, and assuming that a degree of untruthfulness might be permissible, how do we set limits on what a justice can do in failing to be completely truthful? Readers interested in broad, philosophical discussions of truth and (lying), however, might consult BERNARD WILLIAMS, TRUTH AND TRUTHFULNESS: AN ESSAY IN GENEALOGY (2002); and SISSELA BOK, LYING: MORAL CHOICE IN PUBLIC AND PRIVATE LIFE (Vintage Books ed. 1989). I also recommend the discussions of truthfulness in ROBERTO MANGABEIRA UNGER, WHAT SHOULD LEGAL ANALYSIS BECOME? (1996) (emphasizing the importance of truthfulness and candor by a Supreme Court that serves as a facilitator of the People's decisions); and LINDA RADZIK, MAKING AMENDS: ATONEMENT IN MORALITY, LAW, AND POLITICS 97, 189–90 (2009) (emphasizing the importance of truthfulness in atoning for wrongful conduct).

BERNARD WILLIAMS, TRUTH AND TRUTHFULNESS: AN ESSAY IN GENEALOGY (2002), emphasizes that government in particular should be truthful. He insists, for example, that truthfulness protects against an illegitimate government that wishes to conceal its illegal actions; it is a tool of citizens who wish to remain free and exercise true consent. He also argues that truthfulness is antithetical to governments that wish to treat people as a means to an end. Williams links the obligation of governmental truthfulness to the "fiction" that government "is in some sense a trust" and refers to government as an agent of the people, *id.* at 210–11, but he does not develop an extended trusteeship argument.

The costs of deceit are fleshed out in SISSELA BOK, LYING: MORAL CHOICE IN PUBLIC AND PRIVATE LIFE (Vintage Books ed. 1989). Bok argues that lies are used to deprive individuals of autonomy and the power of choice, and that the control exercised by a liar is equivalent to an assault on the person. She notes that lies are not merely coercive; they are *differentially* coercive in that they "affect the distribution of power." *Id.* at 19. Bok also suggests that obligations of truthfulness may be different respecting friends (to whom lying is unacceptable) and enemies (to whom lying is perhaps legitimate). *Id.* at 134–45. Finally, Bok discusses the concept of noble lies, or lies told for the benefit of the public good. For example, we may tell a noble lie to avoid a truth that will be too painful for others to cope with rationally or because we believe they have a superior understanding of what the truth is. *Id.* at 167–68.

Bok reminds us that truth depends on what we are able to remember out of all the things we have forgotten, BOK, *supra* at 5 (recounting the ancient Greek tradition of characterizing truth, or *aletheia,* as those things kept separate from "the river of forgetfulness"). She thus emphasizes how complex the subject of truthfulness can become.

For purposes of justices' obligations, this book asserts that truth must be seen from the perspective of stakeholders in a rights dispute. As suggested in ROBERT A. BURT, THE CONSTITUTION IN CRISIS (1992), justices can only respect the equality and consent expectations of individuals if they define truth in this fashion. See also DAVID LUBAN, LEGAL ETHICS AND HUMAN DIGNITY (2007) (arguing that if one does not allow individuals to present their own stories, without distortion, harm to human dignity will result). Cf. LINDA RADZIK, MAKING AMENDS: ATONEMENT IN MORALITY, LAW, AND POLITICS 91 (2009) (linking empathy to truthful recognition of what has been done from the perspective of the person harmed). For discussions of how difficult it can be for attorneys to convey a truthful account of their client's interests and values to a court, see Anthony V. Alfieri, *(Un)Covering Identity in Civil Rights and Poverty Law,* 121 HARV. L. REV. 805, 828–31 (2008) (discussing the ACLU's misguided strategy of treating homosexuality as a disability and a mental disorder in order to garner favor with courts in antidiscrimination litigation); and William B. Rubenstein, *Divided We Litigate: Addressing Disputes among Group Members and Lawyers in Civil Rights Campaigns,* 106 YALE L.J. 1623 (1997) (describing the difficulty of reaching a consensus on what is at stake when a group's interests are being litigated).

According to BERNARD WILLIAMS, TRUTH AND TRUTHFULNESS: AN ESSAY IN GENEALOGY (2002), truth has two basic features: accuracy and sincerity. The text does not explore justices' sincerity, but readers interested in this topic should consult RUTH GRANT, HYPOCRISY AND INTEGRITY: MACHIAVELLI, ROUSSEAU, AND THE ETHICS OF POLITICS (1997). See also John M. Kang, *The Irrelevance of Sincerity: Deliberative Democracy in the Supreme Court,* 48 ST. LOUIS U. L.J. 305 (2004) (arguing that too much sincerity will lead to too little exchange of opinion and that although lying threatens stability, insincerity does not); and John M. Kang, *The Uses of Insincerity: Thomas Hobbes's Theory of Law and Society,* 15 LAW & LITERATURE 371 (2003) (founding an argument for the virtues of insincerity on Thomas Hobbes's work and asserting that sincerity gets in the way of civil society, which requires insincere gestures of respect).

According to BERNARD WILLIAMS, TRUTH AND TRUTHFULNESS: AN ESSAY IN GENEALOGY (2002), accuracy requires us to be on guard against self-deception or wishful thinking. Readers wishing to explore this idea might be interested in the link between self-deception and ideology made in RUTH GRANT, HYPOCRISY AND INTEGRITY: MACHIAVELLI, ROUSSEAU, AND THE ETHICS OF POLITICS (1997) (arguing that a zealot's adherence to principle in disregard of harm done to others starts him down a path of corruption rooted in self-deception). For examples of how an ideological commitment to doctrine can get in the way of assessing what is at stake in a rights dispute, see Frederick Schauer, *Principles, Institutions, and the First Amendment,* 112 HARV. L. REV. 84 (1998) (arguing that a focus on factual reality rather than doctrinal categories of First Amendment speech might lead to better constitutional analysis and behavior). The text's example of how First Amendment doctrine can obscure the truth of workplace sexual harassment comes from Justice Scalia's opinion in *R.A.V. v. City of St. Paul,* 505 U.S. 377 (1992). See also Anna-Marie Marshall, *Injustice Frames, Legality, and the Everyday Construction of Sexual Harassment,* 28 LAW & SOC. INQUIRY 659 (2003). Chapter 6 will return to a discussion of ideology.

Truthfulness is especially important to theories of rhetorical or dialogic justice, which emphasize the relational aspect of justice. See, e.g., JÜRGEN HABERMAS, BETWEEN FACTS AND NORMS: CONTRIBUTIONS TO A DISCOURSE THEORY OF LAW AND DEMOCRACY 15 (1996) (developing a linguistic theory of justice in which truth is "the vindication of a criticizable validity claim under the communication conditions of an audience of competent interpreters that extends ideally across social space and historical time" and requires an open and cumulative process of deliberation). Cf. ALASDAIR MACINTYRE, WHOSE JUSTICE? WHICH RATIONALITY? 198–99, 203 (1988) (discussing Thomas Aquinas's view that lying is never permissible, for "insofar as I lie I make myself into the sort of unjust person incapable of achieving" a just life, where justice consists of "norms that define the relations of each person to others").

There is general recognition that truth or truthfulness can interfere with the pursuit of a consensus on debatable matters. See, e.g., MARK KINGWELL, A CIVIL TONGUE: JUSTICE, DIALOGUE,

AND THE POLITICS OF PLURALISM (1995) (discussing civility, duplicitous lying, and when it is permissible not to say something in order to achieve consensus); RUTH GRANT, HYPOCRISY AND INTEGRITY: MACHIAVELLI, ROUSSEAU, AND THE ETHICS OF POLITICS (1997) (asserting that because too much honesty can cause dissension, myths and traditions that do not accurately reflect the truth may need to be invoked; hypocrisy and lying, however, can be corrupting and dangerous); MARTHA NUSSBAUM, THE THERAPY OF DESIRE: THEORY AND PRACTICE IN HELLENISTIC ETHICS 10 (1994) (referencing Hellenistic thinkers who tried to teach people to be indifferent to loss because deep attachments and loss could lead to great evil and the desire to inflict reciprocal harm); MICHAEL J. SANDEL, DEMOCRACY'S DISCONTENT: AMERICA IN SEARCH OF A PUBLIC PHILOSOPHY (1996) (arguing that more openness in debates about public issues is needed, but recognizing that candor and openness can be especially destabilizing when moral questions are debated); and Mark J. Osiel, *Ever Again: Legal Remembrance of Administrative Massacre*, 144 U. PA. L. REV. 463 (1995) (arguing that, in the context of criminal prosecutions of state-sponsored murders, consensus may be found in oblivion; therefore, superficiality in the law might be a virtue). The possibility that truthfulness can raise topics for debate that are best forbidden is suggested by the example of Vichy France and the subject of the status of Jews recounted in RICHARD WEISBERG, POETHICS AND OTHER STRATEGIES OF LAW AND LITERATURE (1992).

Perhaps because of reservations about the effects of complete truthfulness, some argue that "law's deliberations should be shallow and not deep," Lawrence B. Solum, *Public Legal Reason*, 92 VA. L. REV. 1449, 1501 (2006), or at least that the general should not be neglected in taking note of the particular, Emily M. Calhoun, *The Breadth of Context and the Depth of Myth: Completing the Feminist Paradigm*, 4 HASTINGS WOMEN'S L.J. 87 (1993). Chapter 9's discussion of judicial minimalism will return to this topic.

Arguments for speaking more truth rather than less as a way to consensus are found in the literature on truth commissions. Readers interested in this topic may wish to read Thomas M. Antkowiak, *Truth as Right and Remedy in International Human Rights Experience*, 23 MICH. J. INT'L L. 977 (2002); and Mark J. Osiel, *Ever Again: Legal Remembrance of Administrative Massacre*, 144 U. PA. L. REV. 463, 542–45 (1995) (discussing the effect of a judicial effort to treat the story of the Argentine junta as collective memory). Cf. Norman W. Spaulding, *Constitution as Countermonument: Federalism, Reconstruction, and the Problem of Collective Memory*, 103 COLUM. L. REV. 1992, 2005–24 (2003) (discussing how the Supreme Court's treatment of the Reconstruction amendments constituted a dangerous exercise in obscuring the historical misdeeds of the nation); and Suzanne B. Goldberg, *Constitutional Tipping Points: Civil Rights, Social Change, and Fact-Based Adjudication*, 106 COLUM. L. REV. 1955 (2006) (discussing arguments for and against judicial candor and proposing that courts be more candid about the facts on which they base their decisions).

Through a discussion of *Rumsfeld v. Forum for Academic and Institutional Rights, Inc. (FAIR)*, 547 U.S. 47 (2006), the text illustrates the difficulty of identifying what is at stake in a rights dispute. To track what various stakeholders argued in *FAIR*, see SolomonResponse.Org, http:// www.law.georgetown.edu/Solomon/solomon.html (last visited June 13, 2009). Yet another perspective on the stakes in the dispute is presented in Emily M. Calhoun, *Academic Freedom: Disciplinary Lessons from Hogwarts*, 77 U. COLO. L. REV. 843 (2006) (discussing the interests of the discipline of law). Although not emphasized in the text, *FAIR* illustrates that justices choose the truth that they wish to discuss, perhaps because of their view of governing constitutional doctrine, perhaps for other less neutral reasons. For example, justices dismissively treated the plaintiffs' assertion that their expression was adversely affected by the Solomon Amendment despite an extensive factual record on this issue. In addition, they focused on the interests of institutional members of FAIR, and those interests were described in monetary terms. See *FAIR*, 547 U.S. at 54 n.3. Thus, much of the constitutional debate was about institutional rather than individual speech, about what law schools may say or be required to say, and about whether institutional choice is coerced by money. There was little discussion about the stakes for individuals, the communicative interactions of members of the legal profession, or the effect of the

Solomon Amendment on the composition of group membership or the integrity of the legal profession.

Another example of an opinion that neglects important stakeholder interests is *Board of Education of Kiryas Joel Village School District v. Grumet*, 512 U.S. 687 (1994). As a result of that neglect, it can be argued that the Satmar Hasidim were treated disrespectfully by justices. See, e.g., Ira C. Lupu, *Uncovering the Village of Kiryas Joel*, 96 COLUM. L. REV. 104 (1996) (questioning the use of the words "sect" and "sub-group" to describe the Satmar Hasidim). For relevant contemporaneous commentary on the case, see, for example, Martha Minow, *The Constitution and the Sub Group Question*, 71 IND. L. J. 1 (1995); Abner S. Greene, Kiryas Joel *and Two Mistakes about Equality*, 96 COLUM. L. REV. 1 (1996); and Christopher L. Eisgruber, *The Constitutional Value of Assimilation*, 96 COLUM. L. REV. 87 (1996). For an account of the controversy that fills in gaps in justices' discussion of what was at stake, see Jeffrey Rosen, Kiryas Joel and Shaw v. Reno: *A Text-Bound Interpretivist Approach*, 26 CUMB. L. REV. 387, 388–401 (1995–1996).

This book offers a number of examples of how women frequently fade into the background in abortion disputes. However, women are not the only stakeholders whose interests can be neglected in an abortion dispute. Even physicians can suffer that fate. In *Hill v. Colorado*, 530 U.S. 703 (2000), for example, neither the majority nor the dissent paid much attention to physicians. The neglect of these stakeholders is surprising considering that sidewalk counselors admitted that they were interested in persuading women to switch physicians. Had physician stakeholders been taken into account, one might have expected justices in the majority to remind dissenters of state laws, professional medical standards, and malpractice liability rules limiting various types of speech in order to ensure that a patient's consent to and choices about medical care and the patient–physician relationship are informed and protected from interference by third parties. That justices did not develop constitutional doctrine along these lines is particularly surprising given their inclination to think about abortion from the perspective of physicians.

Parties can be deliberately effaced in many ways. *Scott v. Harris*, 550 U.S. 372 (2007), for example, was a garden-variety rights dispute in which Victor Harris tried to avoid arrest for a traffic offense and was harmed in a rollover accident resulting from the ensuing police chase. Harris sued the pursuing police officer for using excessive force to make an arrest. The Court's opinion repeatedly referred to the police officer by his name and rank, while the plaintiff was referenced only as "the respondent." Readers may enjoy the discussion of how courts efface or disregard people through rules of law that reduce them to categories in JOHN T. NOONAN JR., PERSONS AND MASKS OF THE LAW (1976).

If readers wish to focus on justices' intent rather than the simple effect of untruthfulness, they should consult Marie A. Failinger, *Not Mere Rhetoric: On Wasting or Claiming Your Legacy, Justice Scalia*, 34 U. TOL. L. REV. 425 (2003) (discussing problematic judicial "assuming, exaggerating and fudging" that assertedly involve clear distortions of the facts or law to achieve a particular outcome).

Even justices who wish to survey the interests of all stakeholders may write opinions that neglect some stakeholder interests and therefore outrage constitutional losers. Consider, for example, *J.E.B. v. Alabama*, 511 U.S. 127 (1994), which held that sex-based peremptory objections to jurors are unconstitutional. Majority justices did review the interests of a variety of stakeholders, but their primary focus was on the effects of peremptory juror strikes on women: they discussed the harms of excluding a class of jurors in terms of sex-based stereotypes historically used to brand women as inferior or ineligible for political participation. This focus infuriated Justice Scalia. He pointed out that the harm in *J.E.B.* was to a male litigant whom justices had deprived of a traditional right to use sex-based peremptory challenges and who, as a result, would be less likely to believe that he had received a fair trial. *Id.* at 157–59, 161 n.3 (Scalia, J., dissenting). Scalia objected that the majority had made "restitution to Paul" (potential women jurors), "when it [was] Peter" (a male litigant) "who [had] been robbed." *Id.* at 159.

For discussions of the presentation of stakeholder interests through amicus curiae briefs, I recommend Paul M. Collins Jr., *Friends of the Court: Examining the Influence of Amicus Curiae Participation in U.S. Supreme Court Litigation*, 38 LAW & SOC'Y REV. 809 (2004); Thomas G.

Hansford, *Information Provision, Organizational Constraints, and the Decision to Submit an Amicus Curiae Brief in a U.S. Supreme Court Case,* 57 POL. RES. Q. 219 (2004); and Kelly J. Lynch, *Best Friends? Supreme Court Law Clerks on Effective Amicus Curiae Briefs,* 20 J.L. & POL. 33 (2004).

As a final word to this chapter, it is important to stress that although truthfulness about stakeholder interests is required of justices, a judicial opinion that permits a discussion of interests to obscure the person holding those interests will breach harm-avoidance and harm-amelioration obligations. See, e.g., ALAN HYDE, BODIES OF LAW 196-99 (1997) (arguing that judicial opinions improperly transform disputes about people into interest debates). This issue is further discussed in Chapter 7.

Chapter 5: Acknowledgment of Harm

The philosophers and theorists whose ideas are discussed in this chapter have offered beautiful and complex arguments that deserve to be read in their entirety. I ask them to forgive me for generalizations that omit nuances in their thought. Moreover, readers should not mistakenly think that the ideas I have emphasized are the only, or even the central, ideas addressed in their scholarship. Finally, this chapter does not address some questions that are important to philosophers. First, there is the question whether harms inflicted by a tragic choice are ever morally justified. This book simply accepts the fact that justices do make tragic choices and, although their choices cause harm, it does not argue that a tragic choice is impermissible. If justices can avoid a tragic choice, so much the better, although they must find legitimate ways of doing so. See, e.g., Martha C. Nussbaum, *The Costs of Tragedy: Some Moral Limits of Cost-Benefit Analysis,* 29 J. LEGAL STUD. 1005, 1024-25 (2000) (arguing that a decision maker should struggle to find a way to avoid tragic choices). This book also does not engage in extensive debate about whether some harms to losers may entail no obligations. It assumes, for example, that harm-amelioration obligations are always owed in the novel but not frivolous claims raised in most rights disputes that reach the Supreme Court.

GUIDO CALABRESI, IDEALS, BELIEFS, ATTITUDES, AND THE LAW: PRIVATE LAW PERSPECTIVES ON A PUBLIC LAW PROBLEM (1985) defines tragic disputes as presenting a conflict between fundamental values that each of us holds dear. He recommends that citizens "recognize the conflict, give some weight to both beliefs, but mediate the clash by limiting the extent of each belief's dominance." *Id.* at 90. In this book, the tragic choice is defined as a choice between *people* holding different beliefs, not as a choice between beliefs per se. This distinction and Calabresi's ideas are further explored in chapter 7.

Some may resist describing choices in constitutional rights disputes as tragic. Nussbaum, for example, identifies tragic choices only in situations in which harm to a fundamental entitlement occurs. See Martha C. Nussbaum, *The Costs of Tragedy: Some Moral Limits of Cost-Benefit Analysis,* 29 J. LEGAL STUD. 1005, 1023-24 (2000). The stakes in the constitutional rights cases discussed in this book, however, typically will concern what Nussbaum thinks of as an entitlement.

I have drawn heavily on the ideas of Martha C. Nussbaum. See, e.g., MARTHA C. NUSSBAUM, THE FRAGILITY OF GOODNESS: LUCK AND ETHICS IN GREEK TRAGEDY AND PHILOSOPHY (rev. ed. 2001); LOVE'S KNOWLEDGE: ESSAYS ON PHILOSOPHY AND LITERATURE (1990); POETIC JUSTICE: THE LITERARY IMAGINATION AND PUBLIC LIFE (1995); and THE THERAPY OF DESIRE: THEORY AND PRACTICE IN HELLENISTIC ETHICS (1994). See also Martha C. Nussbaum, *Valuing Values: A Case for Reasoned Commitment,* 6 YALE J.L. & HUMAN. 197, 212–14 (1994).

Nussbaum shows us that literature offers important insights about law, discourages simple solutions to difficult choices, and prompts us to care about people as equal individuals not as statistics. Her literary perspective is not unique. Nussbaum herself, for example, relies on WAYNE C. BOOTH, THE COMPANY WE KEEP: AN ETHICS OF FICTION (1988), which readers might find of interest. I also highly recommend JAMES BOYD WHITE, ACTS OF HOPE: CREATING AUTHORITY IN LITERATURE, LAW, AND POLITICS (1994), and Sanford Levinson, *Law as Literature,* 60 TEX. L. REV. 373 (1982). RICHARD WEISBERG, POETHICS AND OTHER STRATEGIES OF LAW AND

LITERATURE 143–72 (1992), attempts to give us a description of what a literary jurisprudence would look like. John Fischer, *Reading Literature/Reading Law: Is There a Literary Jurisprudence?*, 72 TEX. L. REV. 135 (1993), however, argues that literary theory's usefulness is limited because, while literature can afford to be experimental, legal texts need to be coercive and authoritative. Compare, Patricia Ewick & Susan S. Silbey, *Subversive Stories and Hegemonic Tales: Toward a Sociology of Narrative*, 29 LAW & SOC'Y REV. 197 (1995) (cautioning that narrative can sustain oppression and authority); and MARK OSIEL, MASS ATROCITY, COLLECTIVE MEMORY, AND THE LAW (1997) (asserting that the proliferation of many little narratives operates against a single tyranny of collective memory). Chapter 8 will return to the subject of the authority of legal texts. Literature discussing narrative in law has been previously referenced in chapter 1. See also, ROBIN WEST, NARRATIVE, AUTHORITY, AND LAW (1993).

The text draws on the insights of JAHAN RAMAZANI, POETRY OF MOURNING: THE MODERN ELEGY FROM HARDY TO HEANEY (1994). Ramazani does not deal directly with law, but he does explore ideas relevant to the proper ethical stance of persons who make tragic choices and inflict harm. He identifies "protocols of bereavement" and concepts of loss important in a diverse society. *Id.* at xi. His discussion of the elegies of Sylvia Plath and other feminists, such as Ann Sexton and Adrienne Rich, who question the idea of inheritance, and of the elegies of William Carlos Williams, Seamus Heaney, and W. H. Auden, are especially relevant to this chapter. According to Ramazani, the modern elegist attempts to compensate for the shortcomings of a bureaucratic society in which decisions are made on the basis of a detached balance of costs and benefits. The modern elegist also questions any demand that those who suffer loss should "get a life," should "get over it." Moreover, the elegist is truthful about even the most painful or violent events. I enjoyed Ramazani's parsing of W. H. Auden's satire of the traditional elegiac form in "The Unknown Citizen," and the discussion of Auden's effort to write an elegy for William Butler Yeats, whose reactionary philosophy Auden deplored but whose poetry he loved and whom Auden viewed as neither an unequivocal hero nor a villain.

Memorials to loss other than the elegy may be of interest to readers. Those who study such memorials often invoke the power of the Vietnam War Memorial. See, e.g., W. J. T. MITCHELL, PICTURE THEORY: ESSAYS ON VERBAL AND VISUAL REPRESENTATION 379–81 (1994) (providing an eloquent description of the Vietnam War Memorial, by way of analogy); and RAMAZANI, *supra* at 362.

In thinking about memorials, I have found ROBERT POGUE HARRISON, THE DOMINION OF THE DEAD (2003), to be helpful. Harrison's observation that the dead do not simply disappear but remain as ghosts with the power to haunt or take revenge is relevant to improper treatment of constitutional losers. *Id.* at 145. See also MITCHELL, *supra*, at 204 n.35 (expressing the idea that if there is no proper recognition of loss, the national memory will be haunted by the unquiet dead). Cf. PAUL W. KAHN, THE REIGN OF LAW: *MARBURY V. MADISON* AND THE CONSTRUCTION OF AMERICA 132 (1997) ("What is suppressed doesn't just disappear. It remains available as a 'hidden truth,' a point from which law's appearance can be challenged."). HARRISON, *supra*, at 69, argues that mourning rituals are constructed to give the dead a proper burial, to appease the dead, and to secure their goodwill. He inspired the idea that justices should write about losers in a way that ensures that future decisions will involve something other than a mere repetition or a mere denial of what has gone before. He is also the source of the idea that winners share the same general fate (over time) as losers. *Id.* at 70. The argument that acknowledging harm can serve to restore important relationships is pursued by George P. Fletcher, *The Storrs Lectures: Liberals and Romantics at War: The Problem of Collective Guilt*, 111 YALE L.J. 1499, 1568–69 (2002), who asks us to imagine "what it would be like to live as African Americans in the United States... [if there were] mass amnesia of the dominant culture toward the crimes of the past." He adds, "The recognition of guilt [or recognition of the infliction of harm] provides a bridge for the victims and those who identify with the victims to enter into normal social relations."

To readers interested in how a judicial opinion might properly memorialize a national undertaking imbued with a sense of tragedy, I especially recommend MARK OSIEL, MASS ATROCITY, COLLECTIVE MEMORY, AND THE LAW (1997). I also recommend JULES LOBEL, SUCCESS

WITHOUT VICTORY (2003) and Austin Sarat, *Rhetoric and Rememberance: Trials, Transcription, and the Politics of Critical Thinking*, 23 LEGAL STUD. F. 355 (1999), who describe how those facing an uphill judicial battle attempt to construct a legacy to history through litigation.

Those who admonish us to remember understand, of course, the dangers of memory (or truthfulness, as discussed in chapter 4). Readers may be interested in the historical account of FRANCES A. YATES, THE ART OF MEMORY (1966), who discusses how different people, from Socrates and Plato to Augustine, thought of the value and danger of memory. See also AVISHAI MARGALIT, THE ETHICS OF MEMORY 5 (2002); Martha Minow, *Breaking the Cycles of Hatred*, in MARTHA MINOW, BREAKING THE CYCLES OF HATRED: MEMORY, LAW, AND REPAIR 14 (Nancy L. Rosenblum ed., 2002); Austin Sarat, *When Memory Speaks: Remembrance and Revenge in Unforgiven*, 77 IND. L.J. 307 (2002). For writings that stress the dangers of forgetting, I recommend Mark J. Osiel, *Ever Again: Legal Remembrance of Administrative Massacre*, 144 U. PA. L. REV. 463, 464 (1995) (quoting Milan Kundera: "The struggle of man against power is the struggle of memory against forgetting"), and Norman W. Spaulding, *Constitution as Countermonument: Federalism, Reconstruction, and the Problem of Collective Memory*, 103 COLUM. L. REV. 1992 (2003) (distinguishing between a collective memory that wants to forget and a "countermemory" that will do justice to persons). Cicero, so influential where the founding generation was concerned, also addresses the topic of memory. MARCUS TULLIUS CICERO, ON GOVERNMENT 221–334 (Michael Grant trans., Penguin Books 1993).

Regarding the moral proposition that proper acknowledgment of harms associated with tragic choices is required, see, e.g., BERNARD WILLIAMS, MORAL LUCK: PHILOSOPHICAL PAPERS 1973–1980 (1981); BERNARD WILLIAMS, SHAME AND NECESSITY (1993); and JUDITH JARVIS THOMSON, THE REALM OF RIGHTS (1990). Cf. AVISHAI MARGALIT, THE ETHICS OF MEMORY 147–82 (2002) (describing the importance of a "moral witness" that does not merely record history but relives the truth of a past event in a revelatory way).

JUDITH N. SHKLAR, THE FACES OF INJUSTICE (1990), is relevant to the proposition that acknowledgment of harm honors the stature of citizens and the more general argument that public decision makers must justify their choices in a particular way. See, e.g., RONALD DWORKIN, LAW'S EMPIRE (1986); JOHN RAWLS, A THEORY OF JUSTICE (rev. ed. 1999); David A. J. Richards, *Public Reason and Abolitionist Dissent*, 69 Chi.-Kent L. Rev. 787 (1994). See also W. Bradley Wendel, *Professionalism as Interpretation*, 99 Nw. U. L. REV. 1167, 1197 (2005) (summarizing conventional ways of thinking about proper justifications for judge's decisions).

The notion that a tragic choice gives rise to compensatory obligations might lead readers in a number of different directions. For a psychological view of the compensatory impulse, see P. S. GREENSPAN, PRACTICAL GUILT: MORAL DILEMMAS, EMOTIONS, AND SOCIAL NORMS (1995) (relying on research in developmental psychology to conclude that an agent will be at odds with himself when he feels guilty and will want to find some way of cleansing himself of that feeling of guilt).

NUSSBAUM, THOMSON, and WILLIAMS, *supra*, suggest that reparation for harm inflicted might take a variety of forms. Monetary compensation is one possibility. Cf., e.g., U.S. CONST. amend. V (accepting the right of society to take someone's property for the public good, but only on condition that the "taking" is followed by "just compensation"); RESTATEMENT (SECOND) OF TORTS § 197 (1965) (permitting a private person to use the property of another under extraordinary and limited circumstances, as long as there is compensation for the appropriation of property); and Richard A. Epstein, *A Theory of Strict Liability*, 2 J. LEGAL STUD. 151 (1973) (arguing that those who cause harm—without regard to blame or wrongdoing—must compensate simply because of the causal connection between the injurer and injured). See also Eric A. Posner & Adrian Vermeule, *Reparations for Slavery and Other Historical Injustices*, 103 COLUM. L. REV. 689 (2003) (discussing unjust enrichment as a theory of compensatory reparations for institutions once owning or trading in slaves, and a concept of "moral taint" linked to blameworthy institutions).

The text suggests that apologies may also be a form of reparation for harms caused by tragic choices. The discussion of the elements of a good apology comes primarily from Kathleen A. Gill,

The Moral Functions of an Apology, in INJUSTICE AND RECTIFICATION 111 (Rodney C. Roberts ed., 2002).

I also recommend LINDA RADZIK, MAKING AMENDS: ATONEMENT IN MORALITY, LAW, AND POLITICS (2009). Radzik discusses the obligation of wrongdoers to "do something about" the harms they have caused. *Id.* at 5. The harms of most interest to Radzik are those that send a message that someone does not count, is of lesser value, or is a means to an end. *Id.* at 76. These harms "reshape the world so that the victim's value is not fully realized," *id.,* and operate as a threat or encouragement to future similar harms. *Id.* at 77. They damage relationships. *Id.* at 78. Atonement that leads to reconciliation in relationships is therefore of special interest to Radzik, *id.* at 21, and atonement encompasses attitudes of regret and humility in addition to making truthful acknowledgment of the harm that has been inflicted. Apologies as a mechanism for atonement require not only acknowledgment of a wrong but also acceptance of responsibility and an expression of respect for the other that restores value to the person harmed. *Id.* at 92–97.

Readers interested in the apology may also wish to consult Roger Conner & Patricia Jordan, *Never Being Able to Say You're Sorry: Barriers to Apology by Leaders in Group Conflicts,* 72 LAW & CONTEMP. PROBS. 233 (2009) (discussing the power of apologies as cultural artifacts); Brent T. White, *Saving Face: The Benefits of Not Saying I'm Sorry,* 72 LAW & CONTEMP. PROBS. 261 (2009) (explaining how a desire to save face can forestall an apology); Erin Ann O'Hara & Douglas Yarn, *On Apology and Consilience,* 77 WASH. L. REV. 1121 (2002) (linking apologies to forgiveness); Mark J. Osiel, *Ever Again: Legal Remembrance of Administrative Massacre,* 144 U. PA. L. REV. 463, 557–59 (1995) (linking tragedy, apology, and forgiveness but focusing on collective memory rather than harm to losers); and Brent T. White, *Say You're Sorry: Court-Ordered Apologies as a Civil Rights Remedy,* 91 CORNELL L. REV. 1261 (2006) (discussing nonjudicial, governmental apologies as a means of healing victims).

Hate speech has generated some discussion of apologies. RICHARD ABEL, SPEECH & RESPECT (1994), for example, proposes that an apology might be a satisfactory remedy for hate speech. Richard Delgado & Jean Stefancic, *Apologize and Move On?: Finding a Remedy for Pornography, Insult, and Hate Speech,* 67 U. COLO. L. REV. 93 (1996), criticize Abel on the grounds that an apology trivializes the hate speech injury, does not operate as a sufficient deterrent, does not take into account difficult issues pertaining to power dimensions, and can even be used as a justification or to drive an insult home a second time. Readers should note that Abel's recommendations address private speech intentionally used to oppress others. Thus, although Delgado and Stefancic's cautions should be taken seriously, there are significant differences between hate speech and the issues addressed in LOSING TWICE.

As the text notes, forgiveness is an important corollary to an apology. I especially recommend the discussion of forgiveness as the victim's prerogative, in LINDA RADZIK, MAKING AMENDS: ATONEMENT IN MORALITY, LAW, AND POLITICS, 116–26 (2009), and in AVISHAI MARGALIT, THE ETHICS OF MEMORY (2002), which addresses forgetting and forgiveness. For discussions of forgiveness in law, see Symposium, *The Role of Forgiveness in the Law,* 27 FORDHAM URB. L.J. 1351 (2000); and Julie Juola Exline et al., *Forgiveness and Justice: A Research Agenda for Social and Personality Psychology,* 7 PERSONALITY & SOC. PSYCHOL. REV. 337 (2003). The latter article sets forth issues that require study, including what forgiveness entails, whether it requires positive feelings toward offenders, whether offenses are invited or deterred through forgiveness, what cannot be forgiven, what motives are at the root of forgiveness, and whether similar factors influence both perceived injustice and forgiveness. MARGALIT, THE ETHICS OF MEMORY, *supra,* discusses the role of remorse as a precondition for forgiveness. He argues that remorse shows that an offender is not evil, enables the wronged party to separate the offender from the wrongful act, and ensures that relationships can be reestablished. RADZIK, *supra,* discusses the limits of self-forgiveness.

For discussion of the transformation of persons who inflict harm without acknowledging or regretting it, see, e.g., NUSSBAUM, *supra;* BERNARD WILLIAMS, SHAME AND NECESSITY (1993); and AVISHAI MARGALIT, THE DECENT SOCIETY 42, 122–37 (Naomi Goldblum trans., 1996). The historical account of ROBERT WILLIAM FOGEL, WITHOUT CONSENT OR CONTRACT: THE RISE AND FALL OF AMERICAN SLAVERY 388–417 (1989), is especially persuasive of the proposition.

LINDA RADZIK, MAKING AMENDS: ATONEMENT IN MORALITY, LAW, AND POLITICS 56–65 (2009), explores the corollary that proper atonement potentially transforms both the wrongdoer and the meaning of the past wrong.

Philosophers of the tragic choice, scholars of apology, and others noted here do not focus merely on procedural obligations that precede the tragic choice; they are also concerned with obligations arising after a choice has been made. It is the latter topic that is relevant to whether justices have an obligation to take proper account of harms to constitutional losers in the very opinions that identify winners and losers and, if so, how justices might satisfy their obligation.

Most procedural theorists do not discuss the harm inevitably inflicted on losers in constitutional rights disputes. But see Cynthia R. Farina, *Conceiving Due Process*, 3 YALE J.L. & FEMINISM 214, 265 (1991) (arguing that due process provides "an assurance of... [fitting] treatment... whenever government finds it must do harm to one of its citizens, treatment in which there is acknowledgment of loss inflicted, and respect for pain incurred" and that "government should deal fairly and humanely with people, especially when it contemplates harming them"). In the event readers wish to learn about different forms of procedural justice, I recommend, e.g., STUART HAMPSHIRE, INNOCENCE AND EXPERIENCE (1989) (arguing that procedural justice ensures that both sides will be heard and positing that canons of self-reflective and imaginative rationality ensure fairness); and MARTHA C. NUSSBAUM, LOVE'S KNOWLEDGE: ESSAYS ON PHILOSOPHY AND LITERATURE (1990) (suggesting that a form of practical reasoning might satisfy obligations associated with making a just but tragic choice). Procedural fairness will surely guard against outcomes that disadvantage disempowered groups, see, e.g., Martha Minow, *The Supreme Court 1986 Term—Foreword: Justice Engendered*, 101 HARV. L. REV. 10 (1987) (arguing that courts would decide civil rights cases differently were they to do a better job of listening to and empathizing with disempowered groups); and some procedural rules can certainly provide a check against the infliction of unnecessary harms. No one will object to justices who give citizens the opportunity of a fair fight in the courtroom, but this book argues that such an opportunity does not fully discharge justices' obligations to constitutional losers.

Chapter 6: The Art of Harm Amelioration

As LINDA RADZIK, MAKING AMENDS: ATONEMENT IN MORALITY, LAW, AND POLITICS 107 (2009) notes, atoning for (or ameliorating) harm is an art. Atonement is no less an art when pursued by justices. See, e.g., RICHARD POSNER, HOW JUDGES THINK (2008), who describes judging as an art rather than a science. Readers might also be interested in WILLIAM H. SIMON, THE PRACTICE OF JUSTICE: A THEORY OF LAWYERS' ETHICS (1998) for an excellent discussion of ethical attitudes and contextual, non-categorical decision-making. See also William H. Simon, *The Ideology of Advocacy: Procedural Justice and Professional Ethics*, 1978 WIS. L. REV. 29. Finally, I highly recommend JAMES BOYD WHITE, ACTS OF HOPE: CREATING AUTHORITY IN LITERATURE, LAW, AND POLITICS (1994). White asserts that "authority [or law] is a subject of art" and "created by an act of art," because "culture [from which law derives] is a collective human artefact." *Id.* at 276.

It is also appropriate, given the commitment of art to truth and the importance of truthfulness to the ethos recommended in this book, to recommend to readers ELAINE SCARRY, ON BEAUTY AND BEING JUST 113 (1999), an elegant exploration of "the ethical alchemy of beauty," which is both destabilizing and restorative. Scarry observes that, at the moment we see something beautiful, we undergo a radical decentering and no longer stand at the center of our own world. *Id.* at 109–24. Decentering "alters consciousness in the direction of unselfishness, objectivity, and realism" and thus prepares us for virtue. *Id.* at 112 (quoting IRIS MURDOCH, THE SOVEREIGNTY OF GOOD OVER OTHER CONCEPTS: THE LESLIE STEPHEN LECTURE 2 (1967)) (internal quotations omitted). More capacious mental acts are possible because "all the space formerly in the service of protecting, guarding, advancing the self (or its 'prestige') is now free to be in the service of something else." *Id.* at 113. Scarry describes this altered state of consciousness as coming into a state of equality with others. See *id.* at 112–17. If one is open to beauty, she says, one will have a perceptual acuity that makes one especially alert toward injustices. *Id.* at 80–82. She characterizes beauty as something that takes place in the particulars, acknowledges its vulnerability, is opposed to injury, inspires replication by people from different times and different perspectives, invites deliberation, causes us to revisit and to test prior judgments for error, and conveys a sense of being unprecedented. See *id.* at 3–33. According to Scarry, an artistic sensibility knows that something unprecedented can be very precious and valuable; it can even cause others to want to confer immortality on something by replicating it. See *id.* at 4–5. I consider the ethical stance described by Scarry to be bound up with the work of attorneys involved in the world of constitutional rights disputes, who work within law to create the conditions for a radical decentering that enables others to see the world anew and persuades judges to break through convention. This ethical stance is also relevant to the art of judging.

The many functions of dissenting opinions have been thoroughly explored by others. I recommend any of the following: ALAN BARTH, PROPHETS WITH HONOR: GREAT DISSENTS AND GREAT DISSENTERS IN THE SUPREME COURT 19 (1974) (giving examples of memorable dissenting opinions); I DISSENT: GREAT OPPOSING OPINIONS IN LANDMARK SUPREME COURT CASES (Mark Tushnet ed., 2008) (presenting thirteen unvindicated Supreme Court dissents and speculating on what would have happened had those dissents been the majority opinion in each case); William J. Brennan Jr., *In Defense of Dissents*, 37 HASTINGS L.J. 427 (1986) (concluding that dissents can be an expression of personal conscience); Stephen Ellman, *The Rule of Law and the Achievement of Unanimity in*, Brown 49 N.Y.L. SCH. L. REV. 741 (2004–2005) (presenting a history of practices of dissent); Stanley H. Fuld, *The Voices of Dissent*, 62 COLUM. L. REV. 923, 927 (1962) (asserting that dissents act as "an antidote for judicial lethargy…[by ensuring] that the bench has done its work under the constant spur of self-criticism" and prevent the courts from imposing a "rule of artificial unanimity"); Maurice Kelman, *The Forked Path of Dissent*, 1985 SUP. CT. REV. 227 (1985) (arguing, somewhat cynically, that dissents provide language that can be used to justify future decisions); John P. Kelsh, *The Opinion Delivery Practices of the United States Supreme Court 1790–1945*, 77 WASH. U. L. Q. 137 (1999) (outlining the history of dissenting opinions in the Supreme Court and how internal changes in the Court led to or obstructed unanimity in Supreme Court decisions between 1790 and 1945); Robert Post, *The Supreme Court Opinion as Institutional Practice: Dissent, Legal Scholarship, and Decisionmaking in the Taft Court*, 85 MINN. L. REV. 1267 (2001) (arguing that the Taft Court used opinion-writing techniques to transform the Supreme Court from a formalized, dispute resolution–focused institution into a coequal branch of government responsible for guiding the development of federal law); Kevin M. Stack, *The Practice of Dissent in the Supreme Court*, 105 YALE L.J. 2235 (1996) (arguing that dissents call into question any notion that there is a uniquely correct answer for rights disputes); Harlan F. Stone, *Dissenting Opinions Are Not without Value*, 26 J. AM. JUDICATURE SOC'Y 78 (1942–1943) (arguing that dissenting opinions are valuable because they can influence the future development of the law); and Karl M. ZoBell, *Division of Opinion in the Supreme Court: A History of Judicial Disintegration*, 44 CORNELL L. Q. 186 (1958–1959) (analyzing the historical underpinnings of the practice of dissenting, and suggesting that justices should write dissents only when the need to correct a wrong decision outweighs the likelihood that a dissent will make the Court appear fractured).

As noted in the text, dissenting opinions can carry judicial dialogue through time. Kevin M. Stack, *The Practice of Dissent in the Supreme Court*, 105 YALE L.J. 2235, 2257 (1996). For a discussion of the future orientation of dissents, see JULES LOBEL, SUCCESS WITHOUT VICTORY: LOST LEGAL BATTLES AND THE LONG ROAD TO JUSTICE IN AMERICA (2003). For an account of how attorneys use lost causes to build a record that will serve as future generations' witness to history, readers should consult Austin Sarat, *Rhetoric and Remembrance: Trials, Transcription, and the Politics of Critical Reading*, 23 LEGAL STUD. F. 355 (1999). See also Mark J. Osiel, *Ever Again: Legal Remembrance of Administrative Massacre*, 144 U. PA. L. REV. 463, 522 (1995) (discussing Justice Frankfurter's dissent in the Rosenberg case, written after the Rosenbergs were executed, where he acknowledged that his dissent might seem useless to some but that "history also has its claims").

In dissents, judges tend to feel free to be somewhat personal in their assertions. Patricia M. Wald, *The Rhetoric of Results and the Results of Rhetoric: Judicial Writings*, 62 U. CHI. L. REV. 1371, 1413 (1995) ("The strategy of personalization in dissent is to separate the dissenter from the cold, impersonal, authoritarian judges of the majority, who impliedly do not take the human condition into account when they mercilessly impose 'the law.'"); and ALAN BARTH, PROPHETS WITH HONOR: GREAT DISSENTS AND GREAT DISSENTERS IN THE SUPREME COURT 4–5 (1974) (noting that because dissenters perceive that they have decisively lost and therefore face no need to secure a consensus, they do not feel constrained to be "judicial" but rather express themselves with more indignation and complaint).

Lani Guinier, *The Supreme Court, 2007 Term–Foreword: Demosprudence through Dissent*, 122 HARV. L. REV. 4 (2008), argues for more rather than less partiality in dissenting opinions and notes that dissents delivered orally, from the bench, have quite a different function and effect than written dissents or majority opinions. According to Guinier, majority opinions are unlikely to change in character because they must clearly inform lower courts and litigants about rules, must offer a rationale consistent with precedent, and are subject to the standards of an inflexible "constitutional law mafia" composed of judges and law professors. *Id.* at 52. In contrast, LOSING TWICE assumes that justices and the constitutional law mafia will find ways of allowing majority opinions to satisfy justices' obligation to avoid or ameliorate harm. Nonetheless, Guinier's recommendations complement those made in this book.

Ideology was discussed in chapter 5. For arguments against ideology, readers might wish to consult Stephen B. Burbank, *Judicial Independence, Judicial Accountability, and Interbranch Relations*, 95 GEO. L.J. 909 (2007) (arguing that the political ideology of the Court threatens the legitimacy and "diffuse support" for the Court); and ROBERT GRUDIN, THE GRACE OF GREAT THINGS: CREATIVITY AND INNOVATION 219 (1990) (discussing how ideology is used tyrannically and displaces responsibility for our actions). For a recent account of how different justices have approached ideology, see JEFFREY ROSEN, THE SUPREME COURT: THE PERSONALITIES AND RIVALRIES THAT DEFINED AMERICA (2006) (exploring how judicial temperament, an ability to sacrifice an ideological agenda in order to protect the institutional integrity of the Court, shapes the success of a given justice).

Humility is a theme of most of the philosophers discussed in chapter 5. For a definition of humility, I especially like Dan M. Kahan et al., *Whose Eyes Are You Going to Believe? Scott v. Harris and the Perils of Cognitive Illiberalism*, 122 HARV. L. REV. 837, 898 (2009), who say humility is the willingness to imagine who potential dissenters might be and, if dissenters are a group who "bear recognizable identity-defining characteristics," the willingness to "stop and think hard." They propose that an attitude of humility is a way to avoid harm in rights disputes. For other approaches to the subject of humility, consult JEFFREY ROSEN, THE SUPREME COURT: THE PERSONALITIES AND RIVALRIES THAT DEFINED AMERICA (2006); and CASS R. SUNSTEIN, A CONSTITUTION OF MANY MINDS: WHY THE FOUNDING DOCUMENT DOESN'T MEAN WHAT IT MEANT BEFORE (2009). ALASDAIR MACINTYRE, WHOSE JUSTICE? WHICH RATIONALITY? (1988), identifies traits of institutions capable of eliciting participation in ongoing discussions about principles. He suggests that such an institution would be willing to acknowledge that a particular approach to resolving a dispute might be flawed, would have some degree of respect and understanding for opposing views, and would commit to being truthful about opposing views. See *id.* at 166–70. MacIntyre's recommendations apply primarily to actions that should be taken before a decision is made, but his ideas are also relevant to how a judicial opinion is presented. He says, for example, that in order to demonstrate intellectual integrity and to avoid injustice, decision makers such as courts should consider the possibility that a nontraditional way of seeing and addressing a problem is superior. See *id.* at 166–67.

Humility is sometimes linked to judicial minimalism, which is discussed in chapter 9. Chief Justice Roberts has stated that justices are intellectually fallible and that they "have to have the humility to recognize that they operate within a system of precedent shaped by other judges equally striving to live up to the judicial oath, and judges have to have the modesty to be open in the decisional process to the considered views of their colleagues on the bench." *Confirmation*

Hearing on the Nomination of John G. Roberts Jr. to Be Chief Justice of the United States: Before the S. Comm. on the Judiciary, 109th Cong. 55 (2005). Michael J. Gerhardt, *Constitutional Humility*, 76 U. CIN. L. REV. 23, 47–48 (2007), however, notes that Chief Justice Roberts's judicial umpire metaphor does not embody an appropriate concept of humility. In Gerhardt's view, doctrinaire approaches to constitutional meaning are inconsistent with humility, which requires justices to be humble in how they speak to each other and to stakeholders. See *id.* at 42–43. But see William E. Thro, *The Roberts Court at Dawn: Clarity, Humility, and the Future of Education Law*, 222 WEST'S EDUC. L. REP. 491, 492 (2007) (arguing that the Roberts Court "practices judicial humility by refusing to intervene, entertain broad challenges, or overrule precedent" in its decisions).

Many persons have made suggestions relevant to how justices might develop better protocols and language for expressing the proper relation between justices and constitutional losers. These suggestions are strongly influenced by insights drawn from the field of rhetoric, which has been previously referenced in the bibliographic essays to the Introduction and to chapters 4 and 5. See, e.g., ANTHONY G. AMSTERDAM & JEROME BRUNER, MINDING THE LAW (2000) (examining how justices use categorization, storytelling, and persuasion in writing Supreme Court opinions); WAYNE C. BOOTH, MODERN DOGMA AND THE RHETORIC OF ASSENT (1974) (presenting law as a rhetorical field on which the nation founds itself); KARLYN KOHRS CAMPBELL, CRITIQUES OF CONTEMPORARY RHETORIC (1972) (presenting a sociolinguistic approach to a rhetoric that induces participation with others); MAROUF HASAIN JR., LEGAL MEMORIES AND AMNESIAS IN AMERICA'S RHETORICAL CULTURE (2000) (positing that rules of law are negotiated constructs of the arguments of winners, losers, and ordinary citizens); MARK KINGWELL, A CIVIL TONGUE: JUSTICE, DIALOGUE, AND THE POLITICS OF PLURALISM (1995) (proposing a theory of dialogic justice dependent on civility and knowing when to focus on the common ground that people share); Marie A. Failinger, *Not Mere Rhetoric: On Wasting or Claiming Your Legacy, Justice Scalia*, 34 U. TOL. L. REV. 425 (2003) (criticizing Justice Scalia from a rhetorical perspective); Austin Sarat, *Rhetoric and Remembrance: Trials, Transcription, and the Politics of Critical Reading*, 23 LEGAL STUD. F. 355 (1999) (asserting that trial manuscripts serve as records of what the law values at a particular point in history and that manuscripts must be read critically to determine what real-world concerns and issues are omitted from the transcript); and James Boyd White, *Legal Knowledge*, 115 HARV. L. REV. 1396 (2002) (arguing that the law is not a distinct object but knowledge of a language). These scholars challenge the argument that rhetoric is purely sophistic and manipulative, rather than a legitimate form of persuasion.

To the extent that protocols and language reflect the audience to whom justices speak, readers will note that some scholarship assumes that justices speak only to an audience of other judges. See James Boyd White, *Law as Rhetoric, Rhetoric as Law: The Arts of Cultural and Communal Life*, 52 U. CHI. L. REV. 684 (1985) (arguing that law is based not in a system of rules but upon a system of rhetoric used by judges). Justices, however, have multiple audiences. They must not ignore judges and attorneys, who rely on and implement their opinions, but they also must not neglect citizens. Scholars interested in directing judicial attention to the audience of ordinary citizens include RICHARD A. POSNER, HOW JUDGES THINK (2008) (complaining about legalistic opinions); and Lani Guinier, *The Supreme Court, 2007 Term—Foreword: Demosprudence through Dissent*, 122 HARV. L. REV. 4 (2008) (arguing that judges should address losers in language accessible to a lay audience). On occasion, justices will directly address parties in their opinions, as Justice Stevens did in *Medellin v. Texas*, 128 S. Ct. 1346 (2008).

An important thread in scholarly literature links rhetorical practices to a process of securing consent. Rhetoric is, after all, about persuasion not intimidation. See generally WAYNE C. BOOTH, MODERN DOGMA AND THE RHETORIC OF ASSENT (1974); MARK KINGWELL, A CIVIL TONGUE: JUSTICE, DIALOGUE, AND THE POLITICS OF PLURALISM (1995). Furthermore, rhetoricians think of the process of attaining community assent as a form of objectivity. In their view, values and subjective concerns—so important in constitutional rights disputes—may be significant factors in choice without destroying objectivity. Objectivity permits, for example, persuasive arguments based on workability. It may also be measured by community acceptance. Cf. THOMAS KUHN, THE STRUCTURE OF SCIENTIFIC REVOLUTIONS (2d ed. enlarged 1970) (discussing and the importance of rationality in attaining scientific truth and how contested scientific paradigms are handled in scientific and academic endeavors that are conventionally seen as highly rational). As noted in STANLEY FISH, DOING WHAT COMES NATURALLY: CHANGE, RHETORIC, AND THE PRACTICE OF THEORY IN LITERARY AND LEGAL STUDIES 486–88 (1989), Kuhn posited that science is rhetorical "through and through" and that the only criterion for successful scientific argument is the assent of the scientific community at large.

For those especially interested in the ethics of language, I recommend W. J. T. MITCHELL, PICTURE THEORY (1994); MARTHA C. NUSSBAUM, POETIC JUSTICE: THE LITERARY IMAGINATION AND PUBLIC LIFE (1995); ALESSANDRO PORTELLI, THE TEXT AND THE VOICE: WRITING, SPEAKING, AND DEMOCRACY IN AMERICAN LITERATURE (1994); RICHARD WEISBURG, POETHICS AND OTHER STRATEGIES OF LAW AND LITERATURE (1992); Martha C. Nussbaum, *Poets as Judges: Judicial Rhetoric and the Literary Imagination*, 62 U. CHI. L. REV. 1477 (1995); and Girardeau A. Spann, *Expository Justice*, 131 U. PA. L. REV. 585 (1983).

For background on *Romer v. Evans* and the values and interests of winning and losing stakeholders in Colorado's Amendment 2 controversy, I recommend Sharon E. Debbage Alexander, *Romer v. Evans and the Amendment 2 Controversy: The Rhetoric and Reality of Sexual Orientation Discrimination in America*, 6 TEX. F. CIV. LIBERTIES & CIV. RTS. 262 (2001–2002). See also Suzanne B. Goldberg, *Through the Looking Glass: Politics, Morality, and the Trial of Colorado Amendment 2*, 21 FORDHAM URB. L.J. 1057 (1993–1994); Stephen M. Rich, *Ruling by Numbers: Political Restructuring and Reconsideration of Democratic Commitments after* Romer v. Evans, 109 YALE L.J. 587 (1999); and Mark Strasser, *From Colorado to Alaska by Way of Cincinnati: On* Romer, *Equality Foundation, and the Constitutionality of Referenda*, 36 HOUS. L. REV. 1193 (1999).

Judge Bayless's opinion in *Romer v. Evans* was delivered orally. Readers interested in the possibility that rendering a decision from the bench might result in decisions that pay greater attention to losers might wish to read ALESSANDRO PORTELLI, THE TEXT AND THE VOICE: WRITING, SPEAKING, AND DEMOCRACY IN AMERICAN LITERATURE (1994). Portelli discusses the indeterminacy of the personal voice, which is intrinsically nonideological and might accommodate various constitutional meanings. According to Portelli, the personal voice is associated with change, fragility, authenticity, openness, a lack of omniscience, ambiguity, and context. It recognizes that different generations will "sing" about the same song [e.g., the Constitution] in a different way, if only because, over time, there has been an "aging of the yellow gourd rattle" or a "shrinking of the skin around the eagle's claw." *Id.* at 216. Cf. ROBERT POGUE HARRISON, THE DOMINION OF THE DEAD (2003) (arguing that literature is about "voice" and is inherently nondogmatic).

For additional examples of the art of harm amelioration, readers might wish to consult JAMES BOYD WHITE, ACTS OF HOPE: CREATING AUTHORITY IN LITERATURE, LAW, AND POLITICS (1994). For example, White analyzes Abraham Lincoln's Second Inaugural Address, which he says artfully achieved the daunting task of conveying the righteousness of the North's position in the Civil War without attacking the losing South or calling its citizens monsters. *Id.* at 294–302. According to White, Lincoln needed to lay the groundwork for the citizens of the North, who were about to win the war, to accept the South as part of the Union. To establish some commonality between winner and loser, Lineoln emphasized (1) the fact that both North and South had criticized the war but had (albeit for different reasons) both entered into it; (2) that citizens of both regions were equally ignorant and self-righteous; (3) that although the North's cause was moral, no one should judge another lest he also be judged; and (4) that citizens of both regions had suffered from the war. *Id.* ACTS OF HOPE is replete with other examples of how literary analysis enriches our understanding of law.

Chapter 7: Harm and Regret in Abortion Disputes

The abortion debate generates passion on all sides, prompted in part by the labels that each side in the debate attaches to its adherents. Throughout this chapter, I use the pro-choice and pro-life labels that each side has chosen for itself. As Reva B. Siegel, *Dignity and the Politics of Protection: Abortion Restrictions under* Casey/Carhart, 117 YALE L.J., 1694 (2008), notes, the labels are misleading in some respects, but readers will know that the labels nonetheless do point justices toward relevant moral worlds, one focusing on the value of life and the other highly valuing moral agency. The important issue is not whether labels are misleading but, as JAMES BOYD WHITE, ACTS OF HOPE: CREATING AUTHORITY IN LITERATURE, LAW, AND POLITICS 166–67 (1994), says, whether the Supreme Court "should seek to understand the larger currents of feeling and attitudes that are at work …." *Id.* at 167. For White, as for me, the relevant questions are "how the Court goes about thinking and talking about" abortion and "who [the Court] makes itself and its various audiences in the process [to be]." *Id.* at 183.

An excellent overview of arguments related to reproductive freedom is THE REPRODUCTIVE RIGHTS READER: LAW, MEDICINE, AND THE CONSTRUCTION OF MOTHERHOOD (Nancy Ehrenreich, ed. 2008). For a history of abortion disputes, and a discussion of the political and cultural contexts in which those disputes have been resolved, I especially recommend WHITE, ACTS OF HOPE, *supra* at 155–65. See also EARL E. POLLOCK, THE SUPREME COURT AND AMERICAN DEMOCRACY: CASE STUDIES ON JUDICIAL REVIEW AND PUBLIC POLICY 123–52 (2009) (discussing the history of constitutional meaning respecting reproductive freedom). This chapter's summary of the standard critique of judicial involvement in abortion disputes is adapted from Michel Rosenfeld, *Book Review: Law as Discourse: Bridging the Gap between Democracy and Rights*, 108 HARV. L. REV. 1163, 1177–79 (1995) (reviewing JÜRGEN HABERMAS, BETWEEN FACTS AND NORMS: CONTRIBUTIONS TO A DISCOURSE THEORY OF LAW AND DEMOCRACY (William Rehg trans., 1995)).

A straightforward account of essential elements of the abortion debate can be found in Jack M. Balkin, Roe v. Wade: *An Engine in Controversy, in* WHAT ROE V. WADE SHOULD HAVE SAID: THE NATION'S TOP LEGAL EXPERTS REWRITE AMERICA'S MOST CONTROVERSIAL DECISION 6–18 (Jack M. Balkin ed., 2005). Balkin offers readers a collection of hypothetical opinions that might have been written in *Roe*. Hypothetical judicial opinions relevant to the arguments made in this book include one written by Reva B. Siegel, *Siegel, J., Concurring, in* WHAT ROE V. WADE SHOULD HAVE SAID, *supra* at 63, which links the right to choose to women's equal citizenship. Two of the hypothetical dissenting opinions make a moral argument on behalf of the State of Texas. Michael Stokes Paulsen, *Comments from the Contributors, in* WHAT ROE V. WADE SHOULD HAVE SAID, *supra* at 239, writes an opinion that rejects decorum, "in the face of evil." He describes abortion as murder, even private mass murder. *Id.* at 196, 212. Paulsen's dissenting opinion accuses *Roe* majority justices of being men and women "of violence." *Id.* at 213. Theresa Stanton *Collett, Collett, J., Dissenting, in* WHAT ROE V. WADE SHOULD HAVE SAID, *supra* at 187, argues that women are harmed by abortion, a procedure that she views as a man's solution to a woman's problem. Instead of seeking a right to an abortion, women should find ways to make society adapt to their unique nature and reproductive capacity. *Id.* at 188–89. None of the hypothetical opinions in Balkin's collection, majority or dissenting, adhere to practices recommended in this book. None develop an argument based on freedom of conscience.

Much has been written about *Roe v. Wade*. Examples of standard critiques are found in GUIDO CALABRESI, IDEALS, BELIEFS, ATTITUDES, AND THE LAW: PRIVATE LAW PERSPECTIVES ON A PUBLIC LAW PROBLEM 92–97 (1985); ROBERT A. BURT, THE CONSTITUTION IN CONFLICT 344–52 (1992); and MARY ANN GLENDON, ABORTION AND DIVORCE IN WESTERN LAW 42–47 (1987). Although these scholars have valuable things to say about abortion disputes, and I am especially indebted to Calabresi's thoughts on tragic choices, I nonetheless disagree with many of their arguments. I point out a few of those disagreements to give readers a sense of the differences between the standard critique of *Roe* and my argument.

I obviously disagree with Glendon that judges should stay out of the abortion debate. The better view is Robert Post & Reva Siegel, Roe *Rage: Democratic Constitutionalism and Backlash*, 42 HARV. C.R.-C.L. L. REV. 373 (2007), which argues that legitimacy depends on whether we recognize the Constitution as ours and that citizen backlash—which challenges the Court—is an act of "political self-ownership." Post and Siegel maintain that justices should not attempt to avoid conflict and should not pretend that achieving mutual respect for outcomes is a workable aspiration.

I also disagree that *Roe* threatened recognition of the fetus in areas outside the context of abortion and reproductive choice. See GUIDO CALABRESI, IDEALS, BELIEFS, ATTITUDES, AND THE LAW: PRIVATE LAW PERSPECTIVES ON A PUBLIC LAW PROBLEM 94–95 (1985). Blackmun himself apparently believed that *Roe* would leave traditional laws affecting the fetus—for example, in cases of inheritance or personal injury—untouched. Furthermore, it is not clear to me that Germany's abortion laws, enacted against a horrifying history of German genocide, necessarily strike the right balance of values and interests of citizens of the United States, contrary to the argument in MARY ANN GLENDON, ABORTION AND DIVORCE IN WESTERN LAW 26 (1987). Suggested distinctions between *Roe* and the Court's similarly controversial decision in *Brown v. Board of Education*, proposed by ROBERT A. BURT, THE CONSTITUTION IN CONFLICT 347–49 (1992), seem weak. The decision in *Gonzales v. Carhart* notwithstanding, I disagree with the assertions of both Calabresi and Burt that it is unlikely that we will be able to put the excessively divisive abortion debate back in the bottle.

More importantly, although equality is central to constitutional stature, I question conventional wisdom that justices might have better approached the abortion debate through substantive equality rather than liberty or privacy principles, an analytical approach proposed in ROBERT A. BURT, THE CONSTITUTION IN CONFLICT 349 (1992), and GUIDO CALABRESI, IDEALS, BELIEFS, ATTITUDES, AND THE LAW: PRIVATE LAW PERSPECTIVES ON A PUBLIC LAW PROBLEM 102 (1985). Justices and citizens have widely divergent views of what the substantive equality principle entails. As MICHAEL WALZER, THICK AND THIN: MORAL ARGUMENT AT HOME AND ABROAD (1994), might say, we are closer to a world of "thin" understandings about substantive equality than we might like to believe. Some take a highly formalistic approach to the equality concept (for example, pregnancy discrimination is not sex discrimination), while others argue that equality embodies a more expansive, anti-subordination concept. Moreover, there will always be debates about what to compare when equality is the frame of reference in the substantive rights abortion debate. According to CALABRESI, *supra* at 102, we should compare men's and women's sexual freedom rather than equality respecting the more broadly defined liberty that *Roe* justices discussed. Justices in *Harris v. McRae*, 448 U.S. 297, 325 (1980), considering a comparison between abortion and other medical procedures, concluded that "abortion is inherently different from other medical procedures, because no other procedure involves the purposeful termination of a potential life." In *Gonzales v. Carhart*, 550 U.S. 124, 163–64 (2007), however, justices insisted that physicians performing abortion are no different from other physicians when it comes to state regulation. The recommendation that justices should endeavor to leave all parties in the abortion debate in the equal status of stalemate—equally happy or unhappy, as suggested in BURT, *supra* at 368, seems unhelpful. For other substantive equality perspectives that emerge in the abortion debate, see, e.g., Pamela Bridgewater, Gonzales v. Carhart: *Continuing the Class Critique of the Reproductive Rights Doctrine and Movement*, 59 S.C. L. REV. 827 (2008) (addressing the class and race effects of the Court's abortion decisions); Casey A. Coyle, Gonzales v. Carhart: *Justice Kennedy at the Intersection of Life Interests, Medical Practice and Government Regulations*, 27 TEMP. J. SCI. TECH. & ENVTL. L. 291 (2008) (asserting that Justice Kennedy improperly equates life interests that are in fact different); Martha F. Davis, *The Equal Rights Amendment: Then and Now*, 17 COLUM. J. GENDER & L. 419 (2008) (discussing state Equal Rights Amendments and public funding for abortions); Rebecca Dresser, *From Double Standard to Double Bind: Informed Choice in Abortion Law*, 76 GEO. WASH. L. REV. 1599 (2008) (arguing that woman-protective justifications for informed consent laws applicable to abortion deny women equal protection); Martha K. Plante, *"Protecting" Women's Health: How* Gonzales v. Carhart *Endangers Women's Health and Women's Equal Right* to *Personhood under the Constitution*, 16 AM. U. J. GENDER SOC. POL'Y & L. 387 (2008) (discussing disproportionate effects of abortion laws on poor, minority women); and Mary Catherine Wilcox, *Why the Equal Protection Clause Cannot "Fix" Abortion Law*, 7 AVE MARIA L. REV. 307 (2008) (arguing that abortion cannot be subjected to ordinary equality concepts because abortion does not affect women as a class). The thin concepts of substantive equality, of course, should be differentiated from the thick procedural understandings of citizen equality at the heart of constitutional stature. See the discussion in Chapter 9.

This chapter argues that justices have improperly neglected moral and spiritual aspects of the abortion debate and have thereby failed in their harm-avoidance and harm-amelioration obligations to citizens of full constitutional stature. JAMES BOYD WHITE, ACTS OF HOPE: CREATING AUTHORITY IN LITERATURE, LAW, AND POLITICS 163–64 (1994), discusses the historical role of organized religion in U.S. debates about abortion. See also Brief for Amici Curiae American Ethical Union et al. at 2a–3a, *Harris v. McCrae*, 448 U.S. 297 (1980) (No. 79–1268), 1979 WL 199986 (taking note of "the heavy institutional involvement of the bishops of the Roman Catholic Church in a campaign to enact religiously-based anti-abortion commitments into law" and "the institutional mobilization of Roman Catholic dioceses, including massive financial contributions by those dioceses to the National Committee for a Human Life Amendment"). Caitlin E. Borgmann, *Judicial Evasion and Disingenuous Legislative Appeals to Science in the Abortion Controversy*, 17 J.L. & POL'Y 15 (2008), discusses the reliance of recent legislators on moral argument rather than science or policy in the abortion debate.

For an informative exploration of religious views pertaining to a woman's right of choice, see Charlton C. Copeland, *God-Talk in the Age of Obama: Theology and Religious Political Engagement*, 86 DENV. U. L. REV. 663 (2009) (including the argument that a truthful account of one religious view would not focus on when life begins but, instead, on who has sovereignty over life, and on the religious imperative to faithfully bear witness to—in religion's own language—issues related to abortion). See also Laurence H. Tribe, *The Supreme Court 1972 Term—Foreword: Toward a Model of Roles in the Due Process of Life and Law*, 87 HARV. L. REV. 1, 18–25 (1973) (arguing that the status of the fetus is essentially a religious question).

For a discussion of justices' reluctance to engage in debate about religious matters, presumably including the religious dimensions of the abortion controversy, see the articles included in Symposium, *The Supreme Court's Hands-Off Approach to Religious Doctrine*, 84 NOTRE DAME L. REV. 793 (2009). In Harris v. McRae, 448 U.S. 297 (1980), justices refused to decide whether a federal statute denying Medicaid to poor women wishing to have an abortion imposed religious beliefs and prevented the exercise of women's freedom of conscience and religious beliefs, in violation of First Amendment prohibitions against an establishment of religion.

Carol Sanger, *Seeing and Believing: Mandatory Ultrasounds and the Path to a Protected Choice*, 56 UCLA L. REV. 351 (2008), argues that the deliberative path women take to making a decision about abortion is as deserving of protection as is the decision itself. That women pay attention to moral (or religious) considerations in making a decision about abortion, and reconcile responsibilities to many different individuals in doing so, is noted in the Brief for the Amici Curiae Women Who Have Had Abortions and Friends of Amici Curiae in Support of Appellees, *Webster v. Reproductive Health Services*, 492 U.S. 490 (1989) (No. 88–605), and is documented in the work of CAROL GILLIGAN, IN A DIFFERENT VOICE: PSYCHOLOGICAL THEORY AND WOMEN'S DEVELOPMENT (1982). The Brief for the Amici Curiae Women Who Have Had Abortions, *supra*, at 43, included a short section on "whether moral or spiritual values" might argue in favor of rather than against abortion. The many statements offered by these *amici* include one characterizing the era when criminal laws led women to jeopardize their lives and health to secure an abortion as "evil" and asserting that it is the Christian thing to fight for safe and legal abortions. *Id.* at 101–2. The evil days of unsafe, life-threatening abortions referenced in the brief are far from past. See, e.g., DEFENDING HUMAN RIGHTS: ABORTION PROVIDERS FACING THREATS, RESTRICTIONS, AND HARASSMENT (CENTER FOR REPRODUCTIVE RIGHTS 2009), available at http://reproductiverights.org/en/feature/defending-human-rights-abortion-providers-under-siege; and Janessa L. Bernstein, *The Underground Railroad to Reproductive Freedom: Restrictive Abortion Laws and the Resulting Backlash*, 73 BROOK. L. REV. 1463 (2008) (discussing the inaccessibility of abortion to many women, given the current state of the law).

The nature of the regret that may accompany a decision either to carry a pregnancy to term or to have an abortion is not easy to define. The text's comparison of regret to a bruise on the soul rather than to a psychological weakness was suggested by JAMES LEE BURKE, RAIN GODS 231 (2009) ("If certain things we do or witness don't leave a stone bruise on the soul, there's something wrong with our humanity."). I highly recommend the discussion of regret in Chris Guthrie,

Carhart, *Constitutional Rights, and the Psychology of Regret*, 81 S. CAL. L. REV. 877, 879 (2008) (objecting to the Court's "privileging of postabortion regret over preabortion choice"). Guthrie takes account of research showing that people who face tough decisions anticipate the possibility that they may later regret a decision, that they tend to overestimate both the intensity and duration of the regret that might result, and that they make efforts to minimize or avoid regret. Regret thus "tends to 'loom[] larger in prospect than it actually stands in experience.'" *Id*. at 891 (quoting Daniel T. Gilbert et al., *Looking Forward to Looking Backward: The Misprediction of Regret*, 15 PSYCHOL. SCI. 346, 349 (2004)). Guthrie concludes that women who anticipate regret may be biased against abortion. Cf. Jeremy A. Blumenthal, *Abortion, Persuasion, and Emotion: Implications of Social Science Research on Emotion for Reading Casey*, 83 WASH. L. REV. 1 (2008) (commenting on the ability of abortion foes to manipulate women's decisions by introducing biasing emotional material into the discussion); and Harper Jean Tobin, *Confronting Misinformation on Abortion: Informed Consent, Deference, and Fetal Pain Laws*, 17 COLUM. J. GENDER & L. 111 (2008) (discussing the effect of Woman's Right to Know statutes). Readers will note that some justices joining Kennedy's *Carhart* opinion have, in contexts other than abortion disputes, contemptuously dismissed psychic well-being related to personal conscience as a trivial interest. *See Hein v. Freedom from Religion Foundation*, 127 S. Ct. 2553, 2574 (2007) (Scalia, J. concurring).

LOSING TWICE argues that even if a substantive constitutional argument must ultimately be rejected, *no* constitutional analysis—First Amendment, Fourteenth Amendment, or other—should rest on a diminished view of women's constitutional stature or moral and political agency. Chapter 3 cautioned that if justices can explain their resolution of a rights controversy only through an analysis that attacks a loser's constitutional stature, they should consider the likelihood that they have made an erroneous decision. For commentary on justices' failure to recognize the full constitutional stature of women because of their reproductive capacity, readers might consult a number of articles, including Emily Calhoun, *The Breadth of Context and the Depth of Myth: Completing the Feminist Paradigm*, 4 HASTINGS WOMEN'S L.J. 87 (1993) (asserting that women become transformed by pregnancy into a new being, a "pregnantwoman," in one abortion decision); Rebecca E. Ivey, *Destabilizing Discourses: Blocking and Exploiting a New Discourse at Work in* Gonzales v. Carhart, 94 VA. L. REV. 1451 (2008) (asserting that abortion decisions rely on stereotypes to portray women as not rational and only maternal); and Nora Christie Sandstad, *Pregnant Women and the Fourteenth Amendment: A Feminist Examination of the Trend to Eliminate Women's Rights during Pregnancy*, 26 LAW & INEQ. 171 (2008) (arguing that *Carhart* illustrates the Court's diminution of women's rights during pregnancy).

The presumption of full constitutional stature accorded constitutional losers has obviously limited applicability to a fetus. For example, it makes little sense to talk about the moral or political agency or consent of a fetus. Nonetheless, readers may be interested in continued arguments that the fetus should be recognized as a constitutional person, as set forth in, e.g., Robert John Araujo, *Abortion—From Privacy to Equality: The Failure of the Justifications for Taking Human Life*, 45 HOUS. L. REV. 1737 (2009). Women justifiably fear the consequences of recognition of fetal personhood, even in local legislation. See, e.g., THE REPRODUCTIVE RIGHTS READER: LAW, MEDICINE, AND THE CONSTRUCTION OF MOTHERHOOD (Nancy Ehrenreich, ed. 2008); CYNTHIA R. DANIELS, AT WOMEN'S EXPENSE: STATE POWER AND THE POLITICS OF FETAL RIGHTS (1993); LAURA E. GÓMEZ, MISCONCEIVING MOTHERS: LEGISLATORS, PROSECUTORS, AND THE POLITICS OF PRENATAL DRUG EXPOSURE (1997); RACHEL ROTH, MAKING WOMEN PAY: THE HIDDEN COSTS OF FETAL RIGHTS (2000); Susan Goldberg, *Of Gametes and Guardians: The Impropriety of Appointing Guardians Ad Litem for Fetuses and Embryos*, 66 WASH. L. REV. 503 (1991).

Although *Gonzales v. Carhart*, 550 U.S. 124 (2007), is a much more recent decision than *Roe v. Wade*, 410 U.S. 113 (1975), commentary on the decision is nonetheless rather extensive. For excellent articles, please consult the references to chapter 3.

Some scholars suggest that the joint opinion in *Planned Parenthood v. Casey* is an exemplar of proper judicial behavior in abortion disputes. See, e.g., JAMES R. STONER JR., COMMON-LAW LIBERTY: RETHINKING AMERICAN CONSTITUTIONALISM 65–77 (2003) (arguing that *Planned Parenthood* respects both sides of the abortion debate); Robert Post & Reva Siegel, Roe *Rage:*

Democratic Constitutionalism and Backlash, 42 HARV. C.R.-C.L. L. REV. 373, 429 (2007) (arguing that *Planned Parenthood* is productively confrontational in its clarity, manages conflict by drawing people into a discussion about the meaning of the Constitution, and seeks to "channel disagreement [both] by acknowledgment" and by adopting a flexible undue burden standard); Neil S. Siegel, *The Virtue of Judicial Statesmanship*, 86 TEX. L. REV. 959, 1028–29 (2008) (arguing that justices in *Planned Parenthood* saw both sides and gave states additional room to limit abortions, but firmly endorsed women's liberty interests). I especially commend JAMES BOYD WHITE, ACTS OF HOPE: CREATING AUTHORITY IN LITERATURE, LAW, AND POLITICS (1994), to readers. His analysis of the joint opinion in *Planned Parenthood* leads him to conclude that the justices were able to talk about religion "without themselves using invidious sectarian language." He added, "[They found] a way to define what is at stake that connects it ... [to] the religious character of the laws prohibiting abortion, and their possible incompatibility without commitments against establishment of religion." *Id.* at 171. Moreover, the joint opinion represents "an extraordinary moment in the history of American law" in that it "turns its mind to the way citizens respond to its decisions, especially to those they disagree with." *Id.* at 177. The justices of the joint opinion directly address people who disagree with the outcome of *Roe* but struggle to accept it. *Id.* at 177–78.

Others question the value of *Planned Parenthood* to those who support women's right of choice. Dawn E. Johnson, *A Progressive Reproductive Rights Agenda for 2020*, in THE CONSTITUTION IN 2020, at 255 (Jack M. Balkin & Reva B. Siegel eds., 2009), for example, argues that despite its rhetoric, *Planned Parenthood* undeniably undermined *Roe*. Johnson also argues against characterizing all abortions as tragedies, because she believes the characterization will stigmatize women and that the "tragedy label ... promotes shame and silence." *Id.* at 265.

I will leave it to readers to reach their own conclusions about *Planned Parenthood* and whether justices properly acknowledged or avoided harms to its constitutional losers. *Planned Parenthood* was as much about the concept of *stare decisis*—and a refusal to overrule *Roe v. Wade*, a decision under political fire—as it was about abortion per se. Moreover, because *Planned Parenthood* both adopted a more permissive "undue burden" test for evaluating the constitutionality of restrictions on abortion and yet affirmed the essential holding of *Roe*, people might even disagree about who won and who lost as a result of the decision.

Portions of the joint opinion have been referenced in earlier chapters. The statements most relevant to this chapter's argument that it is possible for majority opinions in abortion decisions to fulfill justices' harm-avoidance and harm-amelioration obligations include *Planned Parenthood*'s assertion that:

> Men and women of good conscience can disagree, and we suppose some always shall disagree, about the profound moral and spiritual implications of terminating a pregnancy, even in its earliest stage. Some of us as individuals find abortion offensive to our most basic principles of morality, but that cannot control our decision. Our obligation is to define the liberty of all, not to mandate our own moral code. The underlying constitutional issue is whether the State can resolve these philosophic questions in such a definitive way that a woman lacks all choice in the matter, except perhaps in those rare circumstances [of danger to life or health or rape or incest].

Planned Parenthood of Se. Pa. v. Casey, 505 U.S. 833, 850–51 (1992). In addition, the opinion acknowledged the many different "intimate views with infinite variations" of the meaning of procreation and human responsibility. *Id.* at 853. It also asserted that decisions about marriage, procreation, contraception, population control, family relationships, childrearing, education, and medical treatment "involv[e] the most intimate and personal choices a person may make in a lifetime, choices central to personal dignity and autonomy." It further argued: "At the heart of liberty is the right to define one's own concept of existence, of meaning, of the universe, and of the mystery of human life. Beliefs about these matters could not define the attributes of personhood were they formed under the compulsion of the State." *Id.* at 851. Indeed, "the destiny of the woman must be shaped to a large extent on her own conception of her spiritual imperatives and her place in society." *Id.* at 852. Nonetheless, the state has an interest in potential life, and abortion remains a unique act "fraught with consequences for others: for [women]; for the persons who perform and assist in the procedure; for the spouse, family, and society which must confront the knowledge that these procedures exist, procedures some deem nothing short of an act of violence against innocent human life." *Id.* at 852. Moreover, the joint opinion recognized that "an extra price will be paid" by constitutional losers who disagree with, but who struggle to live within, the decision. *Id.* at 867–68. It expressed determination not to breach faith with people who have made an effort to live with *Roe. Id.* It called "the contending sides of a national controversy to end their national division by accepting a common mandate rooted in the Constitution," but simultaneously acknowledged that there will be "inevitable efforts to overturn [the Court's decision] and to thwart its implementation." *Id.* at 867.

A final observation about this chapter's thesis is in order. Supporters of women's rights may fear the consequences of asking justices to pay attention to women's moral and spiritual struggles. As previously noted, some abortion opponents have already seized on that struggle to describe women as emotionally vulnerable and in need of government protection regarding pregnancy in general. Others cite the struggle as proof that women never want an abortion, are in effect coerced by circumstances into getting unwanted abortions, and therefore require protection. See, e.g., Reva B. Siegel, *Dignity and the Politics of Protection: Abortion Restrictions under* Casey/Carhart, 117 YALE L.J. 1694 (2008); Reva B. Siegel, *The Right's Reasons: Constitutional Conflict and the Spread of Woman-Protective Antiabortion Argument,* 57 DUKE L.J. 1641 (2008) (noting the emergence of this argument as a justification for restrictive abortion laws). *Carhart,* however, has already ventured one step in the direction of presuming that women need protection. As a supporter of women's right to choose and someone committed to defending my full constitutional stature, I believe that the best response is to directly take on the understanding and to ask justices to think more deeply about women's spiritual struggles pertaining to abortion. More rather than less debate on this question, as a matter related to equal moral agency and constitutional stature, is in order. See also Caitlin E. Borgmann, *The Meaning of "Life": Belief and Reason in the Abortion Debate,* 18 COLUM. J. GENDER & L. 551 (2009) (arguing that the crucial moral issues underlying the abortion debate must be engaged). Cf. scholarship that has taken up the rights of conscience of medical providers, including Whitney D. Pile, *The Right to Remain Silent: A First Amendment Analysis of Abortion Informed Consent Laws,* 73 MO. L. REV. 243 (2008); Rachel T. Caudel, *What the Doctor Ordered: Balancing Religion and Patient Rights in U.S. Pharmacies,* 97 KY. L.J. 521 (2009); Rebecca Dresser, *From Double Standard to Double Bind: Informed Choice in Abortion Law,* 76 GEO. WASH. L. REV. 1599 (2008).

MICHAEL J. SANDEL, JUSTICE: WHAT'S THE RIGHT THING TO DO? (2009), has stated that "a just society involves reasoning together about the good life," *id.* at 261, and "moral engagement." *Id.* at 268. Sandel offers only a very few suggestions about "what kind of political discourse would point us in this direction," *id.,* especially when it comes to moral disagreements, but his advice about moral engagement should be taken to heart. In particular, engaging with others respectfully and as equals is essential. Cf. *id.* at 267.

Chapter 8: Valuing Precedent Differently

This chapter does not attempt to persuade readers to reject precedent and finality but only to value them differently. Moreover, nothing said here affects the binding effect of any specific decision on parties to a given dispute. Finally, the chapter does not question the binding effect of Supreme Court decisions on inferior courts. It considers only the extent to which justices are controlled by their previous constitutional decisions.

Readers interested in conventional justifications for precedent might wish to consult MICHAEL J. GERHARDT, THE POWER OF PRECEDENT (2008). I also especially recommend Michael C. Dorf, *Legal Indeterminacy and Institutional Design,* 78 N.Y.U. L. REV. 875 (2003) (summarizing how theories of judicial review cope with the inherent indeterminacy of law). The relationship between precedent and original intent theories of constitutional interpretation is explored in Randy E. Barnett, *Trumping Precedent with Original Meaning: Not as Radical as It Sounds,* 22 CONST.

COMMENT. 257 (2005) (arguing that when constitutional text is vague, as with the due process clause, the Court can develop doctrine to help implement text and that doctrine is subject to revision); or Daniel A. Farber, *The Rule of Law and the Law of Precedents*, 90 MINN. L. REV. 1173 (2006) (arguing that tensions between originalism and precedent might be resolved were a decision's binding effect determined through standards rather than rigid rules).

Precedent and finality in constitutional meaning are generally seen as valuable for instrumental reasons. Scholars, however, debate the empirical validity of instrumental claims. See, e.g., LARRY D. KRAMER, THE PEOPLE THEMSELVES: POPULAR CONSTITUTIONALISM AND JUDICIAL REVIEW 234–35 (2004) (noting that the empirical validity of the settlement function of law has yet to be tested). For an empirically based study of precedent, see SAUL BRENNER & HAROLD J. SPAETH, STARE INDECISIS: THE ALTERATION OF PRECEDENT ON THE SUPREME COURT 1946–1992 (2006). For a case-study analysis of precedent, readers should consult RICHARD A. POSNER, HOW JUDGES THINK 272 (2008) (concluding that justices are awash in an ocean of discretion uncontrolled by prior decisions).

Earl Maltz, *The Nature of Precedent*, 66 N.C. L. REV. 367 (1988), argues that instrumental values conventionally associated with precedent do not require a rigid system of precedent. Reliance interests and equality can be protected if new constitutional rules operate only prospectively. *Id.* at 368–70. Judges can resort to means other than precedent to sustain citizens' belief in justice or to avoid an appearance of arbitrary decision-making. Id. at 271. Claims that precedent brings efficiency to the judicial system are weak, and the argument that precedent ensures that judges are law-finders rather than law-makers is based on an assumption that constitutional meaning should not be permitted to evolve to meet changed circumstances. See also Larry D. Kramer, *The Supreme Court 2000 Term—Foreword: We the Court*, 115 HARV. L. REV. 4 (2001).

Readers who want to learn more about justices' authority and whether it will be undermined by the absence of a rigid system of precedent might consult James Boyd White, *What's an Opinion For?*, 62 U. CHI. L. REV. 1363 (1995). For those interested in an alternative disciplinary perspective on the subject, I recommend ALESSANDRO PORTELLI, THE TEXT AND THE VOICE: WRITING, SPEAKING, AND DEMOCRACY IN AMERICAN LITERATURE 118–24 (1994) (discussing the potential consequences of reducing the authority of the narrator of any story). LARRY D. KRAMER, THE PEOPLE THEMSELVES: POPULAR CONSTITUTIONALISM AND JUDICIAL REVIEW (2004), asserts that authoritative constitutional meaning should be less dependent on a single precedent than on the quantity of decisions manifesting popular acceptance. Cf. Richard B. Cappalli, *The Common Law's Case against Non-Precedential Opinions*, 76 S. CAL. L. REV. 755, 767 (2003) (asserting that "the full meaning of the law of a single case, or a group of cases, or a body of case law can only be known through a meticulous study of the opinions which generated their holdings," and that "when case lawyers speak of the reach of a precedent, they mean its authoritative force as known through the hard study of its origins and justification, the cumulative aspirations and concerns of the judges who authored the precedent, and their predecessors whose earlier work was consulted").

The stability that precedent brings is said to need special attention in a pluralistic world. Lawrence B. Solum, *Public Legal Reason*, 92 VA. L. REV. 1449 (2006), reminds us, however, that in a pluralistic world judges resolving hard cases will need to justify their decisions by means other than a resort to precedent. See also Daniel A. Farber, *The Rule of Law and the Law of Precedents*, 90 MINN. L. REV. 1173, 1202 (2006) ("maximizing stability may call for flexibility" and "it is a mistake to expect too much from [precedent]"). Moreover, the wrong type of stability may support tyranny and violence of law. See, e.g., Norman W. Spaulding, *Constitution as Countermonument: Federalism, Reconstruction, and the Problem of Collective Memory*, 103 COLUM. L. REV. 1992 (2003) (arguing that precedent has been used to help unjust moments in a nation's history disappear). As ANTHONY G. AMSTERDAM & JEROME BRUNER, MINDING THE LAW 285 (2002), argue:

> Courts must...manage the law's own special dialectic between continuity and change. They must manage a system of ideas that protects and enshrines old, established balances, yet leaves room for the construction and justification of new ones when the times change enough. The stability of the existing order is, in some significant measure,

in their keeping; but it is also a part of their job to bring into being new worlds of the possible.

See also PAUL W. KAHN, THE REIGN OF LAW: MARBURY V. MADISON AND THE CONSTRUCTION OF AMERICA 221 (1997) (explaining that the written constitution instituted "a tradition of commentary that both sustains and stabilizes conflict"); EDMOND N. CAHN, THE SENSE OF INJUSTICE: AN ANTHROPOCENTRIC VIEW OF LAW 22 (1949) (asserting that, to avoid injustice, a Court must not stand still or leap forward; there must be movement in an intelligible design). Peter Fitzpatrick, *Why the Law Is Also Nonviolent*, in LAW, VIOLENCE, AND THE POSSIBILITY OF JUSTICE, at 142, 154–55 (Austin Sarat, ed. 2001), offers a useful rhetorical perspective on this process: "to 'stay the same,' the [judicial] decision must alter in its relation to what is ever different.... [T]he decision is continually 'conserved' *and* 'destroyed'.... (emphasis in original).

For general discussions of values associated with a lack of finality, I recommend ROBERTO MANGABEIRA UNGER, WHAT SHOULD LEGAL ANALYSIS BECOME? 110 (1996) (arguing that society leaves agreements incomplete for good reason); and CASS R. SUNSTEIN, LEGAL REASONING AND POLITICAL CONFLICT (1996) (incompletely theorized opinions have value). A degree of indeterminacy and lack of finality allows justices to distinguish or even overrule constitutional decisions without seeming to be arbitrary. See, e.g., PAUL W. KAHN, THE CULTURAL STUDY OF LAW: RECONSTRUCTING LEGAL SCHOLARSHIP 52–53 (1999) (stating that courts endeavor to "make present[] something that appears already to exist," because "an interpretation that fails to appear as a rediscovery will appear as an illegitimate construction of new law"). The lack of finality inherent in constitutional common-law methodologies may also enhance law's pragmatic, consent-securing capacity. See, e.g., LARRY D. KRAMER, THE PEOPLE THEMSELVES: POPULAR CONSTITUTIONALISM AND JUDICIAL REVIEW (2004); Richard B. Cappalli, *The Common Law's Case against Non-Precedential Opinions*, 76 S. CAL. L. REV. 755 (2003); David A. Strauss, *Common Law, Common Ground, and Jefferson's Principle*, 112 YALE L.J. 1717 (2003). Cf. RICHARD A. POSNER, HOW JUDGES THINK 253–54 (2008) (describing "constrained" pragmatism, as a preferred method of judicial decision-making).

Some scholars endorse indeterminacy in constitutional meaning because of their faith that good answers will work themselves out over time, or because indeterminacy sustains citizen faith and hope for the future. See, e.g., JAMES BOYD WHITE, ACTS OF HOPE: CREATING AUTHORITY IN LITERATURE, LAW, AND POLITICS (1994); Richard H. Fallon Jr., *Judicially Manageable Standards and Constitutional Meaning*, 119 HARV. L. REV. 1274 (2006) (assuming that the Court has an aspirational function); Sanford Levinson, *Law as Literature*, 60 TEX. L. REV. 373, 402–3 (1982) (expressing faith that continued attempts to find good answers will provide "a common language of constitutional discourse" fit for our nation). Of special interest is Kathryn Abrams & Hila Keren, *Law in the Cultivation of Hope*, 95 CAL. L. REV. 319 (2007). Abrams and Keren argue that government institutions should actively facilitate hope, or the ability to imagine new possibilities, a sense of agency and capability to pursue these possibilities, and adequate resources to implement the possibilities. They also discuss the danger that those whose hopes are not realized will suffer profound disappointment and the risk that hope will be manipulated so as to benefit persons in superior positions of power.

ROBERTO MANGABEIRA UNGER, WHAT SHOULD LEGAL ANALYSIS BECOME? (1996), explores whether the public has the self-confidence to demand ambiguity and indeterminacy from judges. His inquiry is echoed by others. See, e.g., ALESSANDRO PORTELLI, THE TEXT AND THE VOICE: WRITING, SPEAKING, AND DEMOCRACY IN AMERICAN LITERATURE 57 (1994) (asking whether "a textuality accessible to the mob still guarantees the necessary rule of law and order"); Frank I. Michelman, *Judicial Supremacy, the Concept of Law, and the Sanctity of Life*, in JUSTICE AND INJUSTICE IN LAW AND LEGAL THEORY 139, 157 (Austin Sarat & Thomas R. Kearns eds., 1996) (exploring whether a state protects a contestable value best by dictating a right interpretation and forcing us to conform, or by encouraging us to think of a value as contestable and to take responsibility for deciding for ourselves what it means).

Readers may be interested in commentary on precedent from a virtue ethics perspective. Sarah M. R. Cravens, *Judges as Trustees: A Duty to Account and an Opportunity for Virtue*, 62 WASH. & LEE

L. Rev. 1637 (2005), for example, argues that precedent is important whenever a corpus of law reflects a developing tradition, but that blind adherence to precedent is improper. She also contends that a well-developed decision ethic is especially important whenever judicial choices about constitutional meaning are not controlled by prior decisions. *Id.* at 1641–42 (attributing the argument to Aristotle). According to Lawrence B. Solum, *The Supreme Court in Bondage: Constitutional Stare Decisis, Legal Formalism, and the Future of Unenumerated Rights*, 9 U. Pa. J. Const. L. 155 (2006), a distinction should be made between different categories of constitutional precedent. *Id.* at 199–200. He asserts that judges who possess the proper "virtue" will admit that law will evolve and "work[] itself pure" through case-by-case decisions in the common-law tradition. *Id.* at 191. See also Lawrence B. Solum, *Natural Justice*, 51 Am. J. Juris. 65 (2006); and Lawrence B. Solum, *Judicial Selection: Ideology versus Character*, 26 Cardozo L. Rev. 659 (2005).

Discussions of the Roberts Court's treatment of precedent abound. I recommend Ronald Dworkin, The Supreme Court Phalanx: The Court's New Right-Wing Bloc (2008); Michael J. Gerhardt, The Power of Precedent (2008); Pamela S. Karlan, *The Law of Small Numbers*: Gonzales v. Carhart, Parents Involved in Community Schools *and Some Themes from the First Full Term of the Roberts Court*, 86 N.C. L. Rev. 1369 (2008); Christopher W. Schmidt, Brown and the *Colorblind Constitution*, 94 Cornell L. Rev. 203 (2008); and Neil S. Siegel, *The Virtue of Judicial Statesmanship*, 86 Tex. L. Rev. 959 (2008). Readers will find a passionate debate reflecting Roberts Court justices' views of precedent in *Citizens United v. Federal Election Commission*, 2010 U.S. LEXIS 766, 88–93 (January 21, 2010); *id.* at 111–26 (Roberts, C. J., concurring); and *id.* at 169–80 (Stevens, J., concurring in part and dissenting in part).

Readers may be interested in scholarship indirectly related to the discussion of precedent and finality. See, e.g., Penelope Pether, *Inequitable Injunctions: The Scandal of Private Judging in the U.S. Courts*, 56 Stan. L. Rev. 1435 (2004) (criticizing the practice of selecting only some opinions for publication, which results in arbitrariness and a lack of transparency, impedes the development of the law, leads to repeat-player advantage, suppresses dissenting views, and adversely affects litigants on the margins of society); and Gary Lawson, *Controlling Precedent: Congressional Regulation of Judicial Decision-Making*, 18 Const. Comment. 191 (2001) (discussing whether Congress can dictate how precedent must be used).

This chapter's presentation of the ideas of Jürgen Habermas is based on Jürgen Habermas, Between Facts and Norms: Contributions to a Discourse Theory of Law and Democracy (William Rehg trans., 1996). Without endorsing his theory in its entirety, the text concludes that his principles respecting the political branches of government are relevant to the legitimacy of the Supreme Court's law-production in rights disputes.

I am indebted to Christopher F. Zurn, Deliberative Democracy and the Institutions of Judicial Review (2007), who also explores the applicability of Habermas's theory to judicial review. In some respects, Zurn follows the same paths taken in this book. He attempts to break away from stale debates and paradigms; he takes into account the empirical reality of institutions in making recommendations for improved constitutional review; and he parses the language of specific Supreme Court decisions so as to compare juristic discourse and the discourse of public reason. In contrast to this book, however, Zurn questions whether courts are the best vehicle for performing constitutional review, concludes that they are not, and sets forth a complex proposal for restructuring institutions of constitutional review. He concludes that the Supreme Court generally employs a discourse appropriate to an institution that resolves actual controversies, sits at the apex of a complex system of courts, and reasons from precedent.

Zurn offers a nice overview of theories of deliberative democracy, their focus on self-government and their rejection of a purely aggregative conception of democracy. As important theorists, Zurn includes Ronald Dworkin, Law's Empire (1986); Christopher L. Eisgruber, Constitutional Self-Government (2001); John Hart Ely, Democracy and Distrust (1980); Frank I. Michelman, Brennan and Democracy (1999); and John Rawls, Political Liberalism (1993). Zurn notes that deliberative democrats tend to assume that courts should facilitate democratic interactions in other branches of government. Although positing equality among citizens, deliberative democrats also tend to assume that judicial elites with special capabilities are needed for certain functions. Cf. literature addressing a conventional view of the Supreme Court's democratic function, e.g., BRUCE ACKERMAN, WE THE PEOPLE: FOUNDATIONS (1991); BRUCE ACKERMAN, WE THE PEOPLE: TRANSFORMATIONS (1998); and MICHAEL J. SANDEL, DEMOCRACY'S DISCONTENT: AMERICA IN SEARCH OF A PUBLIC PHILOSOPHY (1996).

To readers interested in different ways of thinking about democracy and judicial review, I especially recommend William H. Simon, *Solving Problems vs. Claiming Rights: The Pragmatist Challenge to Legal Liberalism*, 46 WM. & MARY L. REV. 127 (2004). Simon argues that citizens should participate in solutions to problems and that institutions of government should facilitate their participation, *id.* at 175; that there will be no definitive resolutions to conflict and we should thus accept "a rolling rule regime," which permits continuous adjustment to different situations, *id.* at 187; that disputants should focus on common interests and values through a process called bootstrapping, *id.* at 182; and that, when it is impossible to identify something called the common good, institutional legitimacy will turn on whether all views have been expressed and considered. *Id.* at 210. I also recommend advocates of democratic constitutionalism, who insist that the authority of the Constitution depends on its acceptance by Americans. See, e.g., Robert Post & Reva Siegel, *Roe Rage: Democratic Constitutionalism and Backlash*, 42 HARV. C.R.-C.L. L. REV. 373 (2007); and Jack M. Balkin, *Framework Originalism and the Living Constitution*, 103 Nw. U. L. REV. 549 (2009).

Michael C. Dorf, *Legal Indeterminacy and Institutional Design*, 78 N.Y.U. L. REV. 875, 945–46 (2003), argues that courts may be more capable of addressing intractable disputes than political branches because courts have a convening power that elected officials lack, are perceived as neutral and therefore have more prestige and respect, and have a dis-entrenching capacity. Because any institution will have difficulty with intractable disputes, for him "the crucial question... [is] whether whichever institution is charged with the task adopts problem-solving methods equal to the challenge." *Id.* at 979. He argues that we should embrace the transactional, pragmatic judicial role and better design courts to perform it. In his view, "legal culture, despite its association of law with authoritative commands, already has room for a different conception of law as an invitation to problem solving." *Id.* at 961. He pays tribute to Frank Michelman for recognizing that solutions to the problem of indeterminacy turn on how we define democracy, and he encourages us to reimagine our institutions. *Id.* at 904–9.Others who, like Dorf, voice the possibility that courts might better satisfy democratic ideals than ordinary political processes are discussed in CHRISTOPHER F. ZURN, DELIBERATIVE DEMOCRACY AND THE INSTITUTIONS OF JUDICIAL REVIEW (2007). See also RICHARD A. POSNER, HOW JUDGES THINK 304–5 (2008) (asserting that justices may be less partisan than legislators, and noting that others have argued that justices might be better legislators than elected officials if only the institutional judicial setting were improved); Lani Guinier, *The Supreme Court 2007 Term—Foreword: Demosprudence through Dissent*, 122 HARV. L. REV. 4, 127, 131 (wishing to "reviv[e] the Court as a representative body," and characterizing the Court as a "nascent democratic forum that is broader than legislative decisionmaking and potentially less divisive than exclusive reliance on electoral up/down voting"); Dan M. Kahan et al., *Whose Eyes Are You Going to Believe: Scott v. Harris and the Perils of Cognitive Illiberalism*, 122 HARV. L. REV. 837, 897 (2009) (asserting that judges are uniquely able to rise above naïve realism and to be "sensitive to [the potential for] community outrage"). That judicial review is especially important when elected branches have opted out of meaningful public discourse is noted by Marie A. Failinger, *Not Mere Rhetoric: On Wasting or Claiming Your Legacy, Justice Scalia*, 34 U. TOL. L. REV. 425, 442–43 (2003). That justices can model proper discourse is a point developed in Michael S. Kang, *Race and Democratic Contestation*, 117 YALE L.J. 734 (2008). It should be emphasized that none of these scholars suggest that the Court should aspire to rendering decisions based solely on a show of hands. Cf. Hein v. Freedom from Religion Foundation, 551 U.S. 587, 127 S. Ct. 2553, 2573 (2007) (Scalia, J., concurring) (rejecting processes that result in decision-making by show of hands rather than by rule of law); JEFFREY TOOBIN, THE NINE: INSIDE THE SECRET WORLD OF THE SUPREME COURT 237 (2007) (describing Chief Justice Rehnquist's wish to avoid behaving as if only votes matter, not justifications or rationales).

Readers might note that the Supreme Court has itself participated in a certain disabling of the legislative branches of government. See, e.g., Jed Rubenfield, *The Anti-Antidiscrimination Agenda*, 111 YALE L.J. 1141 (2002); Ruth Colker & James J. Brudney, *Dissing Congress*, 100 MICH. L. REV. 80 (2001); and Robert C. Post & Reva B. Siegel, *Equal Protection by Law: Federal Antidiscrimination Legislation after Morrison and Kimel*, 110 YALE L.J. 441 (2001). As a result, the Court has perhaps elevated its own importance as a democratic forum.

This chapter emphasizes that the Supreme Court has a transactional role. Cf. JOSEPH J. ELLIS, AMERICAN CREATION: TRIUMPHS AND TRAGEDIES AT THE FOUNDING OF THE REPUBLIC (2007) (institutions of the United States were set up to facilitate argument and disputation and to transform disagreement into a constructive force). In conceptualizing the transactional role, I have been influenced by conflict resolution theory, notwithstanding that alternative modes of conflict resolution such as mediation are usually seen to be in tension with judicial review. See, e.g., OWEN FISS, THE LAW AS IT COULD BE (2003); Owen M. Fiss, *Against Settlement*, 93 YALE L.J. 1073 (1984); Owen M. Fiss, *Out of Eden*, 94 YALE L.J. 1669 (1985). For explanations of conflict resolution and mediation, readers might enjoy the discussion in BERNARD S. MAYER, BEYOND NEUTRALITY: CONFRONTING THE CRISIS IN CONFLICT RESOLUTION (2004); or BERNARD MAYER, STAYING WITH CONFLICT: A STRATEGIC APPROACH TO ONGOING DISPUTES (2009) (reviewing standard conflict-resolution theory in light of the reality that rights disputes can be intractable and often do not result in true win-win agreements).

The Constitution itself suggests that transactional aspects of the Supreme Court's role deserve further attention. Exploring this topic is well beyond the scope of this book, but readers might consider, in this regard, the right of association and the right to petition government for redress of grievances. Excellent discussions of transactional values enhanced by the First Amendment right of association are found in FREEDOM OF ASSOCIATION (Amy Gutmann ed., 1998); Jason Mazzone, *Freedom's Associations*, 77 WASH. L. REV. 639 (2002); and Seana Valentine Shiffrin, *What Is Really Wrong with Compelled Association*, 99 NW. U. L. REV. 839 (2005). The history of the First Amendment petition right is recounted in THOMAS E. CRONIN, DIRECT DEMOCRACY: THE POLITICS OF INITIATIVE, REFERENDUM, AND RECALL (1989); and EDMUND S. MORGAN, INVENTING THE PEOPLE: THE RISE OF POPULAR SOVEREIGNTY IN ENGLAND AND AMERICA 224–30 (1988). See also James E. Pfander, *Sovereign Immunity and the Right to Petition: Toward a First Amendment Right to Pursue Judicial Claims against the Government*, 91 NW. U. L. REV. 899 (1997).

Transactional aspects of the remedial phase of rights litigation might also be of interest to readers. A classic study of equitable relief is OWEN M. FISS, THE CIVIL RIGHTS INJUNCTION (1978). I especially recommend PETER CHARLES HOFFER, THE LAW'S CONSCIENCE: EQUITABLE CONSTITUTIONALISM IN AMERICA 1–6 (1990), which describes how the Supreme Court drew on an expansive view of equity powers to remedy the wrong of racial segregation in public schools in *Brown v. Board of Education*. For recognition of how the remedial phase of rights litigation offers an opportunity for stakeholders to collaborate regarding proper changes in dysfunctional government institutions that do not work as democratic theory requires, see, e.g., Charles F. Sabel & William H. Simon, *Destabilization Rights: How Public Law Litigation Succeeds*, 117 HARV. L. REV. 1015 (2004). See also Wendy Parker, *The Decline of Judicial Decisionmaking: School Desegregation and District Court Judges*, 81 N.C. L. REV. 1623 (2003); Michael C. Dorf, *Legal Indeterminacy and Institutional Design*, 78 N.Y.U. L. REV. 875 (2003); and Susan P. Sturm, *A Normative Theory of Public Law Remedies*, 79 GEO. L.J. 1355 (1991).

Chapter 9: Losing Twice: The Lottery

Parents Involved in Community Schools v. Seattle School Dist. No. 1, 127 S. Ct. 2738 (2007), has attracted much attention and scholarly commentary. For additional reading, I recommend RONALD DWORKIN, THE SUPREME COURT PHALANX: THE COURT'S NEW RIGHT-WING BLOC 49–59 (2008); Pamela S. Karlan, *The Law of Small Numbers: Gonzales v. Carhart, Parents Involved in Community Schools, and Some Themes from the First Full Term of the Roberts Court*, 86 N.C. L.

Rev. 1369 (2008); Charles Lawrence III, *Unconscious Racism Revisited: Reflections on the Impact and Origins of "The Id, the Ego, and Equal Protection,"* 40 Conn. L. Rev. 931 (2008); Martha C. Nussbaum, *The Supreme Court, 2006 Term—Foreword: Constitutions and Capabilities: "Perception" against Lofty Formalism,* 121 Harv. L. Rev. 4 (2007); and Neil S. Siegel, *The Virtue of Judicial Statesmanship,* 86 Tex. L. Rev. 959 (2008). Most of this commentary is directed at substantive constitutional analysis and outcomes, or goes to Justice Kennedy's argument that the plurality opinion is "inconsistent in both its approach and its implications with the history, meaning, and reach of the Equal Protection Clause." *Parents Involved,* 127 S. Ct. at 2788 (Kennedy, J., concurring in the judgment).

The denial of a tragic choice manifested in *Parents Involved* can be quite useful to justices. Justice Thomas, for example, asserted that rights disputes should have a "culpable party" so that courts will better know how to respond to requests for judicial relief. *Parents Involved,* 127 S. Ct. at 2773. (Thomas, J., concurring). Moreover, it certainly makes life easier for justices if they can treat constitutional losers as blameworthy wrongdoers and do not have to grapple with obligations owed innocent constitutional litigants. If losing parties are wrongdoers, for example, justices do not need to find a way of expressing regret for rejecting values that might be endorsed in another context. Nor do they need to shore up threatened relationships with losing stakeholders.

Another example of the flawed practices evident in the *Parents Involved* plurality opinion is *Ricci v. DeStefano,* 129 S. Ct. 2658 (2009). In *Ricci,* justices determined that a city unlawfully ignored the results of a test that had a disparate and adverse impact on minority firefighters. Although *Ricci* involved Title VII mandates rather than the Constitution, justices hinted that they might be ready to adopt an unforgiving *constitutional* colorblindness principle. Moreover, they evidenced a striking indifference to minority firefighters and their interests. For example, although both minority and white firefighters had studied diligently for the promotion test at the center of the debate, justices commiserated only with white firefighters who had done well on the test. They seemed blind to the plight of minority firefighters who, like their white colleagues, wanted to be judged on the merits of their abilities, and had worked hard and had studied as diligently as their white counterparts, but were put at an unfair disadvantage by the test.

Citizens United v. Federal Election Commission, 2010 U.S. LEXIS 766 (January 21, 2010), was decided more recently than *Parents Involved,* and there are few scholarly assessments of the decision. It is worth noting, however, that a debate about the proper characterization of corporate entities surfaces in other rights disputes. See, e.g., *Monroe v. Pape,* 365 U.S. 167 (1961), and FDIC v. Meyer, 510 U.S. 471 (1994) (addressing the liability of governmental entities for rights violations). Cf. *Ashcroft v. Iqbal,* 129 S. Ct. 1937 (2009) (refusing to recognize supervisory liability for government officials accused of rights violations). Readers will be interested to know that, when considering the status of states under the Eleventh Amendment, justices have suggested that such entities possess dignitary interests akin to those ascribed to human beings. See, e.g., *Federal Maritime Com'n v. South Carolina State Ports Authority,* 535 U.S. 743 (2002). For additional commentary on the status of corporate entities, see the references in the bibliographical essay to chapter 1, where the innocence of corporate entities is addressed.

Although the majority opinion in *Citizens United* made a straightforward albeit mistaken comparison between corporate entities and living beings, concurring opinions added an apparent fallback argument. For example, Justice Scalia encouraged us to focus our attention on the speech rights of the "authorized spokesman of a corporation," who is "a human being who speaks on behalf of the human beings who have formed that association." *Citizens United v. Federal Election Commission,* 2010 U.S. LEXIS 766, *139 n.7 (January 21, 2010) (Scalia, J., concurring). The flaws in Scalia's argument were, as noted in the text, pointed out by Justice Stevens. Commentary on the complicated law of associational rights is referenced in the bibliographic essay to chapter 8.

Neither the Roberts Court nor any individual justice is necessarily an ideological adherent of all tenets of the doctrine of judicial minimalism discussed in this chapter. Justices also do not always agree on how judicial minimalism should affect the outcome of a given rights dispute. For example, according to Cass R. Sunstein, *Burkean Minimalism,* 105 Mich. L. Rev. 353 (2006), Justice Ginsburg is a minimalist in the sense that she favors small steps, but she differs from other minimalists in her distrust of tradition and her demand for justifications. Justice Scalia may stick to his categorical guns when a search for broad constitutional principles comes into conflict with judicial minimalism's case-by-case methodology, see generally *Crawford v. Marion County Election Bd.*, 128 S. Ct. 1610, 1626–27 (2008) (Scalia, J., concurring) (criticizing a "voter-by-voter examination of the burdens of voting regulations [which] would prove especially disruptive ... encourage constant litigation ... [and] provide[] no certainty, and will embolden litigants"), but other justices may not do so. *In Hein v. Freedom from Religion Foundation*, 127 S. Ct. 2553 (2007), for example, Justice Scalia accused Chief Justice Roberts of an analysis that only "pose[d] [as] minimalism," *id.* at 2580 (Scalia, J., concurring) but in reality employed "meaningless and disingenuous distinctions," *id.* at 2582, that "beat [precedent] to a pulp and then sen[t] it out to the lower courts weakened, denigrated, more incomprehensible than ever, and yet somehow technically alive." *Id.* at 2584.

Whether justices are always faithful to their own theory of judicial minimalism is a subject of some debate. See Suzanne B. Goldberg, *Constitutional Tipping Points: Civil Rights, Social Change, and Fact-Based Adjudication*, 106 COLUM. L. REV. 1955 (2006) (arguing that justices try to sustain an illusion of fact-based, contextual decision-making that protects the judiciary by making it seem legitimate, even as justices make significant normative judgments). See also Martha C. Nussbaum, *The Supreme Court, 2006 Term—Foreword: Constitutions and Capabilities: "Perception" against Lofty Formalism*, 121 HARV. L. REV. 4 (2007), who characterizes the decision in *Parents Involved in Community Schools v. Seattle School District No. 1* as an example of a lofty judicial formalism in which "good judgment requires standing at a considerable distance from the facts of the case and the history of struggle that they frequently reveal." *Id.* at 26. Dissenting justices argued in *Citizens United v. Federal Election Commission*, 2010 U.S. LEXIS 766 (January 21, 2010), that the majority deviated from dictates of judicial minimalism. As Heather K. Gerken, *Rashomon and the Roberts Court*, 68 OHIO ST. L.J. 1213, 1213 (2007), notes, we are in a "doctrinal interregnum" in many respects.

Explanations of judicial minimalism can be found in the work of Cass Sunstein. See, e.g., CASS R. SUNSTEIN, A CONSTITUTION OF MANY MINDS: WHY THE FOUNDING DOCUMENT DOESN'T MEAN WHAT IT MEANT BEFORE (2009); Cass R. Sunstein, Legal Reasoning and Political Conflict (1996); Cass R. Sunstein, One Case at a Time: Judicial Minimalism on the Supreme Court (1999); CASS R. SUNSTEIN, RADICALS IN ROBES: WHY EXTREME RIGHT-WING COURTS ARE WRONG FOR AMERICA (2005); and Cass R. Sunstein, *Trimming*, 122 HARV. L. REV. 1049 (2009).

Judicial minimalism has much to recommend it, but its virtues should not be accepted without question. See e.g., Owen Fiss, *The Perils of Minimalism*, 9 THEORETICAL INQUIRIES IN LAW 643 (2008) (using the Guantanamo detainee cases to offer a caution about judicial minimalism as practiced within the Roberts Court). The text argues that judicial minimalism may prioritize deference to legislative judgments to the exclusion of satisfying requirements of harm-avoidance and harm-amelioration obligations. Consider, for example, how an ideological commitment to deference may have resulted in opinions embodying inconsistent assumptions about citizenship capacities associated with constitutional stature. In *Washington State Grange v. Washington State Republican Party*, 128 S. Ct. 1184 (2008), justices explained their decision to uphold a Washington election statute by invoking an assumption that citizens would be well informed and able to make meaningful choices about candidates. Challengers to the statute were told they would have to rebut that assumption with concrete evidence before justices would entertain a constitutional challenge to a statute. In contrast, in *Gonzales v. Carhart*, 550 U.S. 124 (2007), justices explained their decision to defer to Congress and the Partial-Birth Abortion Ban Act of 2003 by portraying women and their physicians as weak and malleable insofar as choices about reproductive issues are concerned.

Judicial minimalism does not invariably result in deference to decisions made by the political branches of government. See, e.g., Robert C. Post & Reva B. Siegel, *Equal Protection by Law: Federal Antidiscrimination Legislation after Morrison and Kimel*, 100 YALE L.J. 441 (2000) (arguing that, when it comes to expansive civil rights legislation, justices demonstrate a determined refusal *not* to defer to majoritarian judgments as to how the Constitution should be implemented). The most recent indication that justices may not defer to civil rights legislation is *Northwest* Austin *Municipal Utility District Number One v. Holder*, 129 S. Ct. 2504 (2009) (hinting that certain provisions of the Voting Rights Act are unconstitutional). See also *Dist. of Columbia v. Heller*, 128 S. Ct. 2783 (2008) (invalidating gun regulations); *Parents Involved* in *Cmty. Schs. v. Seattle Sch. Dist. No. 1*, 551 U.S. 701 (2007) (invalidating school districts' policy of using racial benchmarks to determine whether schools were sufficiently integrated).

Rebecca L. Brown, *Liberty, the New Equality*, 77 N.Y.U. L. Rev. 1491, 1540 (2002), has noted that it is odd that judicial minimalism, a doctrine spawned by deliberative democracy, should hold that courts ought to "defer to legislation that imposes one moral view on others for no reason other than that it is the moral view of a majority of voters." Brown contends that deliberative democracy "rejects simple majority rule as the method for resolving all moral disagreement." *Id.* at 1539. Instead, such disagreements should be resolved by rationales according respect to opposing arguments and narrowing areas of intractable moral disagreement. When judicial minimalism leads to undue deference, however, it will "simply enshrine[ ] the results of a power struggle...resolved by majority rule." *Id.* at 1538. Brown asserts that the current version of judicial minimalism has made courts afraid even to ask meaningful questions about the Constitution. *Id.* at 1540.

That the narrow-ground tenet of judicial minimalism ignores the possibility that an unwavering focus on narrow questions is not necessarily the best way to secure an agreement acceptable to all stakeholders was suggested by William H. Simon, *Solving Problems vs. Claiming Rights: The Pragmatist Challenge to Legal Liberalism*, 46 Wm. & Mary L. Rev. 127, 184 (2004) (noting the benefits of expanding the pie of interests).

I encourage readers to look beyond scholarship dealing with Supreme Court judicial minimalism and to consider the concept of moral minimalism set forth in Michael Walzer, Thick and Thin: Moral Argument at Home and Abroad (1994) (focusing on the international sphere, where one frequently encounters intractable debate among competing values and principles). According to Walzer, moral minimalism is not intended to define a proper role for any governmental institution. It is simply a means of keeping discussion of intractable issues at a level of abstraction that enables diverse groups to participate in the discussion without having to relinquish the particularized, "thick" values that reflect unique backgrounds and understandings of any given group. Resolution of specific disputes involving abstract principles plays out in a highly contextual way. For Walzer, "the value of minimalism lies in the encounters it facilitates." *Id.* at 18. Moral minimalism is a tool that enables us to relate, vicariously, to the quests of others for justice, truth, or liberty, without having our specific experiences and beliefs concerning these ideals get in the way. It helps us in moments when we are asked to stand in solidarity with others who hold fundamentally different views about important matters. It permits us to share an understanding, for example, with all who seek racial equality and justice, although we simultaneously disagree with the precise meaning of racial equality and justice espoused by others. According to Walzer, "moral minimalism...has no imperial tendencies," *id.* at 64, and does not work coercively, for ideological principle and the ideologue are deaf and out of place in a differentiated, pluralist society. See *id.* at 100–1.

As the text notes, Walzer does not consider theories of justice or democracy minimalist if they make assumptions about people and about rules of engagement that are informed by local understandings. He argues, for example, that Jürgen Habermas's assumptions about people could be valid only within a society that already had a non-minimalist or "thick" set of opinions and views about how society should be organized. See *id.* at 26–27. The concept of constitutional stature central to this book is not a minimalist concept. Precisely because the concept is entrenched in understandings that transcend conservative or liberal talking points it is a legitimate foundation for the harm-amelioration and harm-avoidance obligations owed by justices to all stakeholders in rights disputes.

This chapter revisits and adds one more example to the introduction's discussion of judicial activism. Readers may be interested in four relatively recent analyses of judicial activism. See, e.g., The Rehnquist Court: Judicial Activism on the Right (Herman Schwartz ed., 2002) (approaching the subject from an avowedly liberal standpoint); Stefanie A. Lindquist &

FRANK B. CROSS, MEASURING JUDICIAL ACTIVISM (2009) (presenting an empirical study of judicial activism); KERMIT ROOSEVELT III, THE MYTH OF JUDICIAL ACTIVISM, MAKING SENSE OF SUPREME COURT DECISIONS (2008) (offering a scholarly defense against charges of judicial activism); and Lori A. Ringhand, *Judicial Activism: An Empirical Examination of Voting Behavior on the Rehnquist Natural Court*, 24 CONST. COMM. 43 (2007) (offering another empirical study).

For scholarly discussion of the Second Amendment and *District of Columbia v. Heller*, 128 S. Ct. 2783 (2008), readers may wish to consult Reva B. Siegel, *The Supreme Court 2007 Term— Comments: Dead or Alive: Originalism as Popular Constitutionalism in* Heller, 122 HARV. L. REV. 191 (2008); Cass R. Sunstein, *The Supreme Court 2007 Term—Comment: Second Amendment Minimalism:* Heller *as Griswold*, 122 HARV. L. REV. 246 (2008); Mark Tushnet, Heller *and the Critique of Judgment*, 2008 SUP. CT. REV. 61 (2008); Mark Tushnet, Heller *and the New Originalism*, 69 OHIO ST. L.J. 609 (2008); and J. Harvie Wilkinson III, *Of Guns, Abortions, and the Unraveling Rule of Law*, 95 VA. L. REV. 253 (2009).

As a final word to the bibliographic essays of LOSING TWICE, we should recall the commentary of two scholars, one who reminds us that we are lacking Supreme Court guidance on the concept of citizenship, Bruce Ackerman, *The Citizenship Agenda*, in THE CONSTITUTION IN 2020, at 109 (Jack M. Balkin & Reva B. Siegel eds., 2009), and the other who reminds us that we need new ways of imagining the individual person (or body) in relation to the body politic. ALAN HYDE, BODIES OF LAW 201 (1997). LOSING TWICE has proposed one starting point for anyone interested in pursuing these projects.

INDEX